Israel and the Holy Places
of Christendom

Walter Zander

Israel and the Holy Places of Christendom

Weidenfeld and Nicolson
5 Winsley Street London W1

ISBN 0 297 00430 1

Printed in Great Britain
by Ebenezer Baylis and Son Ltd.
The Trinity Press, Worcester, and London

To the memory of my wife
who longed for the Peace of Jerusalem

Contents

Contents

Introduction

Up to the end of the Ottoman Empire the Christian Holy Places were mainly considered under two aspects, one arising from the fact that the government of the country was in non-Christian hands, the other from the division of Christendom. This book tries to deal with both issues as they have developed since on 7 June 1967 the Israeli Forces entered the Old City of Jerusalem and the town of Bethlehem. In doing so it concentrates on the two main Sanctuaries – the Church of the Holy Sepulchre and the Basilica of the Nativity; and the two most important of the Christian communities involved – Roman Catholics and Greek Orthodox. The Sanctuaries of Judaism and Islam are only discussed by way of comparison or contrast.

It is customary at present to speak of the Holy Places in Jerusalem as if they formed one entity, and as if the measures to be taken in their interest were identical. This is misleading. They differ not only in their religious significance, but also in most practical implications. There is first the basic distinction between the Sanctuaries of the *rulers* of the country and those of the *ruled*. The former rarely present any difficulties: thus Catholic rights in the Christian Holy Places were not endangered in the Latin Kingdom of Jerusalem; Moslem shrines were well respected under the Turkish reign; and there are no complaints today from Jewish religious authorities about Jewish rights at the Western (Wailing) Wall.

Conversely the position of the Sanctuaries of the ruled will vary according to the attitudes of the rulers. Two examples may suffice.

When in 1099 the Crusaders conquered Jerusalem, they transformed the Dome of the Rock from a Mosque into a Church – the Templum Domini – and burnt the Synagogue (including the Jews who had sought refuge there). When less than a century later the Moslems regained control of the City, Saladin left the Church of the Holy Sepulchre to the Christians,

A*

1

and in due course the Jews were given permission to rebuild their houses of prayer.

The question of the Holy Places today, concerns essentially the Sanctuaries of Islam and Christianity. Each of the two cases presents fundamentally different problems.

Moslem Sanctuaries

Both the Dome of the Rock and the El Aksa Mosque stand in the grounds of the Temple area, the Haram Al-Sharif. Moslems from the beginning of the Jewish National Movement have been deeply suspicious of Jewish intentions, and have feared that the Jews ultimately aim at the reconquest of the Temple Mount and the destruction of the Islamic Sanctuaries; and although the official spokesmen of Jewry and Israel have time and again protested to the contrary, there were Jewish writers, scholars and visionaries who gave substance to such suspicions.

Moreover, in June 1967, within hours of the conquest of the Old City, the Chief Rabbi of the Israel Army, Brigadier Goren with some of his followers entered the area and conducted Jewish prayers in what the Moslems consider ground holy to Islam[1] and a few weeks later he suggested erecting a synagogue on the esplanade of the El Aksa Mosque. In addition on 17 August 1969, four days before the fire in the El Aksa Mosque, a group of the Jewish National Youth Movement BETAR – against the protest of the Moslem officials – held a ceremonial parade in the precincts of the Temple Mount near the Dome of the Rock, where their leader in his address complained that the Temple Mount was still 'held by aliens', and called for the rebuilding of a Third Temple.[2] Even today the courtyards of the two Mosques which to the Moslems are as holy as the buildings themselves, by order of the Israel government are open to all visitors. All protests of the Moslem Council that 'the whole of the Haram Al-Sharif compound is a Mosque, all of it is holy and all of it is the sole property of the Moslems' and that 'Israel was invading Sanctuaries and desecrating sacred beliefs'[3] were in vain. Thousands of sightseers are pouring into what the Moslems feel is the holy ground of Islam. Each step to them is a desecration which reverberates through the Moslem world.

Jewish Orthodoxy has always held that ultimately – in the days of the Messiah – the Temple will be rebuilt, and the sacrifices reinstated; and the representative of the State of Israel in the debate of the Security Council on 12 September 1969, accepted this belief as the position of his government. He added 'It is inconceivable that we ourselves should make any plans for the rebuilding of the Temple,'[4] but the suspicions on the Islamic side prevail. Jewish messianic expectations therefore clash with Moslem piety on the Temple area.

Christian Sanctuaries

No such problems exist between Israel and the Christian communities. Christians naturally respect the site of the Temple, but they believe that after the Crucifixion 'the veil in the Temple was rent in twain from the top to the bottom'. They hold that the Temple has been destroyed never to rise again, and that the sacrifices have been replaced by a new and higher dispensation. They therefore do not claim the ground upon which the Temple stood. Likewise the Jews do not demand the site of the Holy Sepulchre and the Basilica of the Nativity. Golgotha according to tradition was outside the walls of the city, and Bethlehem anyway is another town. There are no religious aspirations on either side to any Sanctuary which would mutually exclude each other. But there are other issues and these are the subject of this book.

The situation of the Christian Holy Places is determined by three factors. Firstly, the unique nature of the Christian *attachment* to the Sanctuaries which independent from theological controversies, and in spite of the most divergent influences during a history of more than fifteen hundred years, has prevailed unchanged as a living force. Secondly, the *division* of the Christian Churches: this has affected not only the relationship between the communities themselves in the Holy Places but the attitude of each of them to the general political issues facing Jerusalem as a whole. Lastly, and most important: the new movement – now in progress – towards a *reunion* of the Western and Eastern Churches which found its first fulfilment in the meeting of Pope Paul VI and Patriarch Athenagoras I in Jerusalem in 1964.

Against this threefold background the book examines Israel's actions concerning the Sanctuaries, the reactions of the different Churches, and the various proposals which have been made for the future of the Christian Holy Places. It reaches the conclusion that – whatever the general political or strategical necessities in the Middle East may be – the situation of the Christian Holy Places does not require or justify an intervention of the United Nations or any other international organisation, and that the responsibility for the Christian Sanctuaries should rest with the government of the country. It is the personal hope of the author that the government over the Old City will ultimately be based on a condominium between Arabs and Israelis.

As far as the relationships of the Christian communities in the Holy Places are concerned the book proposes that a solution of their conflict will be found not by a continuation of legal and historical arguments about the respective claims and rights, an approach which necessarily is bound to the past, but by the 'spirit of charity' invoked by the leaders of the Roman and the Greek Orthodox Churches which could transform the Sanctuaries from objects of strife into symbols of reunion.

1 The Nature of the Christian Attachment to the Holy Places

The Gospels do not contain any obligation for the Christian to make a pilgrimage to Jerusalem, or indeed to the Holy Land. In this respect Christianity differs both from Judaism and from Islam. At the three pilgrimage festivals the Jews are commanded to appear before the Lord:

Three times in a year shall all thy males appear before the Lord thy God in the Place which he shall choose: in the feast of unleavened bread, and in the feast of weeks, and in the feast of tabernacles. (Deuteronomy XVI. 16 and Exodus XXIII. 14–17).

Similarly Islam enjoins every believer to visit Mecca, the birth-place of the Prophet, at least once in his life:

Pilgrimage to the House is due to God from people, whosoever is able to make the way thither (III, 91).

In both cases the pilgrimages are religious obligations, imposed by explicit commandment upon the whole community. The pilgrimage of a Christian, on the other hand, is voluntary and the result of a personal decision. Such voluntary pilgrimages became popular soon after the sites of Christ's birth and death had been discovered and the first churches had been erected upon them. Many believers from different parts of the world flocked to the Holy Land.

St Jerome (345–413), writing from Bethlehem, gave the following description:

Here one can see the most important people from everywhere . . . the best-known in Gaul . . . the Briton comes to seek a city which he

5

knows ... by what he has read of it in the Holy Scriptures. What shall we say of the Armenians, Persians, peoples of India and Ethiopia, from Egypt, Pontus, Cappadocia, Coeli-Syria, Mesopotamia, and all the crowds from the East.[1]

Thus the question arose whether pilgrimages to the Holy Places established a special spiritual link with Christ which could not be achieved elsewhere, and whether therefore they were a way towards salvation.

Church Fathers

Many of the Church Fathers were called upon to answer this question, and nearly all denied it. St Augustine (354–430) proclaimed: 'God is indeed everywhere, and He who created all things is not contained or shot in by any one place.'[2] He referred to the Gospel of St John:

The hour cometh when ye shall neither in this mountain nor yet at Jerusalem worship.... God is a Spirit and they that worship him must worship him in spirit and in truth. (John IV. 21, 24).

Similarly St John Chrysostomus (349–407):

The task is not to cross the sea, nor to undertake a lengthy pilgrimage. As individual men and women, both when we come to church and when we stay at home, let us earnestly call on God; He will grant all our requests.[3]

And St Gregory of Nyssa (335–94) wrote in a letter to a disciple who had asked for his guidance on this issue:

When the Lord invites the blest to their inheritance in the Kingdom of heaven, He does not include a pilgrimage to Jerusalem amongst their good deeds; when He announces the Beatitudes, He does not name amongst them that sort of devotion. What advantage, moreover is reaped by him who reaches those celebrated spots themselves? He cannot imagine that our Lord is living, in the body, there at the present day, but has gone away from us foreigners; or that the Holy Spirit is in abundance at Jerusalem, but unable to travel as far as us.... Change of place does not effect any drawing nearer unto God, but wherever thou mayest be, God will come to thee, if the chambers of thy soul be found of such a sort that He can dwell in thee and walk in thee. But if thou keepest thine inner man full of wicked thoughts, even if thou wast on Golgotha, even if thou wast on the Mount of Olives, even if thou stoodest on the memorial-rock of the Resurrection, thou wilt be as far away from receiving Christ into thyself, as one who has not even begun to confess Him. Therefore, my beloved friend, counsel the brethren to be absent from the body to go to our Lord, rather than to be absent from Cappadocia to go to Palestine.[4]

St Jerome on the other hand seemed to take a different stand, and he proclaimed the value of pilgrimages to the Holy Land. He himself was one of the most famous early pilgrims, and he spent the last thirty years of his life in Bethlehem. He considered it as 'part of the faith to adore where His feet have stood, and to see the vestiges of the nativity, of the Cross and of the passion'.[5] His reasons, however, are complex. On one side he stresses the emotional aspect, as when he urges a friend in Rome to join him in Palestine:

We shall be able to enter with you the cave of the Saviour, weep at the Sepulchre, kiss the wood of the Cross, and ascend . . . the Mount of Olives.[6]

On other occasions he uses a rational, almost secular argument when he maintains that knowledge of Palestine is as essential for the understanding of the Bible as knowledge of another country is for the understanding of its literature:

Just as one understands the Greek historians better when one has seen Athens, or the third book of Virgil when one has sailed to Troas or to Sicily . . . so we also understand the Scriptures better when we have seen Judaea with our own eyes . . . and discovered what still remains of ancient towns. That is why I myself took care to travel through this land.[7]

St Jerome had studied both Greek and Hebrew besides his native Latin. Anticipating Humisman by well over a thousand years, he was convinced that scholarly knowledge of the country and its languages was essential for the understanding of the Scriptures. To prove his case, he even fell back on Latin pagan antiquity by calling Cicero as witness:

If the great orator [he says] is right in demanding that Greek literature must be studied in Athens, and not in Lilybaeum; and that Latin literature must be studied in Rome, and not in Sicily, how can we consider having reached the summit of our studies without 'Our Athens'?[8]

Seen in this light the pilgrimages to Palestine could hardly be said to have a specific Christian character; the analogy with Greece and Rome was indeed ambiguous, and St Jerome himself describes the split in his heart by a dramatic account of a dream he had in his youth during a serious illness. Whilst the last rites were already being prepared for him, he dreamed that he was suddenly transported from complete darkness into the blinding light of the Last Judgement and found himself facing the Judge:

Questioned who I was, I replied I was a Christian. And He who presided answered: You lie, you are a Ciceronian, not a Christian.[9]

And he was sentenced to torture. But howsoever he combined these two strains of thought, he ultimately declared, with the other Fathers of the Church, that pilgrimages – although valuable – are not essential for salvation. He comforted a friend who could not make the journey that nothing was lacking in her faith because she did not see Jerusalem, and that those who enjoy the privilege of living there are in no way better than those who do not.[10]

The faithful will be judged not according to the places where they are, but on the merit of their faith. The Heavens are equally open over Jerusalem and over Britannia for the Kingdom of God is within you.

St Augustine, St John Chrysostomus, St Gregory and even St Jerome therefore agree that ultimately the place is irrelevant; that a change of place does not bring man nearer to redemption; that the Lord is to be adored not on this or that mountain, but in spirit and in truth; that the Kingdom of God is within us and that the gates of Heaven are open over Britain as over Jerusalem; that if the mind is corrupted neither Golgotha nor the Mount of Olives nor the monument of resurrection can help; and that the true pilgrimage is from the flesh to the spirit and not from Cappadocia to Palestine.

But in spite of this teaching the Holy Places took an increasingly strong hold on the Christian imagination. Even if pilgrimages could not lead to salvation, many felt that in the Holy Land they were nearer to the person of Christ. Few of the pilgrims, of course, followed St Jerome in studying the historical and geographical background of the Bible, let alone the Hebrew language, but they were drawn to the Holy Land by the memory of the sacred events, the persons involved and above all the Redeemer himself. Moreover, the effort and the moral discipline required to face the hardships of so long a journey were in themselves considered meritorious. Many pilgrims went to do penance, frequently to redeem most serious crimes. Others hoped to secure relics for reasons of piety or in the hope that they might possess the power to work miracles. Thus over the centuries pilgrimages to the Holy Land became an essential part of Christian life.

Crusades

At the time when the Church Fathers were debating the spiritual value of pilgrimages, Jerusalem was part of the Byzantine Empire and belonged, therefore, to the Christian world. The issue could thus be discussed on its religious merits without regard to political or military considerations. But the conquest of Jerusalem in 638 by the Arabs under Omar, changed the situation. Since Constantine the Great had accepted Christianity as the religion of the Roman Empire, the Government which controlled the Holy Places had been Christian. Now for the first time the Christian world was faced with the fact that its most sacred shrines were in the hands of the infidels. Could such a state of affairs be tolerated? The answer of the Crusaders was that the Holy Land had to be reconquered by force and to be ruled by a Christian kingdom. But it took several centuries for this attitude to develop. Omar himself had shown great tolerance to the vanquished. He had left the Church of the Holy Sepulchre to the Christians, and Christian services and pilgrimages continued. Later on friendly relations even developed between Charlemagne and Caliph Harum al Rashid who exchanged embassies and presents. The struggle between the Arabs and the West which extended from Spain, over the

Mediterranean, to the borders of the Byzantine Empire, was not conceived at first in religious terms. In the East a change occurred in the tenth century when the Byzantine armies under the Emperors Nicephorus and Jean Tzimesces, advanced into Syria and Galilee, taking Tiberias, Nazareth and Caesarea.

Up to that time, [says Runciman in the History of the Crusades[11]] there was no greater merit in dying in battle for the protection of the Empire against the infidel Arab than against the Christian Bulgar; nor did the Church make any distinction. But both Nicephorus and John declared that the struggle was now for the glory of Christendom, for the rescue of the Holy Places, and for the destruction of Islam. . . . Nicephorus emphasised that his wars were Christian wars . . . he saw himself as the Christian champion, and even threatened to march on Mecca to establish there the throne of Christ.

Similarly Jean Tzimesces, in a letter to the King of Armenia, describing his campaign of 974, wrote: 'Our desire was to free the Holy Sepulchre from the outrages of the Moslems,' and he adds that but for his halt before Tripoli, he would have gone to the Holy City of Jerusalem and prayed in the sacred places.

In the West likewise, up to the beginning of the eleventh century the Christian princes in the North of Spain were hardly conscious of the fact that 'they were involved in the sacred task of defending the Church'.[12] Some, when convenient, were even allied to Moslems, and El Cid, a national Christian hero of Spain, spent part of his life in the service of Moslem princes.

It was the Order of Cluny that brought about a change. Under its influence a Christian renaissance spread through France and Spain, uniting all forces and giving them the dynamic conviction that war against the infidels was a sacred duty for the Christian. The idea developed of a Christian Holy War against the unbelievers, a war which would give the soldiers of Christ forgiveness for their sins and eternal reward. In the beginning the vision did not extend as far as the Holy Land but concentrated on Spain and the sanctuary of St James of Compostella. But the idea of the '*Reconquista*' became an inspiration to Western Christendom and a fire which was soon to spread to the Eastern world.

The occasion came after the invasion of Asia Minor by the Ottoman Turks and the destruction of the Byzantine army at

Manzikert in 1071. The Emperor in Constantinople appealed for help, and Pope Gregory VII agreed to respond. The time seemed to have come for the West to take on the leadership for the defence of Europe.

I call to your attention [Gregory wrote to Henry IV, King of Germany] that the Christians beyond the sea, a great part of whom are being destroyed by the heathen with unheard of slaughter, have humbly sent to beg me to succour these our brethren in whatever ways I can, that the religion of Christ may not utterly perish in our time – which God forbid.

Envisaging the possibility of advancing to the Grave of the Lord, he continued:

Already more than fifty thousand men prepare themselves for this task and if they can have me as a leader and priest in the expedition, they are ready to rise with armed strength against the enemies of God and under the same leadership to advance unto the Grave of the Lord.[13]

No action was taken at that time, but twenty years later a similar situation arose. Emperor Alexius sent envoys from Constantinople to the Western world to ask for support against the Turks, and in November 1095, at the Council of Clermont, Pope Urban II issued his historic call for the First Crusade.

The overriding idea which inspired all was the unity of Christendom; the immediate purpose was to help Christians in the East and to liberate their Churches. It seems that in the beginning Jerusalem and the Holy Places were not the major concerns. In fact, Jerusalem had been in Moslem hands for more than four hundred years, and Christian pilgrimages had never entirely ceased although they had lately become difficult and dangerous. The main issue was the Turkish threat to the whole East, and to meet this threat was the first task of the campaign. The report on Urban's speech, written by Fulcher of Chartres, mentions neither Jerusalem nor the Christian Holy Places:

You must carry succour to your brethren dwelling in the East, and needing your aid, which they have so often demanded. For the Turks, a Persian people, have attacked them, as many of you know, and have advanced into the territory of Romania ... and occupying more and more the lands of those Christians, have already seven times conquered them in battle, have killed and captured many, have destroyed the churches and devastated the Kingdom of God. If you permit them for a time to remain unmolested, they will extend their sway more widely over many faithful servants of the Lord. Wherefore, I pray and exhort, nay not I, but the Lord prays and exhorts you, as heralds of Christ, to urge men of all ranks, knights and foot-soldiers, rich and poor, to hasten to exterminate this vile race from the land of our brethren, and to bear timely aid to the worshippers of Christ. . . . Moreover, the sins of those who set out thither, if they lose their lives on the journey, by land or sea, or in fighting against the heathen, shall be remitted in that hour; this I grant to all who go, through the power of God vested in me. . . . Let not those who are going, delay their journey, but having arranged their affairs and collected the money necessary for their expenses, when the winter ends and the spring comes, let them with alacrity start on their journey under the guidance of the Lord.[14]

In a letter written shortly afterwards to the princes in Flanders, the Pope himself, summarizing the events, refers to the Holy City as one of the victims of the devastation:

I believe you will have heard from many reports how the fury of the heathen has utterly devastated the churches of the Lord in the lands of the East and that they even have thrown into unbearable servitude the Holy City, made illustrious by the passion and resurrection of the Lord, with its churches. . . . In deep sympathy with these sufferings I journeyed to France and have exhorted princes and people to liberate the Eastern churches, and have urged them solemnly at the Council of Auvergne to this enterprise – for the forgiveness of their sins.[15]

Robert the Monk, in a report on the Pope's speech, gives Jerusalem and the Holy Places a central position:

Let the Holy Sepulchre of the Lord our Saviour which is possessed by unclean nations, especially incite you, and the Holy Places which are now treated with ignominy and irreverently polluted with their filthiness. . . . Enter upon the road to the Holy Sepulchre; wrest that land from the wicked race, and subject it to yourselves. That land which as the Scriptures says 'floweth with milk and honey' was given by God into the possession of the Children of Israel. Jerusalem is the navel of the world, the land is fruitful above others, like another paradise of delights. This the Redeemer of the human race has made illustrious by His advent, has beautified by residence, has consecrated by suffering, has redeemed by death, has glorified by burial. This royal city, therefore, situated at the centre of the world, is now held captive by His enemies, and is in subjection to those who do not know God, to the worship of the heathens. She seeks therefore and desires to be liberated, and does not cease to implore you to come to her aid. From you especially she asks succour, because God has conferred upon you above all nations great glory in arms. Accordingly undertake this journey for the remission of your sins, with the assurance of the imperishable glory of the Kingdom of Heaven.[16]

Whatever were the religious or political aims of the First Crusade,[17] it was the name of Jerusalem which resounded in the hearts of the masses, and the Holy Grave became the 'magic word' which drove the peoples forward. The Holy Places were the goal of the popular preachers, and the crusaders themselves were described by contemporary writers as 'Jerusalemites'. But more important still was the fact that the name of Jerusalem itself was linked with apocalyptical and eschatological conceptions.

It was [says Runciman] an age of visions. . . . Medieval man was convinced that the Second Coming was at hand. He must repent while yet there was time and must go out to do good. The Church taught that sin could be expiated by pilgrimage, and prophecies declared that the Holy Land must be recovered for the faith before Christ could come again. Further, to ignorant minds the distinction between Jerusalem and the New Jerusalem was not very clearly defined. Many believed that they would be led out of their present miseries to the land flowing with milk and honey of which the Scriptures spoke. The journey would be hard, there were the legions of Antichrist to be overcome. But the goal was Jerusalem the golden.[18]

On 15 July 1099, Jerusalem fell to the Christian armies. But the messianic expectations were not fulfilled. In the Holy City itself most of the Moslems were slaughtered; the Jews were burnt in their synagogue; the conquerors themselves were far from united; and in Europe – and indeed in the world at large – the Kingdom of God was in no way nearer than before. Moreover Jerusalem, now the capital of the Latin Kingdom, continued to be threatened by enemy forces, and the new task was to defend it against further onslaughts. In these circumstances the intellectual and emotional attachment of the Christian world to the Holy Places became even more intense. The first enthusiasm of the early Crusaders had been full of hope: the Holy Grave had to be liberated, and with that, the task would be completed. Now Jerusalem was in Christian hands but there was no peace and the future was fraught with danger. Thus a new theology of a rather sombre nature developed: with Jerusalem threatened, Christ Himself seemed to be involved in the suffering. But the danger of a new catastrophe presented a unique opportunity ... 'a special time for securing redemption by Christ's abundant grace'.

Bernard of Clairvaux[19] in his letter to the English people (in which incidentally he warns the Crusaders against persecution of the Jews) wrote:

Now is the acceptable time, now is the day of abundant salvation. The earth is shaken because the Lord of Heaven is losing his land, the land in which he appeared to men, in which he lived amongst men for more than thirty years; the land made glorious by his miracles, holy by his blood; the land in which the flowers of his resurrection first blossomed. And now, for our sins, the enemy of the Cross has begun to lift his sacrilegious head there, and to devastate with the sword that blessed land, that land of promise. Alas, if there should be none to withstand him, he will soon invade the very city of the living God, overturn the arsenal of our redemption, and defile the Holy Places which have been adorned by the blood of the Immaculate Lamb. They have cast their greedy eyes especially on the holy sanctuaries of our Christian religion, and they long particularly to violate that couch on which, for our sakes, the Lord of our life fell asleep in death. ... If they do but once lay hands upon these Holy Places, there shall be no sign or trace of piety left.

St Bernard then raises the question why God permits such a catastrophe to happen.

Is the hand of the Lord shortened and is he now powerless to work salvation so that he must call upon us, petty worms of the earth, to save and restore to him his heritage? Could he not send more than twelve legions of angels or even just say the word and save his land? Most certainly he has the power to do this whenever he wishes, but I tell you that God is trying you. ... He looks down from heaven to find one soul that reflects, and makes God its aim, one soul that sorrows for him. For God has pity on his people and has prepared for them a means of salvation. He does not want your death but rather that you should turn to him and live. He puts himself in your debt, so that in return for your taking up arms in his cause, he can reward you with pardon for your sins and ever-lasting glory. . . . I call blessed the generation that can seize an opportunity of such rich indulgence as this, blessed to be alive in this year of jubilee, this year of God's choice.

Such thoughts were repeated in numerous letters and sermons throughout the Western world and appeared as an expression of the true spirit of Christianity. But at the same time similar ideas were proclaimed on the other side in the world of Islam. [20] There too, the war against the 'infidels' from the West was a holy war. Islam, too, thought that victory required a purification of the soul; that spiritual reward could not be given to those who joined the fight for vainglory or material benefits, but was reserved for those who fought for the true glory of God, and like Christianity, Islam was certain that God, if he wished, could vanquish the enemy but that he wanted to test the faithful.

Were such the pleasure of God, [says the Koran] He could himself take vengeance upon the infidels; but He would rather prove the one of you by the other. And whoso fight for the cause of God their works he will not suffer to miscarry. . . . And he will bring them into the Paradise of which he has told them. (Sura, XLVII. 5).

When in spite of all entreaties and efforts, on 2 October 1187 Jerusalem again fell into the hands of the Moslems, the event was conceived by Christians as an insult to God Himself and the call went out to revenge the disgrace and injury which God, Christ and the Christian name had suffered.

Oh that the world would hearken [proclaimed Pope Gregory VIII] and all those who dwell in it, all those born of earth and the sons of men, rich and poor; that they would hearken at once together to one thing and grieve for the reverse which Christ has suffered and remember that they are indebted to Him for their redemption, and refuse to allow this injury to Christ to remain unavenged. [21]

For more than a hundred years writers and preachers repeated the call to avenge the injury which had been inflicted upon Christ, and the spiritual interpretation of the tragic event became more and more complex. Cardinal Henry of Albano, a Legate of Pope Gregory VIII, saw in the fall of Jerusalem a new crucifixion and a repetition of the mystery of the redemption:

Who would not suffer deepest grief for the sake of this holy ground upon which the Lord once has set his foot and which now is abandoned to defilement by the pagans; who would not cry bitterly over the sacrilegious theft of the Cross of the Redeemer trampled upon by the infidels; and who would not burst into tears about the profanation of the Holy Places. . . . How would the Redeemer have tolerated the rape of the Cross by the pagans, unless he was ready to let himself be crucified again by them? Thus the mystery of our redemption repeats itself.[22]

Furthermore, in his treatise *Lament over the capture of Jerusalem by the infidels*,[23] he dealt with the mysterious relationship between the earthly and the heavenly Jerusalem, pointing out that the former would have never fallen into the hands of the infidels if the true faith had not perished among Christians:

Indeed the loss of the earthly Jerusalem and the pollution of the Holy Land by the heathen is to be deeply deplored; but what is much worse is the cause of these events, namely the destruction of the spiritual Jerusalem. Had the faith among Christians not died, and had the scandal of their sins not spread far and wide, they would not have suffered the loss of the earthly Jerusalem and no earthly adversity could have befallen them.

He repeats the lamentations of Matathias in the book of the Maccabees: 'O that I have been born to see the destruction of my people and of the Holy City' (Maccabees I, Ch. ii) and comparing the Jewish and the Christian religions as he sees them, he adds:

If those who only lived in the flesh and revered celebrations in the flesh could bewail the profanation of their sanctuaries so disconsolately, 'what are we Christians to do who serve not in the oldness of the letter but walk in the newness of the Spirit?' (Romans VII. 5, 6.)

The earthly Jerusalem can become a symbol, a means to regain the heavenly city of salvation. The visible can lead to the invisible, the earthly to the heavenly, and the Cross and the Grave of the Lord are such visible sanctuaries.

The inscrutable wisdom of God desired to give to the Christians something visible in order that those who cannot lift themselves to the spiritual spheres may create themselves through the visible a ladder to the invisible.

Thus to him the earthly Jerusalem became a means to reach the spiritual city, a Jacob's ladder to the heavens. The liberation of the Holy Sepulchre, would lead therefore to the recovery of the True Jerusalem, the salvation of the soul.

It was natural that the theologians and preachers who propounded these thoughts took their images and examples from biblical material. The fall of Jerusalem to the Saracens of Saladin was likened to that of the biblical Jerusalem to Nebuchadnezzar, and the Crusaders were admonished to show the courage and determination of the Maccabees. Just as the children of Israel could only reach the Promised Land and could only be successful in battle after atonement for their sins, so the Crusaders would depend on religious and moral regeneration. But not only did the Christian preachers use biblical examples as means of exhortation and encouragement, the Christians felt themselves as successors of Israel and claimed the heir's right to possess the country, the Land of Promise:

We are descendants of the Holy Land [wrote the Dominican Stephan of Bourbon] both according to the flesh and the spirit. According to the flesh, because our father Adam was created here and like the other patriarchs is buried in this country; according to the spirit because our father Christ and our mother the Holy Virgin were born, lived, died and were buried here; moreover here our fathers the apostles were born and brought up, and here our mother the Church had its origin. Likewise the land is ours by the right of succession as far as we are the true children of God. . . .[24]

All these claims to the Land were derived from the Jewish past and based on the presumption that the Church had become the true Israel. But there was an additional argument which did not rest on history or tradition. It was the claim that Christ had bought the land by his blood:

This land belongs to us by the right of purchase and acquisition; for Christ bought it for us by his blood, has expelled the Jewish people from it by the might of the Romans and has handed it to Christendom.[25]

No attempt has ever been made to find a scriptural basis for this claim.

Finally an argument developed which sprang from the Christian medieval world of feudalism and especially from

Germanic concepts which had penetrated the world of Catholic thought. It was the idea that Christ was the supreme feudal Lord and that the Crusaders were his vassals. The Holy Land became the '*patrimonium Christi*', the inheritance of God; and just as the earthly vassal had to fight for his feudal Lord, the Christian knight had to fight for his Lord's restoration.[26]

What would you do, [wrote Bishop Henry of Strassburg] if one of you would witness how his lord was driven from his heritage and suffered violence? Surely you would consider it a disgrace not to take up arms on his behalf? How much more we all who belong as members to the Head of Christ and who owe to Him our whole life, ought to give Him all we are. . . . He who became man for our salvation, calls now for your help . . . the heritage of the Lord is at stake. . . .[27]

Similarly Martinus Parisius:

Therefore you warriors full of strength, hurry to the help of Christ, join the fellowship of His knights. . . . Use all your strength to lead Him back into His heritage from where He was so cruelly expelled. . . .[28]

And the words of Jacob of Vitry are even more exalted:

Christ is your supreme Emperor who invests all Christians with body, soul and earthly goods. When the liege lord has lost his inherited land his vassals are called upon to prove their loyalty. He who breaks faith with the Lord, rightfully loses his life. For he who has a fief from his liege lord and forsakes him, will rightfully be deprived of his fief.[29]

Thus the conceptions of chivalric feudal obligations were added to the ancient links which bound the Christian heart to the Grave of Christ and the Holy Land.

The theology of the Crusaders passed through various stages. In the beginning the thoughts of the Crusaders were directed to the liberation of the Holy Land for the sake of man's salvation, *pro animae salute*, with apocalyptic overtones about the Second Coming. After the conquest, when Jerusalem was threatened again with onslaughts of the unbelievers, the peril of the Sanctuaries was conceived as a unique opportunity, 'the acceptable time', for a supreme sacrifice. When Jerusalem was lost, its fall was felt as an insult to God, and the Crusaders were called upon to revenge the injury. Some even saw in the loss of Jerusalem a new Crucifixion, and the reconquest of the earthly Jerusalem appeared as a Jacob's ladder to the heavenly city of salvation. Lastly the Crusaders claimed the land as their heritage, seeing themselves as the spiritual successors of Israel and the beneficiaries of Christ's sacrifice; they proclaimed their duty to fight for His reinstatement in His patrimony and inheritance. Many of these strands were woven into a prayer, introduced by Pope Innocent III for daily recital after Holy Mass:[30]

Deus qui admirabili providentia cuncta disponis, te suppliciter exoramus ut terram quam unigenitus Filius tuus proprio sanguine consecravit de manibus inimicorum crucis eripiens restituas cultui Christiano, vota fidelium ad ejus liberationem instantium misericorditer dirigendo in viam salutis aeternae.

[O God, who by thy admirable providence disposest of all things, we humbly beseech Thee to restore to Christian worship, the land which thy only-begotten Son consecrated with His own blood; mercifully directing the vows of the faithful, who urge its liberation, upon the way of eternal salvation.]

Mysticism, Reformation, Humanism

The religious basis of the Crusades had been the conviction that the Holy Places of Christendom could not be left in the hands of a non-Christian Power, and therefore had to be restored by force to Christendom. But this conviction was soon attacked from many sides. First there were the mystics who longed for a union of the soul with God and believed that this could be achieved by a complete detachment of the heart from all external matters. Among these external matters – which to them were spiritually irrelevant – they counted sanctuaries and places of pilgrimage including even the shrines of the Holy Land, and they returned to the views of those Fathers of the Church who held that the heavens are equally open over Jerusalem and over Britain and that the Kingdom of God has to be found within man. Thus Master Eckhart (1260–1327) said:

Many are of the opinion that they must undertake much heavy work such as fasting, going barefoot and such like which is called penitence. But the true and best penitence is when man turns away from everything which is not God.

19

Similarly Thomas à Kempis in the *Imitatio Christi* (early fifteenth century) wrote:

They that go much on pilgrimage are but seldom the holier . . . there are many people who run off to various places to see relics of Saints. . . . When men go to see such things it is often out of curiosity and a wish for change of scenery; they come back but little inclined to amend their lives.

And even more striking:

The place wardeth but little if thou lack a fervent spirit; nor shall that peace long stand that is sought from without if the state of the heart be vacant of a right foundation.

Walter Hilton (died 1395) devoted in his *Ladder of Perfection* an entire chapter to pilgrimages to Jerusalem under the title 'How one who wishes to reach Jerusalem must have faith, be very humble and endure troubles of body and soul.'

Jerusalem, [he pointed out] spiritually interpreted is the vision of peace and symbolises contemplation in the perfect love of God. For contemplation is nothing other than the vision of Jesus, who is our true peace. Therefore, if you really desire to attain this blessed vision of true peace and to be a true pilgrim to Jerusalem, I will set you on the right road as far as I can. The beginning of this high road is the reformation in faith, which is grounded in humility, faith and the laws of the Church.[31]

For such pilgrimages to spiritual perfection no outward travel was required.

In this connection the medieval Christian hymn *Urbs Sino Aurea* may be mentioned, which many centuries after its composition conquered the Western world under the name *Jerusalem the Golden*. It was written by a Cluniac monk at a time when the Holy Land was in the hands of the Crusaders. But the whole poem – *Hora novissima* – of which the hymn is a part ignores this fact, and in mystical ecstasy sings only of the Heavenly City, the City beyond time, the Paradise.

In addition to the mystics, there were rebellious movements within the Church such as the Hussites in Bohemia, the Lollards in England, and the Waldensians in Savoy and Piedmont. In 1395 the Lollards summarised their beliefs in the Twelve Conclusions, in which they denounced pilgrimages, among other things, as idolatry:

And we ask you pilgrim when you make an offering to the en-shrined relics of saints in some place, whether you intend to relieve the need of the saint or that of the almshouse for the poor which is so well endowed?

The Reformation in its attitude to sanctuaries and pilgrimages followed similar lines. Luther in his *Appeal to the Christian Nobility of German Nationality*, wrote:

Simple-minded folk are often misled in a wrong illusion and misunderstanding of the Divine Laws. Then they believe that pilgrimages are valuable and good deeds, but if repeated they are evil deeds and God has not decreed them. They are devilish ghosts and the money and the work which are being spent on a pilgrimage should be used a thousand times better for the maintenance of one's family and for the poor.

In the *Confession of Augsburg* of 1538 which was drawn up by Melanchton, pilgrimages were described as 'childish and useless works'. Zwingli, in his sixty-seven Articles said: 'Time and place are subject to the Christian man and not man to them; therefore those who bind themselves to time and place, deprive the Christian of his freedom.' (Article 25). And Calvin in numerous sermons fulminated against pilgrimages, main-taining that the pilgrimages favoured by the Papacy were without value, and that they had no foundation in the Scriptures.

Apart from these religious attitudes there were developments of a different kind. In 1453 the Ottoman Turks had conquered Constantinople, and in 1517, took Jerusalem from the Egyptian Mameluks. Their position had become unassailable and there was no longer any question of a reconquest of the Holy Places. Moreover, the loss of the Holy Grave, although lamented by many, was no longer felt as a 'new Crucifixion'; men no longer believed that the liberation of the Holy Land was essential for their salvation or happiness, and gone were the apocalyptic ideas of the great preachers. The European mind had turned to other ventures. The Americas were discovered, the Cape was circumnavigated. Commerce developed between Europe and the Middle East. Palestine was seen not so much as the Holy Land but as part of the Levant; and the Turks were no longer the 'accursed race' described by Pope Urban, 'utterly alienated from God, degenerate and despised', but had become a member

21

of the family of nations. It was under these changed conditions that Francis I, King of France, after his defeat at Pavia by the German Emperor, turned to Turkey, and in 1535 concluded an alliance between France, 'the eldest daughter of the Church' and the Ottoman Empire, the leading Islamic power of the time.

Francis I did not share the eschatological visions of the Crusading era. His world was that of the Renaissance. He had brought Benvenuto Cellini and Leonardo da Vinci to his court. He and his friends did not long for pilgrimages to Jerusalem. They were attracted and fascinated by the intellectual rediscovery of the ancient world; and this included a new understanding of the biblical writings through the study of Hebrew and Greek, the languages in which the Holy Scriptures had been written. Like St Gregory of Nyssa, they did not want to go from 'Cappadocia to Palestine'. Instead they wanted to proceed from the 'translation' to the 'original source'. Up till then, Latin had been the language of scholarship and learning in Europe. Now Greek and Hebrew were brought to the fore. In 1518, under the influence of Erasmus, the first Trilingual College had been established in Louvain for the study of Greek, Latin and Hebrew, and in 1530, Francis I – five years before his treaty with Turkey – appointed the first *Lecteurs Royaux* in the fields of Hebrew, Greek and Mathematics – who, independent from the University of Paris and its theological faculty, pursued their work under the protection of the King himself. They maintained that the knowledge of Greek and Hebrew was essential for the full understanding of the Holy Writ, an opinion which the theologians of the Sorbonne condemned as '*scandalosa et ridiculosa*'. These latter felt that mere grammarians were in no way qualified to understand religious writings and maintained that what was required was a '*spiritus mysticus*'. This conflict between the Scholastic and the Renaissance world was in 1534 brought before the Court in one of the most extraordinary cases of legal history in which Parliament was asked to decide whether or not the knowledge of Hebrew and Greek was essential to the understanding of the Bible, and the controversy became a *cause celèbre* of the time.[32] This was the intellectual atmosphere in which in 1535 the first treaty between a European state and the Ottoman Empire was concluded. It opened a new era in the relationship between the Christian Powers and Islam, and became the pattern for a long series of treaties or 'capitulations' extending over several centuries.*

The Early Capitulations

Essentially all these treaties were concerned with commerce and politics. But at the same time they revealed a new attitude to the Holy Places. Western Christians no longer aimed at the re-conquest of the sanctuaries. They were satisfied with the right to visit them; and in the beginning they did not even claim this right.

The treaty of 1535 consisted of seventeen articles, sixteen of which deal with commerce and business. It laid down that the subjects of both countries should freely and safely, with their belongings, navigate or travel on land, for the purposes of trade, to their respective countries. They should be free to buy or sell and move from one country to another all kinds of merchandise and should not be subject to paying more than the ordinary customs' duty. The treaty contained detailed regula-tions concerning jurisdiction, the fulfilment of contracts, and the right to dispose of property by will. It protected French merchants and their agents from being pressed into military service, and arranged that ships of both countries should show the usual courtesy on the high seas when meeting each other by lowering the sails and hoisting the flags of their rulers. One article only, Article 6, referred to religion and read as follows:

Likewise as regards religion it has been expressly promised, concluded and agreed, that the said merchants, their agents and servants, and all other subjects of the King shall never be molested nor tried by the *cadis, sand-jak-beys,* or *soubashis,* or any person but the *Sublime Porte* only, and they cannot be made or regarded as Turks (Mohammedans) unless they themselves desire it and profess it openly and without violence. They shall have the right to practise their own religion.[33]

The right of trading merchants to practise their own religion was all that remained of the far-reaching and glorious aims of the Crusades. The Holy Places were not mentioned in the treaty, nor were Jerusalem and Bethlehem. The treaty of 1535 was followed by two more agreements with France. The first, of

*The word 'capitulation' derives originally not from the contents of the Treaties but from their form, i.e. the succession of 'little chapters' or *'capitula'*.

1569, was entirely devoted to commerce. It concentrated on cotton, wax, skins, shipwreck, and jurisdiction.

The second, of 1581, had similar contents. But it contained an item which for a long time to come played a dominant part in French policy, by establishing the right of precedence for the Ambassador of France. Whilst the true Crusaders had approached the Holy Land with penitence and profound humility, the spirit of the new age was expressed in the following Clause, often to be repeated in the future:

Whereas the above-mentioned Emperors of France, whose family and race is supreme and recognised above all Princes of this world who adore the Messiah, and whereas the Emperor is the Most Ancient and the Most Exalted of all Kings, and besides this since the days of our Illustrious predecessors up till the present, there has never been anybody greater at our Sublime Porte, nor has shown greater friendship to us. . . . Ambassadors of France who come to our Imperial and Divine Council, shall be above the Ambassadors of Spain and the other Princes and Kings of Christendom. And the Ambassadors of France shall have forever precedence at Court.[34]

During the same century the Republic of Venice, too, entered into three treaties with Turkey. Here again religion played no part and the Holy Places themselves were not mentioned. The Netherlands, too, entered a treaty in 1598, likewise without any reference to religious issues.

The seventeenth century saw a slight change in the situation. France concluded a new capitulation in 1604, and this time it was laid down – among a large number of commercial items – that the subjects of the Emperor of France should be entitled to visit the Holy Places:

It is our wish and command that the subjects of the Emperor of France and those of the Princes who are his friends or allies may visit under his protection freely the Holy Places of Jerusalem without any hinderance being put in their way.

At the same time a completely new element was introduced by the addition of the proviso that the monks residing in Jerusalem should be entitled to continue with their services . . . 'that the monks who live in Jerusalem and serve in the Church of the Holy Sepulchre of our Lord Jesus Christ, may stay there, come and go securely without any trouble or disturbance.'[35]

In 1612 the Netherlands concluded a new treaty with Turkey. One of its sixty-four Articles referred to religion and stipulated that Dutch subjects and their servants should be entitled to visit Jerusalem, although they were Protestants:

Neither the monks in the Church of the Holy Sepulchre nor anyone else is to hinder them and to say: 'You are Lutherans, we do not want to let you see the places!' But they must show them the places which it is customary to see without any opposition or excuse.[36]

The issue to them therefore was not so much to worship at the Holy Places, but to see them; and when in 1680 the treaty was renewed this was made even clearer by the use of the word *'besichtigen'* which may well be translated as 'sightseeing'. A treaty concluded in 1675 between Britain and Turkey did not make any allusion to religion in its seventy-five Articles.

When in 1670 Louis xiv had seized Lorraine and prepared for war against Holland, the German philosopher Leibnitz, who at that time was in the service of the elector of Mainz, submitted a memorandum to the French King in which he suggested that France instead of attacking the Netherlands should undertake the conquest of Egypt and join the German Emperor in a crusading war against Turkey which would unite European Christendom.[37] Relations between France and Turkey at that time were strained, and for some time Louis xiv seems to have considered the proposal. But ultimately the French Secretary of State, Simon Arnauld de Pomponne wrote: 'I have nothing against the plan of a holy war but such plans since the days of St Louis have ceased to be the fashion'. In 1673 France concluded a new capitulation with Turkey, leaving the Christian nations divided as before. Neither this new capitulation nor any other treaties which between 1535 and the French Revolution were concluded by a Western Power with Turkey contained a single clause about the Christian minorities in the Ottoman Empire.

Enlightenment

During the eighteenth century the influence of the Western Powers and particularly France in the Ottoman Empire reached unprecedented proportions, and Turkey had to grant valuable privileges in many fields. In the religious sphere the rights of

Christian pilgrims were solemnly assured. But paradoxically by that time the movement of Western pilgrims had nearly come to an end. There were, according to a contemporary traveller, in 1697 still 'some Popish pilgrims in Jerusalem' but they seem to have died out altogether in the eighteenth century.[38] This was not due to any difficulties created by the Turks, but to the profound change of mind which had taken place in France itself. Christianity was no longer the dominant force. On the contrary, in the era of Bayle, Montesquieu, Diderot and Voltaire, it became fashionable to deride its teaching and to jeer at the Christians 'who quarrelled about a Grave; although they all agreed that the Grave was empty'. But, Christianity was not only derided, it was attacked and made responsible for the existing ills of men and society.

It was more than a reformation that the eighteenth century demanded. It was the total overthrow of the Cross, the utter repudiation of the belief that men had ever received a direct communication from God, of the belief in other words, in Revelation. It was nothing short of an attempt to achieve the total defeat, the complete annihilation of religion that was now the object.[39]

Men did not thirst any longer for Salvation, but for earthly happiness; and happiness was to be found through Enlightenment. The light however was not that of which St John had spoken – 'the light which shineth in the darkness, and which the darkness comprehendeth not' – the new light was Reason, and Reason was proclaimed by the Revolution as the legitimate successor of Christianity and the ultimate guide of man.

Napoleon I

On 1 July 1798, Napoleon landed his troops at Alexandria. It was the first time since the Crusades that a French Army set out to conquer Egypt and Palestine. This time however, the goal was not the Holy Grave. The Order of the Day, issued a few days before the landing, made the purpose of the expedition clear: it was to deal 'a mortal blow at England'. But the order also contained instructions concerning religion:

The people amongst whom we are going to live, are Mohammedans; the first article of their faith is: 'There is no other God but Allah and Mahomet is his prophet'. Do not argue with them: behave

26

towards them as we behaved towards the Jews and the Italians! show respect to their *muftis* and *imams* as you have to rabbis and bishops. Have for the mosques and the ceremonies prescribed by the Koran the same tolerance that you showed for convents and synagogues, for the religions of Moses and Jesus Christ. The Roman Legions protected all religions. You will find here customs different from those of Europe; you must get used to them.[40]

A proclamation to the people of Egypt read as follows: 'You will be told that I have come to destroy your religion, do not believe it ... more than the Mamelukes I respect God, his Prophet and the Koran.' On 3 July the following order was issued: 'The Commander-in-Chief wishes the Turks to carry out their acts of worship in the mosques, as in the past; he expressly forbids all Frenchmen, military or otherwise, to enter the mosques or to collect at the door of a mosque.'[41]

According to one of his biographers Napoleon considered all religions as sacrosanct, particularly because of their stress on obedience and authority. He even wrote once: 'In religion I see the mystery of the social order.' But the full benefit from a people's religion could only be gained if he convinced those whom he was ruling that their religion was also his. 'It was by making myself a Catholic,' he said, 'that I won the war in the Vendé, by making myself a Moslem that I established myself in Egypt. ... If I were to govern a nation of Jews I would rebuild the Temple of Solomon.'[42]

To his soldiers he gave the example of the Roman legions who in supreme indifference had protected all religions alike, and he made great efforts to convince the Moslems that if he personally did not share, he at least greatly respected their religion. And as if this was not enough, he proclaimed himself proudly an enemy of the Pope:

Cadis, sheiks, imams, tell the people that we are friends of the true Moslems. Is it not we who have destroyed the Pope, who called for war against the Moslems? Is it not we who have destroyed the Knights of Malta, because these madmen believed God wished them to fight the Moslems? Is it not we who have been through the centuries the friends of the Sultan – (may God grant his desires) – and the enemies of his enemies?[43]

At the Feast of the Prophet, he took part in the celebrations with great pomp and issued the following order of the day:

Governors of Provinces will make known by means of a circular in Arabic, which will be sent to all villages, the pomp with which the Feast of the Prophet has been celebrated in Cairo. In living memory there has been none more brilliant. All troops in Cairo marched by torchlight to visit the Sheik El-Bekry. The Commander-in-Chief dined there, together with Mustapha Pasha and all the principal officers. The Commander-in-Chief was present at the reading of Arabic poems in honour of the prophet, after which, in the midst of the great sheiks, he had prayers said and the genealogy of the Prophet recited.[44]

In February 1799 he set out for Palestine. He explained the reasons in a report to the Executive Directory in Paris:

I have three aims in the operation: 1 to assure the conquest of Egypt by the establishment of a strong point beyond the desert.
2   to force the Porte to take up a position supporting negotiations.
3   to prevent the English cruisers from drawing supplies from Syria.[45]

Christianity and its sanctuaries certainly were not his motives for the expedition, and when he was at Ramle, the ancient Arimathia, on 1 March he declared, 'Jerusalem does not lie on my line of march'.[46]

Napoleon spent three months in the country, in cruel battles both against the Turks and the plague, conquering Gaza, Jaffa and Haifa, and laying siege to Acre. In his efforts to rouse all possible opponents against the Turks, he apparently also tried to enlist the support of the Jews. The *Gazette Nationale*, a paper issued in Paris by the French Republican Government, reported from Constantinople under the 28 Germinal of that year:

Bonaparte had a proclamation issued in which he invites all Jews of Asia and Africa to come and place themselves under his colours; in order to re-establish ancient Jerusalem. He has already a great number of them armed and their battalions threaten Aleppo.

How far the last sentence in this report is true may be doubtful. But he seems to have considered at that time even further steps towards a restoration of the Jews to Palestine.[47]

One night he slept at Nazareth. 'Before entering the village' says Comte de Lavallette, then Bonaparte's aide-de-camp, 'he stopped at an ancient fountain where a number of cattle were drinking. There the chief personages of the village met him;

everything recalled the ancient scenes that are so naively described in the Bible. The French were received with much joy by the Christian population and General Bonaparte and his staff spent the night at the monastery of Nazareth.'[48]

Some of the soldiers – Voltairians or atheists – joked about Nazareth. But others, in the words of the biographer, 'suddenly remembered that they were born Christians. Nazareth revived their childhood memories of the Gospels, of First Communion, of the church bells that had been silenced in France for six years, and on the morning their victories were celebrated by a solemn *Te Deum.*'

The next day Napoleon returned to the siege of Acre. But when all attacks on the fortress had failed, he returned to Egypt with the remnant of his army, without ever having tried to enter Bethlehem or the Holy Sepulchre. Jerusalem indeed did not lie on his line of march.

Romanticism

The scene changed with the rise of the Romantic Movement. Whilst the thinkers of the Enlightenment and of the French Revolution had placed their hopes in the future, the Romantics looked back on the lost Paradise of the past; and whilst the former trusted in progress through the spread of Reason, the latter longed for a revival of a Universal Christendom, and the medieval world appeared to them as a golden age of mankind. 'Those were beautiful and glorious times,' wrote the German poet Novalis[49] in 1799, 'when Europe was one Christian country, when one Christendom inhabited this humanely civilized Continent. . . . Rome itself had become Jerusalem, the sacred capital of Divine Government of Earth.' And as a hope for the future he added: 'only religion can re-awaken Europe, give security to its peoples and restore Christendom visibly in renewed glory.' In his novel, '*Heinrich von Ofterdingen,*' he described how in a German castle the knights spoke of the Holy Land, of the miracles of the Holy Grave, the adventures of their campaign and expressed their indignation that the Heavenly birthplace of Christendom still was in the sacrilegious hands of the infidels; and in his '*Kreuzlied*' (Song of the Cross) he wrote:

> *Das Grab steht unter wilden Heiden;*
> *Das Grab worin der Heiland lag,*
> *Muss Frevel und Verspottung leiden*
> *und wird entheiligt jeden Tag.*
> *Es klagt heraus mit dumpfer Stimme:*
> *Wer rettet mich von diesem Grimme?*
> *Hinueber zu der heilg'en Staette,*
> *Des Grabes dumpfe Stimme toent*
> *Bald wird mit Sieg und mit Gebete*
> *Die Schuld der Christenheit versoehnt*
> *Das Reich der Heiden wird sich enden*
> *Ist erst das Grab in unseren Haenden.*

[The Grave stands among savage pagans, the Grave of the Redeemer must suffer sacrilege and mockery and is defiled day by day. From it a sombre voice laments – Who will save me from this rage? Forward to the Holy Place, sounds the sombre voice of the Grave. Soon will the guilt of Christendom be redeemed with Victory and Prayer, the Realm of the pagans will pass away once the Grave is in our hands again.]

In their imagination the Romantics relived and idealised the events and deeds of the Middle Ages. It was an era of fairy tales, of '*Maerchen*,' folk songs and knightly ballads, culminating in the stories of the Crusades with their mystique of chivalry, piety and oriental magic. Chateaubriand published *Le Génie du Christianisme* and himself made a pilgrimage to Jerusalem. Victor Hugo wrote his *Notre Dame de Paris* which extolled the mysteries of the Cathedral itself. Sir Walter Scott was attracted by the Crusades throughout his whole literary career, and it is reported that a Russian count, one of his readers, was so impressed by his stories about Richard Coeur-de-Lion and Saladin that he set out to the Holy Land himself; and there were probably others who acted likewise. But the new pilgrims, in the words of the historian Temperley 'were often only travellers who went to write books and to paint pictures. The Holy Places were objects of sentiment rather than of devotion, and pilgrimage was a mode rather than a passion.'

Chateaubriand had 'wreathed his pilgrim's cross with lilies', but he himself in the *Itinéraire de Paris à Jerusalem* said 'I went to search for images, that is all'; and his biographer, Friedrich Sieburg, adds:

His desire was for distant lands, sea voyages, signs of antique greatness and holy places. He wanted to see Athens and seize the spirit of antiquity in its haunted ruins, but he wanted even more to visit Jerusalem and bow down before the Holy Sepulchre, as the second of his name to do so, the first having trodden the sacred soil as a Crusader.[50]

But he intended to return via Spain to meet there his beloved who secretly had travelled from Paris to the rendezvous. Chateaubriand writing of it later did not conceal the fact that the whole journey from Paris via Corfu, Athens and Constantinople to Jerusalem – where he, the author of *Le Génie du Christianisme* had been received solemnly into the Order of the Holy Sepulchre – was merely a detour to Granada.

Did I visit, [he wrote] the tomb of Christ as a penitent? I was preoccupied by one thought alone. I counted the moments impatiently. On board my ship I kept my eyes on the evening star and begged it for favourable winds and fame, for the sake of being loved.

Interlude: The Holy See for Jerusalem

A strange, if not bizarre, post-Romantic suggestion concerning Jerusalem was made during the struggle for Italian independence and unification. The existence of the Papal States with their temporal power appeared to many as incompatible with the fulfilment of the national hopes. The 'Roman Question' became a central issue of European politics, both in the political and the religious sense. In France which at that time maintained troops in Rome to protect the Pope the debate was passionate. Numerous pamphlets were issued by both sides, many of them anonymously, although some of the authors were leading figures in French political, intellectual and religious life. There will be no possibility, proclaimed one of the pamphleteers, for the Papacy to maintain its position in Rome.

Rome has ceased to be a Christian city. The Papacy will perish there, suffocated by the circle of its enemies which is drawing tighter and tighter. The moment has come when the successor of the apostles must leave the Vatican which he had filled with his greatness and saintliness, to make room for a Garibaldi whose followers undoubtedly will flock to town in search of revolutionary benedictions which will be dispensed *urbi* and *orbi*.[51]

31

He then investigates whether any other Catholic country could offer refuge and security to the Supreme Pontiff and reaches the conclusion that the spread of the revolution will make this impossible.

In the whole of Europe there does not exist one nation where the Holy Father could wear his tiara in security; there does not exist one single people which might not one day consider the Papacy as a burden and a hindrance for the realisation of its revolutionary hopes. Whereto will Pius IX carry the tomb of St Peter? Whereto will he summon the Sacred College of his Cardinals? From which holy mountain will he spread his hands to bless the world?

The author of the pamphlet gives the answer:

There is only one city in the world which by its position, its past, its future, its conditions, its memories, and by its universal influence can replace for the Christian world Rome, invaded by the revolution: this is Jerusalem, Cradle and Tomb of Christ, Mother of all true religions. Jerusalem is the city of God, the Holy City above all.

Comparing Rome with Jerusalem he continues:

In Rome, secular antiquity always mingles with the great souvenirs of Christianity. True, she is the capital of the Christian world. But she is even more the city of the emperors, the great Roman world altogether. Her catacombs belong to the saints and martyrs; but her temples, her ruins, her Colosseum, all that attracts the scholar and artist are her pagan ruins and her pagan dust. Rome is the city of the confessors and martyrs. She guards the tomb of the first Pope, but she also guards the Arch of Titus, the Temple of Vesta, the baths of the emperors and their triumphal columns. If you rake up the Roman ground there may rise a Venus or a Jupiter, some shameless Leda or even some infamous deified Caesar like Heliogobale. Ask Jerusalem and Palestine and you will find nothing but the idea of God.

And reminding his readers that only a year ago France had participated in the war against China to avenge the murder of Western missionaries he called for a new crusade:

Yesterday we carried the war into the capital of the Chinese Empire in order to free our commerce from the Chinese extortions and to restore to the Christian cult the buildings which had been seized. How can we hesitate today to liberate Jerusalem and to restore to her her glorious and saintly past by installing there the Holy See which the European revolution threatened at its source in Rome. . . . May the Mazzinis and Garibaldis establish themselves in Rome. But let us open Syria to the Sovereign Pontiff of the Christian world. Let us detach Syria from the Ottoman Empire and fulfill the great idea of the crusades: the emancipation of Christendom on the tomb of the Redeemer.

Russia

From the middle of the nineteenth century onwards Christian missionary and educational activities throughout the Middle East – and in particular in Palestine – multiplied. Catholics, Anglicans, Protestants of many sects, and Orthodox emulated each other. Churches, monasteries and convents were built, and hospitals, schools and colleges were established. But nowhere at that time was the religious interest in the Middle East deeper and more intense than in Russia. Since the fall of Constantinople to the Turks in 1453 Russia had considered herself the heir and successor of Byzantium. She had added to her ancient coat of arms the Byzantine double eagle and in some mystical vision saw in Moscow the 'Third Rome'. Already in the early sixteenth century the monk Philothey had proclaimed Moscow's sacred role in a famous letter to Basil III, Grand-Prince of Moscow (1505–33):

The Church of old Rome fell for its heresy; the gates of the second Rome, Constantinople, were hewn down by the axes of the infidel Turks; but the Church of Moscow, the new Rome, shines brighter than the sun over the whole universe. . . . Two Romes have fallen, but the third stands fast; a fourth there cannot be. Thy Christian Kingdom shall not be given to any other ruler.[52]

Russia soon felt herself responsible for the existence and the defence of Eastern Christendom; and at a time when in the West rationalism and religious indifference dominated the scene, Russia experienced some of the spirit of the Crusades. She would restore Constantinople to its glory as a Christian city with the Hagia Sophia as the crown of Christendom. But more than that: her action would lead to a reunion of the Orthodox Churches and indeed of Christendom as a whole. Her mission was messianic.

B*   33

Sooner or later, [wrote Dostoevsky] 'Constantinople must be ours. It is not only the famous harbour, not alone the way to the seas and oceans, not even the unification and the awakening of the Slav peoples that links Russia so closely to the portentous question. Our task lies deeper, infinitely deeper. We Russians are really indispensable for Christendom in its entirety in the East and for the future of Orthodoxy on earth. . . . In one word, this terrible Eastern question contains nearly the whole of our destiny; it contains all our tasks, above all our only way into the fullness of world history. And there lies at the same time our ultimate conflict and our ultimate reunion with Europe. . . . Sooner or later Constantinople must needs be ours, even if we have to wait until the next century. . . .[53]

Such visions were very different from those prevailing in the West; and this difference reveals itself in the nature of the pilgrimages of that period. In the West pilgrimages had become largely matters of sentiment and inspiration. But the masses of Russian pilgrims who under most difficult conditions flocked to the Holy Land searched for salvation. Laurence Oliphant in his *Land of Gilead* in 1880 described these pilgrims:

Every year about four thousand Russian pilgrims, composed largely of discharged soldiers, make painful and laborious journeys to visit the sacred shrines, and it is impossible not to be struck by the air of fanatical superstition which characterises them.

And dealing with the possibility of a Holy Russian War, he adds:

The Congress of Berlin amounted to a European coalition against Russian aggression on Turkey in Europe, which must put an end, henceforth and ever, to the designs on her part of Constantinople . . . she can henceforth concentrate her energies on conquest in Asiatic Turkey and in accomplishing even more effectively the objects which she had proposed to herself. The temptation to the Russian population would be the fascination of a religious war which should have for its object the conquest of the Holy Places at Jerusalem. Russia at Alexandretta could not stop there; an advance on Jerusalem would be imperatively demanded by the religious sentiment of the country; and indeed, to judge by the site which she has chosen for the Hospice (in Jerusalem) she seems to have anticipated the contingency. It commands the whole town and is thought by many to be in a position designedly of military strength.[54]

Whilst Oliphant stressed the political and military aspect of the pilgrimages, Stephen Graham, in his book *With the Russian Pilgrims in Jerusalem*[55] described the human side:

The Russian pilgrims feel that when they have been to Jerusalem the serious occupations of their life are all ended. They take their death-shrouds to the Jordan, and wearing them, bathe in the sacred river. All in white, on the banks where John baptised, they look like the awakened dead on the final Resurrection Morning. They spend a night in the sepulchre of Christ, and, receiving the sacred Fire, extinguish it with caps that they will wear in their coffins. They mostly hope to die in the Holy Land, preferably near the Dead Sea where the Last Judgement will take place. If indeed they must return to their native villages in Russia, it will be to put their affairs in order and await death.

I suppose, [he continued] the Russian pilgrims read the gospel every day in Lent. Those who could read, read it aloud; and those who could not read, listened. They lived the evangel. I felt the mystery when an aged beggar came and sanctified our wooden beads every morning before dawn in the Holy Week, burning incense in an old tin-can on a stick and making the sign of the Cross over us with the dense fragrant smoke ... or when a woman all in laughing tears kissed our feet and asked our forgiveness seeing that she, a sinful woman, had reached Jerusalem.

The Revolution of 1917 brought Russian expansion and munificence in Palestine, and the stream of Russian pilgrims to the Holy Grave to an end – at least for the time being. Another tomb was built in Red Square in Moscow which is visited annually by millions, and which probably has been seen in the few decades of its existence by more visitors than the Holy Sepulchre since the day of the Crucifixion.

Jet Pilgrimages

Today pilgrimages by aeroplane from almost every country are available to multitudes at moderate prices. It is possible to visit within a few days nearly all the Sanctuaries. A leading travel agency, which specialises in this field announces that 'one may leave London on Tuesday afternoon and be back on Sunday afternoon'. 'Based in Jerusalem, you will visit all Holy Places including Galilee, Nazareth, Tiberias, Capernaum, Bethlehem, the Dead Sea, Jericho, the River Jordan, Mount of Olives, Garden of Gethsemane, Bethany, the Pools of Siloam and Bethesda, the Wailing Wall, the Golden Gate, the site of Solomon's Temple, Pilate's Courtyard, and the Way of the Cross leading to Calvary and the Holy Sepulchre.'

In the past a pilgrimage required infinite time and an almost complete abandonment of earthly interests. The 'jet pilgrim' of our era can fit his pilgrimage easily into the routine of his normal life.

Conclusion

Through all changes and divisions of Christian history certain fundamental attitudes towards the Sanctuaries have remained untouched and are held by all. Firstly, Christianity – contrary to Judaism and Islam – does not know a duty of the faithful to visit any sanctuary. Christian pilgrimages are voluntary and are not considered as essential for salvation. This is true even for the era of the Crusades. For the call to liberate the Holy Land from the rule of the infidels did not go out to Christians as such, but to the soldiers of Christ. The purpose of the Crusades was not so much a pilgrimage but to make pilgrimages possible again for all who wanted to undertake them; and even after Jerusalem had been conquered and the Latin Kingdom had been established, pilgrimages did not become an obligatory part of the Christian faith.

Secondly, Christians of all denominations at all times have felt with St Jerome the urge 'to adore where His feet have stood and to see the vestiges of the Nativity, of the Cross and of the Passion'. The cause of this urge is not the belief that prayers in the Holy Land have a greater spiritual power than prayers elsewhere. Nor is it the assumption that the divine presence there has a particular intensity. For to the Christian 'the heavens are equally open over Jerusalem and over Britain'. The attachment to the Holy Places springs from another source, namely the love of the faithful for the person of Christ; love for Christ the human being – *homo factus est* – and this love is shared by many who cannot be considered Christians in the strict sense of the word. Just as in ordinary life, we are drawn to the places associated with those who were dear to us, and visit their graves to be near to them, thus the Christian is drawn to the Sanctuaries for the sake of his love for Christ, and he seeks in the place His person. This love which to the Christian is eternally new and fresh, runs like a golden thread through the whole texture of Christian history and is running also through the

present period of doubt, indifference and contradictory ideo-
logies. It is the ultimate root and essence of the Christian
attachment to the Holy Places, and independent from theology
and dogmatic controversies will prevail as long as Christianity
itself.

2 The Holy Places and the Division of the Church

The history of the Christian Holy Places has been dominated by the division of the Church; and in many ways this division has influenced their fate more profoundly than the fact that Palestine has been under Moslem rule for more than a thousand years. For the Moslems during the whole period of their reign only very rarely interfered with the Christian shrines. The colourful descriptions of alleged desecrations of Christian Sanctuaries by the Moslems 'a people who do not know God' – which were spread by preachers and writers of the Crusading era were on the whole unfounded and were the products of imagination. In principle, Moslems treated the Christian populations under their control in accordance with the prescriptions of the Koran, as a 'people of the Book', and accepted them as a recognised minority; and whilst the status of the Christians (like that of the Jews) was inferior to that of the followers of Mohammet, it was based on established rights and duties and in that respect at least was stable. The division of the Church on the other hand, led to continued struggle, sometimes even violent strife, between the Christian communities, and created a permanent tension among them with ever-repeated efforts to exclude each other from the Sanctuaries.

The schism of the Church had not started at the Holy Places. Nor were the Sanctuaries the original objects of the conflict. But whilst Catholic Rome and Orthodox Byzantium were separated by nearly a thousand miles, Western and Eastern Christians faced each other in the small space of the Sanctuaries in permanent confrontation. Accordingly the Holy Places became the meeting ground if not the battlefield of the opposing parties. Moreover there was no framework in existence in which the Churches could discuss the dogmatic and liturgical issues which divided them. As a result the conflict expressed itself in a struggle for the physical possession of the Holy Shrines. The Sanctuaries became the objects of the conflict and almost the symbol of the schism; and up to the present day the attitudes of the different Churches to the general political issues concerning Jerusalem and the country as a whole, are largely determined by their position in the internal Christian conflict about the rights on and within the Holy Places. The roots of the schism between the Western and Eastern Church reach back beyond the origin of Christianity to the tensions between the Latin and Greek worlds of antiquity. 'It would be a mistake,' wrote Sherrard,[1] 'to treat pre-Christian Greek and Roman culture as a single unity, to describe it as pagan and to assume that that term covers a common spiritual orientation.' And Runciman[2] similarly says: 'Throughout the history of the Roman Empire there had been a latent struggle between East and West.' Christianity, of course, established a new all-embracing unity in the sphere of the spirit, but gradually far-reaching differences developed. Some were of ancient origin: the difference of language which affected the formulation of theological thought; the Roman tendency to legal conceptions and the Greek inclination to philosophical speculation. But the overriding issue was theological. It centred on the question of supreme authority which Rome claimed for the Pope, whilst for the Eastern Churches it rested with the five Patriarchs and the Ecumenical Councils. To Rome the position of St Peter to whom 'the keys of the kingdom of heaven' have been given is paramount. He and his apostolic successors carry the responsibility for the Church as a whole, and the 'holder of the keys' determines the salvation of all. This to the Orthodox is abhorrent. They do not claim a similar position for the Patriarch of Constantinople, nor for any other Patriarch, nor even for an assembly of Patriarchs. Their eyes are fixed, not on any individual apostle or bishop, but on the Revelation itself, as embodied in Christ, the teaching of the Saints and Fathers in the Creed, as formulated and affirmed by the ancient Councils. To them no human being, whoever he may be, can add to, detract from, or change the word of God. The addition to the Creed of any single word like the '*filioque*', introduced by Rome to indicate that the Holy Spirit proceeds not only from God the Father but also from God the Son – quite apart from the merits of the arguments – is preposterous, a heresy and anathema. Whilst Rome stresses guidance and leadership by the Apostle Peter and his successors, Byzantium glorifies the self-sufficiency and perfection of the Revelation. Accordingly for the Orthodox, the antithesis is not Rome or Byzantium, but Rome or Orthodoxy; not West or East, but West or Universal Truth; and the counterpart of the Church of St Peter in Rome is not a church dedicated to any other Apostle in Constantinople, but the supreme cathedral of Divine Wisdom, the Hagia Sophia.

The exact moment at which the division was completed is difficult, if not impossible, to define. The alienation was a long complicated process. But to the East and West alike the schism has always been symbolised by the dramatic events of the year 1054, when Cardinal Humbert, Ambassador of Pope Leo IX, placed on the altar of the Hagia Sophia in Constantinople a Bull of excommunication of Patriarch Michael Cerelarius, and the latter in turn condemned the ambassador and his associates.

The Crusades as Attempt at Reunion

The first attempt to overcome the schism – if necessary by force – was made in the Crusades. For the Crusades aimed not only at the liberation of the Holy Places from the rule of the Infidels but they were also inspired by the hope for the reunification of the Churches under Rome. When in 1074 – about twenty years before the first Crusade – Pope Gregory VII responded to the appeal of the Byzantine Emperor Michael VII Dukas for help against the Turks, and offered to lead personally the faithful of the West to liberate the Christian brethren in the East, he intended to secure first in the capital of the Byzantine Empire, the reward which the Emperor had offered for the help: the submission of the Eastern Church under the papacy.[3] In a letter written on 7 December of the same year to the Emperor Henry IV he explicitly said:

What stimulates me most to this task is the fact that the Church of Constantinople which disagrees with us about the Holy Spirit expects unity with the Apostolic See. Moreover, nearly all Armenians deviate from the Catholic faith, and almost the whole Eastern world awaits that the faith of the Apostle Petrus will decide their differences.[4]

So deeply was he convinced of Rome's orthodoxy in the dogmatic conflict that he believed the devil himself (*'diabolus per se ipsum'*) was diverting the Eastern Christians from the true faith.

Accordingly he encouraged and sanctioned the attack by the Normans under Robert Guiscard on the Byzantine Empire. He even commanded the Catholic clergy of Southern Italy to urge the knights of their dioceses to join the enterprise and to promise them forgiveness of their sins;[5] and when Robert Guiscard victoriously invaded the Balkans, the Pope sent him his congratulations, and attributed the glorious deeds of the Catholic Normans against the schismatic Greeks to the protection and favour granted by St Peter. At the actual beginning of the Crusade the issue of the schism was in the background. The appeal of Emperor Alexius in 1095 for help against the Turks, submitted to the Council of Piacenca, did not offer a union of the Churches as reward for the desired support. It only spoke of the defence of the sacred Church (*'pro defensione sanctae ecclesiae'*) and the Church was conceived as united in Christ. Nor did Pope Urban II demand submission of the Greeks under the Papacy before Roman Catholics would draw their swords.[6] Whether he considered the liberation of the Holy Grave as paramount above all other issues, or whether he felt that the defence of the Western world against the onslaught of Islam had to have priority, the division of the Churches was not mentioned in the Pope's call for the Crusade. On this point all versions of his famous speech at Clermont agree, 'you must carry succour to your brethren dwelling in the East,' says Fulcher of Chartres; 'let the Holy Sepulchre of the Lord especially incite you,' writes Robert the Monk, and nowhere is it mentioned that the Eastern Christians have deviated from the true faith; Eastern and Western Christians alike are described as 'radiant in the name of Christ'.

It was in accordance with these principles that the leaders and Princes of the Crusades on their way to the Holy Land solemnly swore loyalty in Constantinople to the Byzantine Emperor and promised to restore to his jurisdiction the regions which they

41

would liberate. But as the campaign proceeded the division began to appear again.

When Antioch was conquered by the Crusaders they wrote to the Pope urging him to come himself to the East to bring the Crusade to a successful conclusion.

> For we have been able to conquer the Turks and pagans, but we were not able to conquer the heretics, the Greeks and the Armenians, the Syrians and the Jacobites. . . . We therefore urge you as father and head of the Church that you may come to the seat of your authority and that you, the Vicar of Blessed Petrus, may sit in his chair, that you may have us your sons, who in all matters of authority are obedient, and that you may eradicate and destroy all heretics of whatever kind they may be by your authority and by our fortitude.[7]

When on 15 July 1099 Jerusalem fell to the Christian army, the Crusaders proceeded immediately to establish Latin supremacy in the City. For centuries a Greek Patriarch had presided over the Christian community in the Holy City. Now for the first time a Latin was elected Patriarch. Whether at that time Symeon, the legitimate Greek Patriarch of Jerusalem, was still alive in his exile in Cyprus, as orthodox writers maintain,[8] or whether he had died a few days before the fall of Jerusalem, as Western writers claim[9], he was replaced by a Latin ecclesiastic and as long as the rule of the Crusaders over the Holy City continued no Greek was elected Patriarch. In the words of Runciman:

> Throughout the duration of the Latin kingdom every Patriarch without exception was a man who had been born and brought up in the West, and none of them had any sympathy for the Orientals.

Meanwhile the conflict between the Crusaders and Byzantium continued. In the beginning of the twelfth century, the Norman Prince Boemund, a son of Robert Guiscard, who in violation of his oath to the Emperor had annexed Antioch for himself, set out to attack Constantinople and received the full support of Pope Pascal II, just as his father had been supported by Pope Gregory VII in a similar enterprise. Like that of his father, however, the attempt failed and Boemund had to accept humiliating terms for peace. The second and the third Crusades passed by Constantinople without damage, although both Louis VII and Barbarossa seriously contemplated the capture of the city. But the ultimate catastrophe in the relationship between the Churches occurred when in 1204 the army of the fourth Crusade, instead of moving towards Jerusalem, attacked Constantinople. During the siege the Crusaders had been divided about the righteousness of their cause, particularly after their attacks had been repulsed. 'But the Bishops and the clergy in the army decided that the war was a righteous one and they certainly ought to attack the Greeks. For formerly the inhabitants of the city had been obedient to the laws of Rome and now they were disobedient and called all who believed in it "dogs" and the bishops said for this reason one ought certainly to attack them and that it was not a sin but an act of great charity.'[10] Thus the Christian city of Byzantium with the Hagia Sophia, the Cathedral of Divine Wisdom, was sacked with utmost cruelty and defiled by a Christian army of the West which had assembled to free the Holy Grave from the rule of the Infidels.

From the beginning the Crusades had been characterised by an inherent ambiguity; on one hand they had aimed at the defence of the Christian world against Islam – a task in which the liberation of the Holy Places played a dominant part; on the other hand there had been an attempt by Western Christendom to restore the unity of the Church by bringing Byzantium – if necessary by force – under the authority of Rome. Both elements had been uneasily combined and the emphasis shifted from one to the other as the movement proceeded.

The Ottoman Empire: Political and Diplomatic Manœuvres for Positions

When the Crusades had finally failed the Western nations gave up the hope of reconquest and concentrated on the expansion of their commercial interests. Religious questions, including the conflict between the Christian Churches, receded to the background, at least for the time being. The early capitulations, as has been shown above, were in the main concerned with questions of trade and commerce, and where religion was mentioned at all it was limited to the rights of the foreigners to maintain their own faith and to visit and worship at the Holy Places. Meanwhile the struggle between the Christian Churches

43

about the Sanctuaries was conducted on a local level by the resident communities who tried to secure control of the shrines by favourable decisions (firmans) of the Turkish authorities with whom the ultimate power rested. In this struggle the Latins increasingly secured the support of external powers such as Venice, France, Poland and Austria who interceded on their behalf, whilst the Greeks – until the emergence of Russia at the end of the eighteenth century – had to rely on the indigenous Christian population and their connections at the court in Constantinople. As a result there developed a political and diplomatic manœuvring for positions, and the pre-eminence in the Holy Places changed time and again according to the power or the influence of the contending parties and their protectors. During the years 1630–7 control of the Sanctuaries as a result of local and external influences changed hands no less than six times. The distinguished Catholic writer Mgr B.Collin has given a striking description of the events and the forces involved which can be summarised as follows:[11]

In 1630, as a result of the intercession of the French Ambassador Count de Cesy, Sultan Mourad IV issued a firman according to which the Holy Sepulchre, the two Domes, the Stone of the Unction, the Church of Bethlehem and the Grotto of the Nativity belonged to the Latins.

In April 1632, this decision was reversed by two decrees issued by the Cadi of Jerusalem. Through these decrees the Greeks obtained the Entrance to the Grotto and the right to place in the Grotto four lamps and two candelabras. The Cadi also gave them permission with the consent of the Sultan to erect in the Church of the Holy Sepulchre two candelabras at the Stone of the Unction. The Franciscan Custos of the Terra Sancta, however, enlisted the support of the Consul of Venice and the latter obtained in May of the same year, a new firman which re-established the Latins' rights.

In 1634 the Greek Patriarch Theophanes, having gained the favour of the Sultan by a gift of forty thousand gold coins, submitted to him several documents of alleged antiquity which confirmed the rights of the Greeks; and the Sultan, 'probably more influenced by the gift of the forty thousand gold coins than the documents', granted the Greeks a decree by which practically all the Sanctuaries in the Holy Sepulchre and in

Bethlehem were handed back to them. Based on this decision the Greeks removed from the Holy Places all traces of the Latin presence.

In the following year the scene changed again. The Latins claimed that the documents of alleged antiquity which the Patriarch Theophanes had submitted to the Sultan had in fact been forgeries. Pope Urban VIII appealed to all Christian courts of the Western world. France and Venice approached the Sublime Porte in order to obtain 'the restitution of the stolen goods', and the *démarches* of the Ambassadors were not without effect. On 21 March 1636, the Latins were re-established in their position. 'I decree,' said the firman, 'that the Franciscans shall again have and possess the Grotto of Bethlehem where Christ was born and the two keys of the Grotto, the Stone of the Unction of Christ in the Church of the Holy Sepulchre, the arches of Calvary, the seven arches of St Mary and the two Domes which cover the Sepulchre of Christ.' Even so, the Latins had to pay twenty-six thousand piastres to the Sultan and his subordinates. But one year later on 5 October 1637, the Greeks on their part obtained a new firman, instructing the Turkish authorities in Jerusalem to turn the Holy Places over to them and to expel the Franciscans; the Greeks then excluded all those from pilgrimages to Jerusalem who had not obtained the permission from the Greek Patriarch.

At about the same time the treaties between the European powers and Turkey begin to reflect the division of the Churches. Religious and imperial interests become more and more intertwined. The powers increasingly take sides in the conflict within the Church itself and the Western states come forward as protectors of the Latins. Already in 1642 Austria secured special rights for the 'ecclesiastics, monks, Jesuits and priests' of the 'papal religion' (*'religionis papae'*) which were confirmed in 1649 and 1681.[12]

France in the treaty of Adrianople[13] of 1673 stipulated privileges for the bishops and other ecclesiastics of the 'Latin Sect' (*'les évêques ou autres religieux de Secte Latine'*) and especially the Franciscans in Jerusalem.

Poland in a treaty with Turkey concluded in 1676,[14] went even further and imposed a clause upon the Turks by which they had to undertake to return the Holy Grave to the Franciscans and to exclude from it in future all schismatics. '*Stipulantur Turcae vigore presentis tractatus Franciscanis Sanctum Sepulchrum se reddituros eoque ipso Schismatibus omnibus exinde ortis finem imposituros.*' In other words: Catholic Poland forced Islamic Turkey to expel from the Holy Grave the members of the Orthodox Churches.

In 1699 Austria in the Treaty of Carlowitz[15] established special rights for the 'Christian religion according to the rites of the Roman Catholic Church,' and in addition her legate was entitled to speak at the court of the Sultan on behalf of the Christian interests: 'concerning the Faith and the places of Christian pilgrimage in the Holy City of Jerusalem, and to bring his demands before the Imperial Throne.'

The Peace Treaty of Passarowitz of 1718[16] confirmed all previous rights of the Roman Catholic Church and confirmed that the legate of the Emperor should be free to fulfil his mission in all matters which concern the Holy Places of Jerusalem and in all other places where the Catholic monks have their Churches.

The height of Catholic influence was reached in the middle of the eighteenth century. In 1735 a new war had broken out between Turkey and the combined forces of Austria and Russia. The Turkish armies had not been successful. But France interceded on Turkey's behalf and in 1739 brought about the Peace Treaty of Belgrade. In this Treaty Turkey recovered Belgrade itself and in addition nearly all the territories which Austria had conquered during the war. In the following years France received her reward in the capitulation of 1740[17] which represents the high-water mark of French influence in the Ottoman Empire. The treaty confirmed that the Emperors of France held 'sovereign authority' among the most renowned Kings and Princes of the Christian nations, and that the Ambassadors of France 'according to ancient practice' should enjoy at the Sultan's Court absolute precedence before the Ambassadors of Spain and the other Kings. The treaty contained eighty-five articles. Seventy-eight of these deal with political and commercial matters. Seven concern religions; and all of these are limited to Roman Catholics. The previous capitulations which France had secured are confirmed. In addition, Article 32 stipulates that:

The Bishops who are dependent on France and the other ecclesiastics who profess the French Religion ('*la Religion Franque*') shall not be disturbed in the exercise of their functions in those places of our Empire where they have been for a long time.

Concerning the Holy Grave Article 33 reads as follows:

The Franciscans who according to ancient customs are established in and around the city of Jerusalem, in the Church of the Holy Sepulchre, called Kamana, shall not be molested regarding the places which they inhabit and which are in their hands and which shall remain in their hands further on as before.

This clause came to be considered a kind of Magna Carta of Latin rights. In practice, however, it was of very short duration. Local opposition against the new arrangements was strong and after some bitter fighting within the Church the Latin rights were greatly curtailed, and the Greek pre-eminence was re-established and ratified in a firman of 1757. When the French Ambassador, Comte de Vergennes, protested against this change the Grand Vizier replied: 'These places, Sir, belong to the Sultan and he gives them to whom he pleases; it may well be possible that they always were in the hands of the Franks, but today his Highness wishes that they belong to the Greeks.'[18]

The same century saw the gradual emergence of Russia on the scene; and in the treaty of Kutchuk-Kainardi,[19] signed in 1774, Turkey promised Russia to protect for ever the Christian religion and its churches in her territory. She permitted the establishment of a Russian Church in Constantinople and authorised the Russian Minister to make representations to the Sultan's court whenever he wished on behalf of this church and of those who officiated in it. All Russian subjects, ecclesiastic or secular, were given the right of free and undisturbed passage to Jerusalem and the other Holy Places and were granted the same privileges as those enjoyed by the most favoured nations. Lastly, Russia restored to Turkey Bessarabia and the two principalities Walachia and Moldavia, whereas Turkey undertook to grant to the population of these territories full freedom to live a Christian life. The Ministers of Russia were authorised to speak on behalf of the principalities and the Sultan pledged himself to receive their representations in a spirit of friendship and mutual respect. This treaty in due time became the basis of the

Russian claim to speak on behalf of and act as protectors of all Orthodox Christians in the Ottoman Empire.

When Napoleon invaded Egypt and Palestine, both Russia and Great Britain entered into treaties of alliance with Turkey, but although the war was partly fought in the Holy Land, no religious issues were mentioned.

At the end of the Napoleonic wars, however, the question was raised again, and Russia in a note to the Congress of Vienna renewed her claim to protect the Orthodox in Turkey, in the same way as France protected the Catholics. The claim was not accepted by the other states but the interest of the Great Powers was henceforth linked to the parties within the divided Church.

Meanwhile, tensions and sometimes even actual fighting continued in the Church of the Holy Sepulchre and the Basilica of the Nativity in Bethlehem. At certain periods both Russia and France tried to achieve a reconciliation between the religious groups. Thus Tzar Alexander I gave instructions that everything possible should be done to arrive at an agreement between the major powers and to hold the Greeks back from any violent action, as he was convinced that the King of France would do the same concerning the Latins. 'The task is not' he wrote personally, 'to discuss the hateful principle of exclusion, but to find a mode of coexistence for the different rites of this church.' And the Duke of Richelieu on behalf of France likewise expressed the wish for a peaceful settlement.[20] But the attempts did not succeed.

The Greek war of independence brought about a grave crisis in the Patriarchate in Constantinople which was bound to affect the position of the Christian communities in Palestine. Under the Turkish Millet system the religious head of a community was responsible for actions of every member, and when the Greek freedom fighters under Alexander Ypsilanti invaded Moldavia, the Patriarch Gregory V was arrested by Turkish police and on 22 April 1821 hanged at the gate of his palace, to be followed by two metropolitans and twelve bishops of the Greek Orthodox Church. The new Kingdom of Greece soon insisted on complete religious autonomy under the Archbishop of Athens and with the power of the Patriarch in Constantinople waning, the Orthodox Christians in the Holy Land began to feel that their protection ultimately depended on Russia.

During the war against the Greeks the Pasha of Egypt, Mehmed Ali, had given the Turks valuable assistance. But when he was offered as a reward by the Sultan the administration of Crete he considered this inadequate and proceeded to conquer Syria which he held with the approval of France till 1840, when an alliance between Austria and Prussia, and an intervention of the British Fleet restored the situation.

In the ensuing negotiations King Frederik William IV of Prussia submitted a memorandum which contains the first suggestions in history for an international agreement on the Holy Places of Jerusalem, Bethlehem and Nazareth. The characteristic element of the proposals is that they did not aim at a territorial internationalisation of the towns in question – as most later proposals do – but at the personal exterritoriality of the Christian population living there. The Christian residents of these towns were to cease to be subjects of the Sultan, but to retain their right of domicile against the payment of an annual tax. They were to form three independent communities on a personal religious basis: a Catholic, a Greek and a Protestant. Each of these communities was to be directed by a Resident. The Resident of the Catholics was to be appointed by Austria and France; that of the Greeks by Russia and that of the Protestants by Great Britain and Prussia. The ownership of the Holy Places in Jerusalem, Bethlehem and Nazareth – not the towns themselves – was to be transferred to the 'five Great Christian Powers, Austria, Russia, France, Great Britain and Prussia', who would make special arrangements with those who were in their actual possession.[21] Needless to say, the Prussian proposals were not accepted, and in particular Russia did not wish to see the Holy Places under a joint protection of the European Powers.[22]

Meanwhile the conflict became more intense and the following years saw increased activities both in the religious and political field. In 1843, the first French Consul arrived and was made – like Chateaubriand before him – a Knight of the Holy Sepulchre in a solemn ceremony at which the spurs and the sword of Godfrey of Bouillon were used. Likewise the Russian Archimandrite Porphyri Ouspenski, sent by the Holy Synod with the consent of the Tzar himself, reached Jerusalem and soon reported that the Orthodox Church there could only be

saved by Russian intervention. In the same year the Orthodox
Patriarch in Jerusalem died. For several centuries it had been
customary for the Patriarch to reside in Constantinople and his
election usually took place there in the presence of the Ecumenical Patriarch. Under Russian influence, however, this time
the election was held in Jerusalem. Cyril, the newly elected
Patriarch, took up residence there, and soon became, with his
splendid receptions, a dominant figure in Jerusalem society. In
1846 the Tzar approved the creation of a Russian Mission in
Jerusalem. In 1847 Pope Pius IX appointed a new Latin Patriarch
and whilst this office had been for many centuries merely titular
and had been held in Rome, the Pope now gave it increased
reality by sending the holder of it to reside in Jerusalem.

Theological Conflict on the Highest Level

The conflict now moved into the sphere of theology. On 6
January 1848, Pope Pius IX issued his encyclical '*In Suprema
Petri*' to the Eastern Christians in which he urged 'the strayed
sheep' to rejoin without further delay the communion with the
Holy See of the Apostle Peter, 'the rock of the true Church of
Jesus Christ'. On 6 May of the same year, the Patriarchs of
Constantinople, Alexandria, Antioch and Jerusalem in a joint
statement utterly rejected the proposal and condemned the
Church of Rome for heresy. Both communications spring from
the depth of the religious convictions of their authors and each
of them reveals already in its opening sentence the essence of its
theological position.

'Since I was raised to the Supreme See of St Peter and to the
care for all Churches,' the papal encyclical begins, 'I have
turned my thoughts to the different Christian nations of the
East. For it was in the East that the Incarnation and the
Crucifixion took place, that the Gospel of peace and light was
announced, that the Bishops, Martyrs and Fathers of the
Church flourished during the first centuries, that the ancient
Ecumenical Councils were held, under the chairmanship of the
Bishop of Rome, and that the Catholic Creed was formulated
and affirmed.' The encyclical then recalls that in more recent
times a great part of the Eastern Christians have 'separated
themselves from the communion with this Holy See and

therefore from the unity of the Catholic Church'. It notes with satisfaction that nevertheless many have preserved their links with Rome maintaining their 'Eastern rites', and assures them that Rome will 'continue to keep intact and honour their ancient liturgies although they differ in certain respects from the liturgy of the Latin Church.'

The encyclical then turns to the Orthodox Christians themselves, to 'the Orientals who serve Jesus Christ but who are strangers to this Holy See of the Apostle Peter ... and as strayed sheep on precipitous paths without escape need help to rejoin the flock of the Lord'. It stresses the need for unity and continues: 'Our Lord Jesus Christ has built His Church on Peter, the Head of the Apostles to whom He has given the keys of the kingdom of heaven. He has entrusted to Him the whole Church ... and all these prerogatives belong to the Supreme Pontiffs of Rome, the successors of Peter.' It gives several examples from the history of the Church claiming that they confirm the 'first rank, the authority and the supremacy of the Bishops of Rome' and concludes by exhorting the separated communities to return to the communion with the Roman Church.

We open our arms with tenderness and paternal goodwill to your return ... we shall not impose any burden upon you besides what is necessary. You will naturally join us in the confession of the true Faith and maintain the communion with the Church and this Holy See of Peter. As regards your sacred ritual, it will be necessary to reject all that which has been adopted after the separation and what is in contradiction to the Faith and Catholic Unity. After these additions have been eliminated you will be able to keep your venerable ancient liturgy. As for those in Holy Orders, the priests and Bishops who return to the Catholic Unity, we have decided to follow the example of our predecessors and to recognise their rank and dignity so that we may use their help to maintain and develop the cult of the Catholic religion among their peoples.

To this the Patriarchs replied as follows:

It is certain that the divine Revelation must be preserved intact and pure. But as in the garden of Eden the spiritual enemy of man's salvation adopted the role of a good counsellor to make man transgress the word of God, so in the intellectual Eden of the Church the tempter deceives many by poisoning with heresy the clear waters of Orthodoxy. In the past one of the leading heresies was Arianism, today it is Papism. The former has passed away, and so will the latter. Only the Orthodox Church which is the true 'One Catholic Apostolic Church' will prevail eternally.

The new doctrine according to which the Holy Spirit proceeds from the Father and the Son is contrary to the Creed, and insults the Fathers of the Councils who have prohibited any addition or change under penalty of eternal damnation. The change initiated by Rome naturally has led to other alterations and reprehensible innovations culminating in the claim for papal infallibility. The early Bishops of Rome, particularly Leo III and John VIII have condemned the change as heresy, but most of their successors have been seduced by the prerogatives which the heresy gave them, in the hope for absolute power over the Catholic Church and a monopoly of the Grace of the Holy Spirit. The See of Rome never had the right to put itself above the judgement of the Holy Scriptures and the decisions of the Councils. We must not judge Orthodoxy according to the insinuations of the Holy See, but must judge the Holy See and him who occupies it, according to the Holy Scriptures and Orthodoxy of eternal revelation. We are as anxious as His Holiness to see mutual charity reign among all Christians, but with the one difference that we make it a condition to preserve intact and pure the perfect Christian Creed, whilst His Holiness sees in that union but the means to strengthen and increase the power and preeminence of those who occupy the Pontifical See. This, in essence, is the main issue of the discussion, this is the wall of separation between them and us. . . . One day a successor to the See of Rome will repent, turn his heart, and like the Apostle Peter himself, will weep bitterly. May it be the will of Heaven that this true successor of St Peter will be His Holiness himself. In olden days the Bishops of Rome followed the strictest Orthodoxy. Today Rome is the demon of innovation. The precedence which the Fathers of the Church granted to Rome was based on the fact that Rome was the seat of the Imperial government. It had nothing to do with St Peter and was subject to the Orthodoxy of the holder of the See.[23]

The Orthodox Patriarchs treat the canonical precedence of the Bishop of Rome at present as vacant. 'For the Universal Church is always ready to receive again the shepherds who have deserted her with their flocks.' They had hoped that the Pope's encyclical letter would open the way to reunion. 'But they have seen to their unspeakable sorrow that it is written in the language of innovation, the language used already by Leo IX in his letter to blessed Michael Cerularius.' The request of the Pope that the Orthodox Christians should eliminate from their liturgies 'what had been adopted after the separation' is based on a complete reversion of the facts. For the texts of the Orthodox are the unchanged original, whilst Rome herself has introduced heretical innovations. 'With us innovations could not have been introduced, neither by Patriarchs nor by Councils. For with us the safe-guard of religion rests in the People itself which wishes that its religious dogma remains eternally unchanged.' Every onslaught upon the unimpeachable Faith is justly condemned in Council as error and a danger to the salvation of the souls. 'We proclaim in the universal Church that the encyclical letter to the Christians of the East by the Bishop of the ancient Rome, Pope Pius IX, belongs to this category.'

The Creed is marked by the seal of perfection. It is not open to detractions, additions or to changes, and whoever dares to undertake such an act, has already denied the faith of Jesus Christ and has subjected himself willingly to eternal damnation, as blasphemer of the Holy Spirit.

Measured against the depth of this spiritual conflict the struggle over the physical control of the Holy Places appears almost trivial. But the intensity of the struggle on the spot increased. There were repeated skirmishes and even hand to hand fighting in the Sanctuaries between the monks who used candlesticks and crosses as weapons; and during one of these frays the famous silver star in the Grotto of Bethlehem, placed there by the Latins, was wrenched from its foundations and disappeared. In the international sphere, France and Russia, the respective protectors of the Latins and the Orthodox, now faced each other openly. In the middle of May 1850, General Aupick, the French Ambassador in Constantinople, formally demanded the return of the Holy Places to the Franciscans in accordance with the capitulation of 1740. Russia made it clear that she could not tolerate an expulsion of the Greek monks, and both sides threatened military action.

Status Quo

At the height of the crisis the Sultan once more appointed a commission of learned lawyers to decide 'the disputes which from time to time arise between the Greek and Latin nations respecting certain Holy Places in and around the City of Jerusalem and which have now been again revived'. As a result of the Commission's researches and the deliberations in his Cabinet Council, the Sultan issued in February 1852 the final firman[24] on the Holy Places 'to serve constantly and for ever as permanent rule'. The firman defines the places in dispute, investigates the conflicting claims, pronounces a blessing over Jesus and the Virgin Mary whenever their names are mentioned and decides on the main issue 'that all these places must be left in their present state'. It therefore confirmed in essence the status which had existed since 1757.

Soon afterwards the Crimean War began, not in order to defend the Christian Holy Places against the Infidels, nor to liberate them from Islamic rule, but as a war between the Christian protectors. When at last peace was restored the conquered territories were mutually evacuated, and the position of the Sanctuaries, which had played so great a part at the outbreak of the conflict, was left unchanged. Napoleon III himself, a few years later, described the issue of the Holy Places as '*une affaire sotte*'.[25]

The Treaty of Berlin which in 1878 concluded a new war between Russia and Turkey, laid down that 'no alterations can be made in the status quo in the Holy Places'. The division of the Church was not allowed to disturb once more the precarious balance between the European Powers. The Holy Places, therefore, remained under the shadow of the schism.

3 The Struggle about a Legal Investigation

The end of the First World War brought the opportunity of an international legal investigation into all claims, rights and titles to the Christian Holy Places. During the war England, France and Russia had each put forward reasons why the administration of the Sanctuaries was to be entrusted to them[1] whilst Germany, on the other side, had even suggested to her Turksih ally that the Sultan should hand over the Church of the Holy Sepulchre as a present to the emperors of Germany and Austria who in turn would donate it to the Pope.[2]

When the Ottoman Empire ultimately disintegrated the dispute between the Churches over the Sanctuaries which had been dormant for decades burst into the open again. By that time Russia, the protector of the Orthodox, was powerless and her new leaders appeared to be utterly indifferent to places of Christian worship. Amongst Catholics in the West hopes were running high, and a new Latin pre-eminence in the Holy Land, almost as complete as that at the end of the first Crusade, seemed imminent.

A New Latin Pre-eminence?

Pascal Baldi, one of the leading Catholic writers in this field, set the tone by combining jubilation over the end of Islamic supremacy with indignation over the usurpations which, he felt, the Greeks had committed in the past, and both issues became for him indissolubly interwoven. In a brochure on the 'grave controversies between the various Christian communities in charge of the Holy Places' which was printed in 1919 in Rome by the Institute Pio IX, he exclaimed:

To hope under Turkish rule for a re-assertion of the Latin element, a triumph of Catholicity in the Holy Land, would have exceeded human foresight and would have appeared as something more than an illusion, an insanity.

Today the improbable has become a fact; today, by a wonderful combination of events, which we look upon as providential, Italy, France and England, three nations which had such a large part in the Holy Wars, have Jerusalem in their power; today the Catholics of the whole world may justly expect the hour of justice finally to strike; today they may finally hope that for the Sanctuaries of Palestine may return the splendour of the era of Constantine, the splendour of the first century of the Crusades.

Spelling out the claim for the restoration of the Latins to the positions which existed before the present status quo and using the term 'usurpers' for Moslems and Orthodox alike, he added:

At last the day is about to break which the Fathers of the Holy Land have awaited more than a century and a half, the day on which they will regain possession of the usurped sanctuaries and the exercise of their violated rights.'

And equating Latin Christendom with Christendom as a whole he concluded:

It is now seven centuries since Christian Jerusalem, Latin Jerusalem, fell into the power of the followers of Islam, who by right of conquest possessed themselves of the sacred monuments existing there, and disposed of them at will. Today the nations of Christianity, the Latin nations, have taken revenge on the usurpers; today the warrior-descendants of the Crusaders of the twelfth century have reoccupied the Holy City. They therefore retake what belongs to them; they re-enter the Sanctuary of the Resurrection erected by their own forefathers and restore it to Catholic worship.[3]

Such apotheosis of the West was in full harmony with the thoughts of the Neo-Catholic movement which at that time flourished in France under the leadership of such writers as Paul Claudel, Francis Jammes, Georges Bernanos, and Henry Massis who a few years later called for the 'Defence of the West' against the onslaught of Asia, in which he included not only Dostoevsky but even some of the German writers of the post-war period. Even Clemenceau seems to have followed the general trend of looking to the Middle Ages and the Crusades as an inspiration for the future.[4]

The conflict over the Holy Places became a major issue at the Peace Conference. The attempts which were made then to solve the problem are still relevant and the memoranda which the Latins and Greeks submitted to the Assembly contain the respective claims of their Churches maintained up to the present day.

The Memorandum of the Latins[5]

The Latins presented their case in a historical perspective. They greatly stressed the help which they had received throughout the centuries from Western Powers (remembering perhaps the influence of the West in the Peace Assembly); they described the legal titles they had acquired and the infringements they had suffered; they asked for an examination of all the controversies between the Christian communities about the Holy Places, and being sure about the outcome of such examination, demanded the return of all Sanctuaries to the state which existed in 1740.

The opening sentence already referred to the Crusades:

> From the day when after the heroic but unfortunate era of the Crusades, Moslem domination was re-established in the East, the question of the Holy Places has not ceased to be one of the great issues of European public law and at all times has occupied the diplomacy of the Western powers. . . . Kings and republics have emulated each other to establish their protectorate over the sanctuaries of Christendom . . . and have considered it an honour to protect the Holy Places and the Latin monks who were installed to guard them and to assure for them the free exercise of the cult and to watch over the safety of the pilgrims who visited the fatherland of Jesus.

The memorandum then describes the history of the Holy Places from the beginning of the fourteenth century, when the Kings of Aragon, France and Naples made their *démarches* to the Sultan of Cairo; how in 1333, after long and difficult negotiations and at the cost of enormous sums, the Kings of Naples and Sicily obtained for the Franciscans the exclusive ownership of the Cenacle on Mount Zion and the right to remain permanently in the Church of the Holy Sepulchre and there to celebrate religious services. It adds that, at the same time, the Franciscans took possession of the Basilica of the Nativity in Bethlehem and

C

the Grotto, and, slightly later, of the Grave of the Virgin and other Sanctuaries. It surveys the ups and downs of four hundred years of Ottoman rule and in particular the different Treaties entered by the Sultans with Venice, Genoa and France; it mentions in particular the Capitulations of 1604, 1673, and 1740, and refers to the numerous firmans issued by the Sultans of Egypt and Constantinople in favour of the Custodians of the Holy Land. It then turns to the various acts of 'usurpation by dissident sects', beginning with one in the year 1633; complains that 'the intrigues of the Greeks have always triumphed over justice', and says about the changes of 1757, the last ever to occur:

When in 1757 a new and very grave usurpation was completed to the detriment of the Franciscan monks, the Catholic powers, especially France, Venice, Austria and Naples, who had their representatives in Constantinople, did their utmost to secure from the Sublime Porte redress of the great injustice which had been committed, but their efforts were without success because of the influence of the Christians of the Greek rite which dominated in Turkey.

Having dealt with the events of the nineteenth century the memorandum sums up:

The great question of the Holy Places has not yet been solved; it has merely been referred – for political reasons – to more favourable times. Now having waited for more than a century and a half, Palestine has been liberated from Turkish rule. . . . The Catholic world hopes for and demands an exact clarification of the rights and possessions of the different Christian communities which officiate in the Sanctuaries of Judea. Today the Custodian of the Holy Land, as often before on the eve of great peace treaties between Turkey and the Western powers, addresses his requests to the representatives of the nations which are assembling in Versailles. He addresses his requests to them in the name of Justice which has been trampled under foot for too long; in the name of the whole Catholic world which must have in the Sanctuaries of the Redemption that place which legitimately belongs to it; in the name, finally, of the civilized world. . . .

The Custos of the Holy Land demands nothing but the justice which is due to him. What he demands is that one examines once and for all the controversies which have taken place throughout the centuries between the different Christian communities which are entitled to officiate in the Holy Places: that one verifies the value of the historic documents produced by each of them, and that each should be put into definite possession of that part to which each is entitled.

Having thus demanded an independent and impartial enquiry into the rights and wrongs of the situation by the Supreme Tribunal of the Nations, the memorandum concludes by formulating its claims:

What the Custos demands is exactly the same that in the middle of the last century the Catholic Powers demanded from Turkey, i.e. the return of the Holy Places to the status quo which existed at the moment of the usurpations committed by the heterodox in 1757, that is to say the return to the status quo which was established legally in the course of the fourteenth century, after the ultimate fall of the Latin Kingdom of Jerusalem. The Custos of the Holy Land demands, therefore, that one accedes to the demands which General Aupick, the representative of France at Constantinople by his note of May 28 1850, presented in the name of his Government and in the name of the Governments of Sardinia, Belgium, Spain and Austria, demands which he specified in detail in the month of August of the same year in submitting to the Ottoman Government the status quo of the Sanctuaries which in 1740 were in the possession of the Latins.

The Memorandum of the Greeks[6]

The Greeks in their reply expressed their sorrow about the conflict between the Churches, and deplored that as a result the Christian communities in the Holy Places had adopted 'a hostile character towards each other by which the monks, who are serving in the Sanctuaries, have been changed in their real nature and mission to soldiers'.

In the matter itself they contested the basic assumption of the Latins and claimed instead that from the beginning of Christian history the Holy Places had belonged to the Greeks; that for the first eight hundred years – from their discovery in the fourth century to the Crusades in the twelfth – the Sanctuaries had been under their uncontested control; that during the Crusades the Greeks had been reduced to a secondary position but that after the fall of the Latin Kingdom they had been restored to the original state:

The Greek monks, as possessors and masters of the Holy Places, by virtue of possessory rights and reasons of ethnological nature, from the fourth century till the period of the Crusades at the twelfth century, have been exclusively the rulers and masters of the Holy Places, erecting, repairing, ornamenting and serving in them. During the period of the Crusades, however, the position of the Greeks in the Holy Places has been changed into a secondary one ... but after the expulsion of the Crusaders the Greeks, by virtue of an official political act of Saladin, were recognised as the only rulers and masters of the Holy Places and they continued their mission and traditions.

The memorandum admits that from the fourteenth century onwards the Franciscans did secure certain rights in the Holy Places, but holds that in spite of fluctuations of the possessory status, the Greek position has in substance been maintained.

Whilst the Latins in their statement stress the legal side of their position, pinpointing, as it were, the individual acts on which their claims are based, such as purchase, firmans of the Sultans, and capitulations concluded between the Ottoman Government and the Western powers, the Greeks rely on the coherent and continued course of what they consider 'organic history'. They attach fundamental importance to the history of the first twelve centuries and particularly to the Byzantine period. They maintain that this era is essentially Greek, and although the Emperor Justinian in Constantinople used Latin as the language of his great legal codification, the *corpus juris*, they point out that he himself built there the Cathedral of Christendom, the Hagia Sophia, which not only was given a Greek name but is the sublime expression of Greek spirituality and art. They add that all the ancient monasteries of Jerusalem are in their hands, and that the Byzantine emperors continued to support and maintain the Holy Places even during the period of the occupation by the Western Crusaders.

Against this indigenous position of the Eastern Church, the Latins – according to the Greeks – were only maintained by the external influence of the Western powers. This they consider true not only for the Crusades, but for the long series of inter-cessions or interventions by Catholic states since the fourteenth century, and they link every extension of the Franciscan position to Western influence in Constantinople.

They feel that throughout the centuries the West has tried to reduce if not to destroy their position, and believe this is due to a deep hostility of Latinism to everything Greek. They refer to the anti-Greek attacks during the Crusades against Constantinople:

In 1147 French barons and bishops, incited by national and religious motives, requested the King of France, Louis VII, in alliance with the King of Sicily, Rogerus, to conquer Constantinople. The same project occupied the mind of Frederic I in 1190 and afterwards of his son Henry VI, and at last the 'Hateful Byzantium' was conquered on 12–13 April 1204, with a terrible destruction and devastation and great indecency which is beyond any description.

And they see in almost every action of the West – down to the *démarche* of General Aupick in 1850 – the continuation of the efforts to bring about the expulsion of the Greeks.

The capitulation of 1740 appears to them as the height of Western usurpations. They do not admit that in the long series of fluctuating events any special significance should be attached to this particular act except that it represented the high-water mark of Western penetration. They feel that if any historical investigation is necessary this must extend to the whole sixteen hundred years of history. They maintain that the status quo which exists today has been established by two official firmans of the Sultans and recognised and confirmed by two European Conferences, one in Paris – at the end of the Crimean War – and the other in Berlin, at the conclusion of the war between Russia and Turkey. The firm maintenance of the present status quo, they proclaim, is the only way to establish peace.

The Greeks agree that the history of the Holy Places should be examined and studied:

From this study we can see what was the position of the Greeks, and what historical, legal and political documents they have in their possession, and on the other hand, when and how the Franciscans entered into the Holy Places and by what means they had taken the places which are now in their possession.

They are confident that the ancient customs and the daily services which are held by the Greeks in the Church of the Holy Sepulchre and in the Basilica of the Nativity in Bethlehem leave no ground to the Franciscans claims. They therefore 'request the wise men, who will give their decision about the Holy

Places, to take into consideration these facts, containing long history, and to grant to everyone his own right'.

Finally they call on all Christians to work for reconciliation:

It is the supreme duty of every Christian nation, whatever might be its sect or doctrine, to do its utmost, in order to cause peace and love to reign in the Holy Places, between the custodians there, viz. Greeks, Fransciscans, Armenians and other smaller Christian communities, so that all the Christians might take from these Holy shrines the best example of Christian love and practise it in deeds in their own life.

They conclude by expressing their earnest desire 'that the Greeks and the Franciscans may live together in the Holy Places with mutual respect and love'.

The Attempts at an Investigation

Both sides had asked for an impartial investigation, and the procedure for this was set in motion. Into the Treaty of Sèvres, by which Turkey gave up her rights over Palestine in June 1920, a special clause was inserted according to which the Mandatory Power should appoint with the least possible delay a special Commission to study all questions and claims concerning the different religious communities and issue the appropriate regulations (Article 95). The treaty itself was never ratified owing to the revival of national resistance in Turkey under Kemal Pasha, but the clause was incorporated into the Mandate for Palestine. Article 13 of the Mandate decreed that:

All responsibility in connection with the Holy Places and religious buildings or sites in Palestine, including that of preserving existing rights and of securing free access to the Holy Places . . . and the free exercise of worship . . . is assumed by the Mandatory . . . [and the draft of Article 14 added] The Mandatory undertakes to appoint as soon as possible a special Commission to study and regulate all questions and claims relating to the different religious communities. In the composition of this Commission the religious interest concerned will be taken into account. The Chairman of the Commission will be appointed by the Council of the League of Nations.

This Article 14 which was to fulfil the demand of both the Latins and the Greeks for an impartial investigation into the existing rights itself became an object of long and bitter controversy. But besides the question of how such investigation could be conducted, the statute of the Mandate contained two other issues of fundamental importance which met with opposition. One was the fact that the Mandate over the Holy Land was to be entrusted to Great Britain, a Christian Power which was neither Catholic nor Orthodox. The other was the promise to establish in the country a Jewish National Home.

Pope Benedict xv viewed both prospects with grave misgivings which he expressed with bitterness in the allocution '*Causa Nobis*' of 13 June 1921. As far as England was concerned he warned against the 'nefarious activities of alien non-Catholic sects who call themselves Christians' and who exploit the misery created by the war. ('*Quod conquerabamur a peregrinis acatholicorum sectis, Christianam appellationem prae se ferentibus, ibi nefaris effici.*')

As for the Jews, he feared that they would 'deprive Christendom of the position which it had always occupied in the Holy Land', and in relation to the Holy Places themselves, he even added 'many people work with intense efforts in order to divest the Holy Places of their sacred character, and to transform them into pleasure grounds by importing there all the lures of sensuality and frivolity . . .'

In the same year the *Union Catholique d'études internationales* submitted to the League of Nations a memorandum[7] in which they deplored the proposed powers of the Mandatory, and suggested that the protection of the Catholic sanctuaries should be left, as in the past, with France in accordance with the capitulations of the seventeenth and eighteenth centuries, and that the general control of Christian affairs in Palestine should be entrusted to a permanent international commission consisting of the Consuls of 'the four or five [European or American] powers who count a considerable number of Christians in Jerusalem and Palestine under their jurisdiction'.

Against this Balfour expressed surprise that anyone could imagine Christian interests might suffer from the transfer of authority from a Moslem to a Christian power – particularly when this power was Great Britain. It was true that Britain was a Protestant country, but there was hardly any country – Protestant or Catholic – where Catholicism was treated more justly and generously than in the British Isles. It was impossible therefore that the Holy Places could be adversely affected by the change.[8]

The Battle of Procedure

The issue came before the Council of the League of Nations in the Spring of 1922. The case of the Vatican was presented by Cardinal Gasparri in a letter dated 15 May,[9] which was written in a tone very different from that of the allocution *'Causa Nobis'*. To begin with, it declared that the Holy See did not oppose the decision of the League to entrust the Mandate over Palestine to Great Britain 'which had given proof of her spirit of justice and impartiality'. The Holy See however suggested changes of the mandate in two fields.

The first concerned the Jewish National Home. Pope Benedict xv in his allocution had stressed what he felt was a danger to Catholics and Christians in general. The Cardinal extended the issue beyond the religious into the national sphere and expressed apprehension for the future of the non-Jewish population of the country. He appreciated the clause in the Balfour Declaration by which nothing should be done which may prejudice their civil and religious rights, but thought that the project intended to establish in course of time 'an absolute preponderance of the Jewish element in the economic, administrative and political field to the detriment of other nationalities' and this would be a violation of the established rights of the local inhabitants. He also felt that the project contradicted the very idea of a mandate as defined in Article 22 of the Covenant of the League. A mandate had to serve the interest of peoples who are not yet capable of ruling themselves 'in the particularly difficult conditions of the modern world' and this task had rightly been called 'a sacred trust of civilisation'. It was therefore inadmissable to use the mandate as an instrument for the subordination of one people to another.

The other suggestion concerned the Christian Holy Places, and in particular the Commission which in accordance with Article 14 of the mandate was to be established to investigate the claims of the different religious communities. The Holy See, the Cardinal wrote, would never accept the right of the proposed Commission to investigate the ownership of Catholic Sanctuaries; and although the memorandum of the Latins had complained that Catholic rights had been affected for centuries by grave usurpations by dissident sects, he added that nearly all the Sanctuaries had for centuries been in the peaceful possession of the Catholics:

The Holy See states once and for all that it could never admit that such commission should claim the right to put under discussion the ownership of the Sanctuaries, almost every one of which has been for many centuries, even under the Turkish domination, in the peaceful possession of Catholics.

Even more important, the Cardinal declared, the proposed Commission could not achieve any concrete results since a meeting of the Christian denominations to discuss the Holy Places would without fail lead to a bitter struggle (*'une lutte acharnée'*) among them, which would make it impossible to reach any impartial judgment:

The Holy See observes that the Commission could never reach any concrete results. In fact, as all religious denominations must be represented on that Commission, a fierce struggle would undoubtedly follow, with the inevitable result of a coalition of all the other members against the denominations in actual possession of the Sanctuary in question, from which no serene judgment could ensue.

The Holy See therefore suggested – in accordance with the proposals submitted by the *Union Catholique d'études internationales* that the Commission should be formed by the local Consuls of the Council members.

Finally the Cardinal demanded that voting power in the Commission should be reserved exclusively to Catholics. 'The Holy See does not oppose the representatives of the various religious denominations taking part in the Commission *as long as their vote is only consultative.*' The 'impartial enquiry' into the controversy between the Latins and the Greeks was therefore to be decided by the Catholics alone.

In response the British Government assured all concerned that nothing would be done which could be construed as negligence or indifference to Christian sentiment.[10] In order to meet all objections the Government now suggested that the composition of the Commission should be subject to approval by the Council and that every report of the Commission should be laid before the Council for confirmation.

On 22 July the matter came up again for discussion. Article 14 was still the subject of doubt and controversy. The British Government therefore proposed one more alteration in the text by which the method of nomination, the composition and the functions of the Commission should be submitted to the Council of the League for approval and no action concerning the Commission should be taken until the Council of the League agreed. This at last allayed the apprehensions. Balfour once more proclaimed:

> The British Government never have had, have not now, and never can have any desire with regard to the Holy Places but that of administering historic justice between all the great communities concerned. The last thing we wish is to deprive any man, any community, any nation, of the rights to which they have a claim, and our solitary wish is that all these ancient rights shall be carried on with decency and order in the future, and in a manner which will prevent any religious interest feeling that it has been unjustly treated by those who possess authority.[11]

Thus the British Mandate over Palestine was accepted. Only the final formulation of Article 14 was deferred. In preparation for this debate Cardinal Gasparri submitted on 15 August a new memorandum[12] which contained some changes in the position of the Holy See:

1. The proposed Commission was to be *permanent*, a suggestion which Great Britain had refused since it would create a kind of Executive Power within the Mandate.

2. The Holy See no longer insisted that only Catholics should have voting power in the Commission, but demanded that they must form a *majority*.

> It is beyond doubt that in the Commission the majority must be assured for the representatives of the Catholic nations ... especially Belgium, France, Italy, Spain and Brazil must have in this Commission an equitable representation.

3. The prohibition to discuss Catholic rights in the Commission was now formulated as follows:

The Commission cannot consider itself authorised to discuss any rights on the Holy Places which have *already* been acquired by the Catholics.

This last demand far transcended any previous statement. The introduction of the word 'already' made it clear that the Cardinal considered the question of Catholic rights not as static, but as a dynamic process of continued expansion. It is obvious that this demand – added to the condition that the majority of the Commission must be Catholics – ended all hope for an agreed settlement. The British Government still struggled on, and Balfour made one more and last attempt to save the Commission of investigation.[13] It was now to be divided into three Sub-Commissions, one Christian, one Moslem, and one Jewish. Each Sub-Commission should have its own President; and there should be a Chairman to preside over the whole Commission. For this he suggested 'a prominent American of high standing and judicial temperament', and felt that such an appointment would be particularly suitable, as it would enable representation to be given to the Protestant communities who would not otherwise be represented on the Commission.

The Christian Sub-Commission was to have a French president; three Catholic representatives (an Italian, a Spaniard and a Belgian); three Orthodox (a Greek, a Russian and an Armenian); and one or possibly two representatives of the Abyssinians and the Copts. Unanimous reports of any of the Sub-Commissions should be definitive. In cases where no unanimity could be achieved, the final decision was to rest with the Chairman of the whole Commission.

The proposal as a whole was received by the Catholic world with indignation and the suggestion that a Protestant may have the decisive vote was felt to be 'preposterous'.

The rights of the Catholics, [wrote the *Osservatore Romano* on 6 September 1922] run the risk of being trampled under foot. After having held the quasi-totality of the Sanctuaries in the Holy Land in their possession for centuries, they would now have in the Sub-Commission only a tiny minority (four against ten) against a majority which, as one can foresee, could be too easily united against them, since this majority consists of elements which for centuries have been at the root of the continued strife against the Catholic Church. It must be noted that, since unanimity is required for each decision, and such unanimity cannot be achieved in a Sub-Commission which is formed by so incongruous and opposite elements, the final decision will practically rest with the Chairman of the Commission, in other words a Protestant. This is simply preposterous.

Since no agreement could be reached, the British Government asked the Catholic powers to make their own suggestions. But the replies from Italy and France were contradictory.

The Investigation is Abandoned – Britain Takes Responsibility

Thereupon Great Britain decided to give up any further attempts to secure agreement among those concerned, withdrew the proposals she had made in the course of the negotiations and took upon herself the full responsibility for the administration of the Holy Places which had been entrusted to her in the Mandate. In practice this meant the decision to maintain the status quo, as it had existed under Turkish rule since 1757. In a final address of historic vision Lord Balfour summed up the situation:

As the Mandatory Power, it is the business of my country not merely to do its best to find a solution which shall reconcile differences of opinion within the Catholic community, but it is its business also to see that justice is done as between Catholic and Orthodox ... indeed between all the various sects of Christians who have for centuries disputed certain points in connection with the Holy Places. ... Next to the great Catholic body in the world stands the Orthodox. It is not very strongly represented in the League of Nations. I think there are only about four other nations among our colleagues in which the majority of Christians belong to the Ortho-dox: Greece, Bulgaria, Old Serbia, and Roumania. This is not a very large percentage of the nations belonging to the League, but the populations concerned are very large. They have taken for centuries a very ardent interest in these subjects. Indeed, I suppose, historically, the Orthodox Church may be said to be more intimately connected with them than the Catholic, although I am well aware that there was no division between the two in the earlier days in which these sacred places began to be officially reverenced by large ecclesiastical communities. There is no representative of the Orthodox Church on the Council and it has few representatives in the League of Nations itself. Therefore, no system can be accepted by the Mandatory Power which does not give these nations justice. Therefore as I see the question, these are the two difficulties which present themselves. There is a difficulty within the Catholic Church itself, which I beg the representatives of the countries in which the majority of Christians are Catholic to do their best to solve. There is also the difficulty of settling disputes on a perfectly fair basis when they arise between Catholic and Orthodox.

The Mandatory Power is most anxious to arrive at a solution. The solution which it first suggested is one that has to be abandoned. We ask for the cooperation of our colleagues around this table to help us to solve their own difficulties, and to help us to arrive at a solution which shall be regarded as equitable by all the world, whether it be Catholic, whether it be Orthodox, whether it be Protestant, or whether it be indifferent to all these religions and only desirous that justice shall be done, that peace, order and decorum be preserved within the limits of Palestine, of which we have become the Mandatory Power.[14]

Thus the attempts to examine 'once and for all the controversies between the Christian communities who officiate in the Holy Places' had come to an end. Britain had done her utmost to bring about a settlement 'in the spirit of justice and impartiality' for which Cardinal Gasparri had praised her. She had not been herself directly involved in the conflict, and had shown understanding and sympathy for 'matters so near the hearts and traditions of mankind . . . affecting the most sacred sentiments'. But it was impossible to reach any solution without the active cooperation of the Churches themselves; and as long as the Churches lived in the 'darkness of the schism' – to use a phrase shaped by a great Christian leader nearly half a century later – all attempts were doomed. In reality, the conflict about the Holy Places was but a symptom of the illness, not the illness itself. The day had not yet come for the Churches to meet each other. Until then, the only course to take was to maintain the status quo and to wait for the dawn.

In Rome Pius XII once more repeated the demand that 'the rights of the Catholic Church in view of their obvious superiority must be given priority before all – Jews, Infidels and the non-Catholic denominations'[15] and in Palestine, Great Britain as Mandatory Power took on full responsibility. In the next year her first report to the Council of the League, submitted in accordance with Article 24 of the Mandate contained the following passage:

The Administration of Palestine has assumed responsibility for the Holy Places and religious buildings and sites as successor to the Turkish Government. In all specific cases that have arisen it has strictly maintained the status quo and has postponed the final determination of any disputed questions until the establishment of the Holy Places Commission.

As has been described, the Holy Places Commission never came into existence, and on 25 July 1924, The Palestine (Holy Places) Order-in-Council transferred all power concerning the Holy Places to the High Commissioner. No dispute about them could be brought before any Court, and the High Commissioner himself was to decide finally.

Notwithstanding anything to the contrary in the Palestine Order-in-Council 1922, or in any Ordinance or Law in Palestine, no cause or matter in connection with the Holy Places or religious buildings or sites or the rights or claims relating to the different religious communities in Palestine shall be heard or determined by any Court in Palestine.

If any question arises whether any cause or matter comes within the terms of the preceding Article hereof, such question shall, pending the constitution of a Commission charged with jurisdiction over the matters set out in the said Article, be referred to the High Commissioner, who shall decide the question after making due enquiry into the matter in accordance with such instructions as he may receive from one of His Majesty's Principal Secretaries of State.

The decision of the High Commissioner shall be final and binding on all parties.

A few years later the Mandatory Government produced a confidential memorandum on the Status Quo in the Holy Places for the officers of the Government of Palestine who had to administer and give decisions upon the interpretation of the status quo. It gives a detailed account of the share of the different Christian communities in the Sanctuaries and a succinct description of the complicated practice of the most important services in the Basilica of the Nativity and the Church of the Holy Sepulchre. According to Sir Harry Luke, then Chief Secretary to the Government of Palestine, who wrote an introduction to the memorandum, it is the only collection extant of the rulings and decisions taken since 1918 and a 'valuable *vademecum* to those charged with the delicate duty of applying one of the most fluid and imprecise codes in the world'.

But it does more than help the civil servants. By giving the most minute description of the details which have to be attended to in order to maintain the status quo – ranging from the allocation of time for the service of the different communities, the ownership and the use of space in the different parts of the Churches, the questions of repairs and replacements, the position of lamps, vessels, candelabras and candles, icons and hangings, down to the issues of cleaning, dusting and washing of steps and floors, the number of persons to be employed for the purpose and even the implements to be used – it reveals to what extent the division of the Church permeates the Sanctuaries everywhere, in all things and at all times. This is true not only when services of the various denominations are held simultaneously in mutual disregard of each other, but also in the permanent awareness of the silent presence of the heterodox dissenter; and this awareness of the schism may affect the freedom of religious experience and service more deeply than any interference by hostile forces from outside. Yet, as the whole panorama of the division in all its manifestations is unfolded, it can be felt that the separated parts of the Church – in spite of the many tensions between them – are directed towards the same aim and united in the hope for ultimate reunion.

The Memorandum of the Government was kept for internal use only, and not available to the public. It can, however, now be published, and in view of its significance for the rulers of the country, the religious communities themselves, and a general understanding of the situation, its essential parts are added as an appendix. (See Appendix 6).

4 Government for the Sake of the Holy Places: First Attempts at Internationalisation

As the Mandate over Palestine drew to its end, a new international conception developed according to which the government of Jerusalem ought to be organised – not for the sake of the local inhabitants, but for that of the Holy Places. The Prussian suggestions of 1841 about an international agreement on Jerusalem, Bethlehem and Nazareth had laid the main emphasis on the Christian populations of these cities. They provided that these populations would maintain their domicile in the places where they lived, but would become independent from Ottoman rule and have an organisation and a government of their own. As far as the territory of the three cities was concerned, the proposals limited interference with Turkish sovereignty to a minimum. They aimed at internationalisation not of the cities but of the Christian Holy Places only, leaving the towns themselves – including the Moslem and Jewish Sanctuaries – to the Turks.

The suggestions at the end of the Mandate were of a different kind. They gave first priority to the territories involved and showed much less concern for the populations living in them. Already the Peel Commission which, in 1937, proposed the partition of Palestine by the creation of a Jewish and an Arab State, envisaged a special regime for the towns and districts in which the Holy Places are situated.

'The partition of Palestine,' the report said, 'is subject to the overriding necessity of keeping the sanctity of Jerusalem and Bethlehem inviolate and of securing free and safe access to them for all the world.'[1] Therefore an enclave was to be demarcated comprising both cities, and access to the sea was to be provided by a corridor including the towns Lydda and Ramle and terminating at Jaffa. In addition, the Commission felt 'it would accord with Christian sentiment in the world at large if Nazareth and the Sea of Galilee (Lake Tiberias) were included in the scheme'. To preserve the sanctity of these places was 'in the fullest sense of the mandatory phrase "a sacred trust of civilisation", a trust on behalf not merely of the peoples of Palestine but of multitudes in other lands to whom those places one or both, are Holy Places.'

The Commission apparently assumed as obvious that the local populations were unable to fulfil this task. In fact, such a possibility was not mentioned in the whole report with one single word. Perhaps the Commission feared that the continued hostility between Jews and Arabs would make any cooperation between them – even in this limited and unpolitical field – impracticable, or they were convinced that a matter of such universal significance ought to be handled by an international body.

Possibly even the plan was just a remnant of a colonialist mentality. Whatever the reasons, the Peel Commission suggested that a new mandate should be given to Great Britain for the administration of the territories in question 'with the execution of this trust – i.e. the preservation of the sanctity of Jerusalem, Bethlehem and Nazareth – as its primary purpose'. The legal basis of this suggestion, however was doubtful; because Article 22 of the Covenant of the League of Nations on which all mandates are founded, laid down that mandates could only be created for the sake of '*peoples* not yet able to stand by themselves under the strenuous conditions of the modern world' and that the purpose of the tutelage was 'the well-being and development of such peoples'. It did not provide for the creation of mandates for the sake of *religions*, particularly if the adherents of the religion in question in their overwhelming majority lived outside the territory to be mandated. Moreover the aim of a mandate was undoubtedly self-government by the local population. Nobody could deny that the Jewish part of the population was 'able to stand by themselves'; and as for the Palestinian Arabs the Peel Commission itself admitted 'that they were as well qualified for self-government as the Arabs of neighbouring countries' (Ch. xx, para. 10). Nevertheless self-government was to be denied to the local inhabitants, not because of their incapacity but for religious considerations.

'It might frankly be stated,' the report said, 'that while it would be the trustees' duty to promote the well-being and development of the local population, *it is not intended* that in course of time they should stand by themselves as a wholly *self-governing* community.'

The local population, therefore, was asked to renounce for ever – for the sake of the Holy Places – their title to self-government, a fundamental and inalienable right, often described as sacred, which to assert for all nations had been one of the noblest aims of the Allies in the First World War; and this demand was made although the populations in question had never given the slightest indication that they would be unwilling or unable to administer the Holy Places adequately themselves. Obviously here was a conflict between the right to self-government and a religious interest of the world at large, and this conflict certainly required a fuller examination than the simple statement – contained in one single sentence – that the sanctity of Jerusalem and Bethlehem is 'an overriding necessity'.

As far as the Holy Places are concerned the report of the Peel Commission in spite of its general excellence showed insufficient regard for the rights of the populations involved; and this lack of sensitivity to their feelings found the most striking expression in the suggestion (Ch. xxII, para. 13) that the only 'official language' in Jerusalem, Bethlehem, Nazareth and even on the Lake of Tiberias – for the fishermen of Galilee – should be English, the language of the Mandatory Administration. The Prussian suggestions of 1841 had been more considerate.

Enforced Sanctity or Self-determination?

The matter was taken up by the United Nations immediately after the end of the Second World War. The first body to deal with it, was the United Nations Special Committee on Palestine

(UNSCOP).[2] They agreed unanimously on the need for Free Access to the Sanctuaries, Freedom of Worship and the Preservation of the Holy Places. Thus far they were in accordance with all other committees and commissions who before or after them had dealt with the Holy Places. All have accepted these principles in the same or similar formulations, and they can indeed be described as essential for the continued existence and satisfactory functioning of the Sanctuaries.

Difficulties however arose in the Committee on the question how the 'essentials' were to be put into practice. Had the application to be enforced or could it be left to the free decision of the local inhabitants? The majority of the Committee felt that force had to be used and therefore suggested that – independent from the will of the population – an *international regime* under the Trusteeship Council had to be established. The minority however, consisting of the representatives of India, Iran and Yugoslavia, were willing to entrust the responsibility for the administration of the Holy Places to the peoples in the territory. They accordingly suggested the creation of a federal state with Jerusalem as its capital and advised at the same time *supervision* by a permanent international body.

The General Assembly in its famous Resolution of 29 November 1947 followed the main lines of the majority report. Accordingly they recommended the partition of Palestine and proposed the establishment of Jerusalem as a *corpus separatum* under a special international regime, to be administered by the United Nations. The special objectives of the Administration Authority, as far as they are relevant here, were defined as follows:

> To protect and to preserve the unique spiritual and religious interests located in the city of the three great monotheistic faiths throughout the world, Christian, Jewish and Moslem; to this end to ensure that order and peace, and especially religious peace reigns in Jerusalem.

A Governor was to be appointed to represent the United Nations in the City and to exercise on their behalf all powers of administration. He was to be selected on the basis of special qualifications and without regard to nationality. He was, however, not to be a citizen of either State in Palestine.

The Trusteeship Council was instructed to elaborate a Statute of the City. Concerning the Holy Places it had to incorporate the generally accepted 'essentials' (free access, free exercise of worship and preservation of the Holy Places) to which freedom from taxation was added. Furthermore the following provisions were laid down.

The protection of the Holy Places in the City of Jerusalem was to be a special concern of the Governor. He was also to be empowered to make decisions on the basis of 'existing rights' in cases of disputes between the different religious communities or the rites of a religious community in respect of the Holy Places; and was entitled to call for assistance in this task by a consultative council.

The regime was to remain in force in the first instance for a period of ten years and then be subject to re-examination in the light of the experience acquired. The residents of the City were then to be 'free to express by means of a referendum their wishes as to possible modifications of the regime of the City'.

The Trusteeship Council submitted its draft of the Statute for the City of Jerusalem on 21 April 1948. Soon afterwards fighting between Israel and the Arab States began, and when on 11 June the first armistice was concluded, Jerusalem was divided, and the Old City containing most of the Holy Places as well as Bethlehem were in Arab hands. Already on 28 May, King Abdullah had entered the Old City and sent a cable to the Pope, assuring him that the Christian Sanctuaries would be protected. The international debate about the settlement, however, continued.

The Holy See Joins the Plea for a Corpus Separatum

In October Pope Pius XII issued the Encyclical *In Multiplicibus Curis*[3] about Palestine and in particular the Christian Holy Places. The facts upon which it was based naturally were the same as those which had faced the United Nations, but they were seen in a very different perspective. The United Nations – comprising adherents of all religions as well as unbelievers – had spoken as a political body. The Encyclical was a voice of Christendom. The United Nations were concerned primarily with the political aspect of the struggle between the two nations

– the Church saw the conflict against the background of the Christian drama; and whilst to the worldly observer the issue of the Christian Holy Places appeared almost incidental to the Arab-Israel conflict, to Rome the Holy Places naturally were a central issue. The most urgent task was to preserve the sanctity of the Holy Land.

No event [the Encyclical said] neither joyful nor sad, can mitigate the sorrow of Our Soul at the thought that in the Land where our Lord Jesus Christ shed His blood to bring redemption and salvation to all mankind, the blood of men continues to flow; and that under the heavens where the first angelic message of peace resounded in the Christmas night, men continue to fight.

The destruction which the Holy City had suffered in the fighting of the preceding months intensified the sorrow by the fear of worse things to come:

We do not believe that the Christian world can remain indifferent or satisfied with sterile indignation, seeing this Holy Land which was so sweet for all to visit and which one only approached with profound respect to kiss the sacred soil with ardent love, being devastated today by iron and fire of armies at war, ruined and laid waste by air bombardment. It seems to us utterly incredible that the Christian world will allow the Holy Places to be ravaged and the Tomb of Christ be destroyed. On the contrary we have full confidence that an order will be established which guarantees to each party public and private security and at the same time creates the preconditions of a spiritual and social life which can form the foundations of a normal and true well-being.

Thus, the Encyclical joined the plea for the establishment of an international regime for Jerusalem.

It is entirely appropriate to give Jerusalem and its surroundings where so many precious souvenirs of the life and death of the Saviour are to be found, an international regime, legally established and guaranteed.

But the Encyclical did not comment on the sacrifice which the establishment of such a regime would entail for the local populations, largely non-Christian, who would have to be deprived of their right of self-government.

Realising that an international regime, as such, does not

77

necessarily create the conditions for the preservation and satisfactory functioning of the Sanctuaries, the Encyclical incorporated the universally accepted 'essentials' for this purpose, and in doing so even referred to the established customs and religious traditions:

It will be equally appropriate to secure by international guarantees free access to the Holy Places, freedom of cult for the different Christian denominations and lastly the respect for the customs and religious traditions inherited from the past.

The Pope had spoken for Christendom as a whole and the Encyclical did not refer with any word to the internal Christian conflict about the Holy Places. In fact, the reference to the cults of the different Christian communities and to the 'customs and religious traditions inherited from the past' almost gave the impression that the Holy See now accepted the status quo.[4] But such assumption was rectified by the Encyclical '*Redemptoris Nostri*'[5] which was issued a few months later, at Easter 1949.

The Corpus Separatum *and the Division of the Church*

The Encyclical '*Redemptoris Nostri*' reaffirmed and strengthened the position which '*In Multiplicibus*' had taken. The Christian link with the Holy Land was stressed again:

During these days of the Holy Week the thoughts of the Christians, imbued with profound respect, turn to this land which by the design of divine Providence was chosen to be the fatherland of the Word Incarnate, and in which Jesus Christ spent His earthly life and died after having poured out His blood.

It reaffirmed the need of giving Jerusalem and its surroundings 'where the venerable souvenirs of the life and death of the Saviour are to be found a regime which is established and guaranteed by international law'. Like its predecessor it did not mention what such a regime might mean for the local inhabitants. But it stressed, perhaps more than had been done before, that under the existing conditions of war and tension an international regime might be more suitable to guarantee preservation and protection of the Sanctuaries than any other government. Apart from this, the Encyclical extended the demands of the Church in two directions: firstly it claimed that the international guarantee should not be limited to the Sanctuaries in Jerusalem and surroundings but should comprise all Christian Sanctuaries in Palestine, wherever they might be situated. Secondly, it made special claims concerning the rights of the Catholic Church. The Encyclical '*In Multiplicibus*' had not mentioned Catholics, it had spoken for Christian interests as a whole. '*Redemptoris Nostri*' put forward Catholic interests in three fields: it urged that the 'freedom of Catholics' should be assured at the same time as the preservation and protection of the very Holy Places. It pleaded ardently for the numerous Catholic establishments in Palestine in the field of charity, education and pilgrims' welfare; and most important of all, it reserved all Catholic rights to the Holy Places:

We do not wish to pass over in silence that it is necessary to preserve intact all rights to the Holy Places which the Catholics have acquired since long centuries, which they have valiantly and repeatedly defended, and which our Predecessors have proclaimed solemnly and efficiently.

This reference to the rights of the Catholics naturally did not concern the Arab-Israel conflict, nor even the security and protection of the Holy Places. It only had a meaning with regard to the internal Christian rivalry between the Latins and the Orthodox. Thus far it was a reminder of the claims which Cardinal Gasparri had made nearly thirty years earlier in the deliberations of the League of Nations; and this was confirmed when on 1 September 1949, the Vatican Radio proclaimed that 'the rights of the Catholic Church over the Holy Land and the Sanctuaries which are spread over it have priority before those acquired by other Christian denominations'[6].

Meanwhile the General Assembly in its session on 11 December 1948, had established a Conciliation Commission and confirmed that the Holy Places – including Nazareth – should be protected and free access to them assured, in accordance with existing rights and historical practice; that arrangements to this end should be under effective United Nations supervision; that the Conciliation Commission in presenting its proposals should include recommendations concerning the Holy Places; and that, in view of its association with three world religions, the Jerusalem area should be placed under effective United Nations control.

At the end of November 1949 the reports of the Conciliation Commission were considered by the Ad Hoc Political Committee of the General Assembly. The representative of Jordan expressed the hope that no form of internationalisation would be adopted which was detrimental to the safety, integrity and interest of his country. Internationalisation, he protested, would serve no useful purpose, since the Holy Places under the control of his Government were safe, and there was no need for a special regime.[7] But the Committee remained unmoved and recommended to the General Assembly to proceed with the scheme. In the Assembly the nations were now divided on different lines than in November 1947 when the basic decision on the internationalisation of Jerusalem had been passed. Among those who upheld the principle were Argentine, Australia, Brazil, Cuba, Egypt, El Salvador, Greece, Haiti, Iraq, Lebanon, Pakistan, Peru, Syria and the Soviet Union. The Arab members of the group declared that 'in justice and equity Jerusalem should remain an Arab city, but since, regrettably, the Arab point of view did not prevail in international politics, they were forced to accept full and complete internationalisation as the lesser evil'. The Catholic countries considered internationalisation in keeping with their wishes. The representative of Greece felt that no solution could be regarded as satisfactory which did not protect the Holy Places from any temporal power which at any moment, by a unilateral act, might invalidate the most solemn guarantees[8] and the Soviet Union expressed the belief that internationalisation would ensure peace and security in Jerusalem and would meet the interests of the population of the City and of all religious groups.

Among those who now opposed internationalisation were Canada, Denmark, Guatemala, Israel, the Netherlands, Norway, Sweden, South Africa, Great Britain, the United States and Yugoslavia. Jordan had informed the Assembly that she would oppose the execution of any decision contrary to its rightful wishes. The representative of Israel declared that the plan was 'an attempt to fly in the face of legitimate and unalterable realities which would end in fiasco and leave the Holy

Places without adequate provision'. The Canadian representative stated that to adopt a solution which would not work would be a disservice to the United Nations and an act of irresponsibility towards the Holy Places. Others stressed the difficulties and dangers of the project. The Netherlands and Norway felt that the scheme could not work without the support of the two Governments most concerned, and since both Israel and Jordan had rejected it, an internationalised Jerusalem and its Holy Places 'would be surrounded by hostile forces and a population hostile to the international agreement'. South Africa warned against disregarding the 'legitimate rights and interests of those States in which Jerusalem was situated'. Great Britain thought that 'as a theoretical exercise the scheme might be impeccable, but that it was removed from reality'; and the representative of the United States considered that the adoption of the plan would involve the United Nations in countless difficulties and responsibilities.

At the end of the debate, on 9 December 1949, the General Assembly restated its 'intention that Jerusalem should be placed under a permanent international regime, which should envisage appropriate guarantees for the protection of the Holy Places, both within and outside Jerusalem; that the City of Jerusalem should be established as a *corpus separatum* under a special international regime and be administered by the United Nations'. At the same time the Trusteeship Council was asked to complete the preparation of the Statute of Jerusalem giving due regard to the changed conditions.

On 19 January 1950, Mr Roger Garreau, then President of the Trusteeship Council, submitted his proposals. They were based, of course, on the principle of internationalisation, but in view of the fact that Jerusalem was actually divided, they suggested that not only was Palestine to be partitioned into three units, but Jerusalem itself thould be subdivided into three parts: an Israeli and a Jordanian zone and an 'International City'. Practically the whole of the new New City was to be under the sovereignty of Israel; the Arab Quarters of the Old City, including the Temple area, would remain under the sovereignty of Jordan, and the International City was to include all the Christian Holy Places covered by the Status Quo of 1757.

The Council consulted the major religious communities

concerned, and their replies were most characteristic: Catholic organisations representing seventy-one countries in five continents fully supported the scheme for the internationalisation of Jerusalem and 'expressed their confidence that the Trusteeship Council would ensure its full and faithful implementation'.

The representatives of the Greek Orthodox and the Armenian Patriarchates of Jerusalem stressed, first and foremost, the need for maintaining the status quo, as if they feared that the internationalisation of the City might lead to a change of the internal balance between the Christian Churches in favour of the Latins. Perhaps the encyclical '*Redemptoris Nostri*' had created such a suspicion. In any case, both made the preservation of the status quo the precondition for their agreement to the scheme.

The fundamental principle [the statement of the Orthodox Patriarchate said] adhered to until today with regard to the Holy Places, religious buildings and sites in Jerusalem and the surrounding area has been the maintenance of the existing rights. It is deemed essential further to adhere to this principle of the Status Quo and to find the way to express it in an unambiguous form, *thus laying the basis for the international status of the Holy City*.

Similarly the Armenian Patriarchate proclaimed:

The Armenian Church firmly believes that it is absolutely necessary to maintain the principle of the Status Quo in the Statute to be drawn by the Trusteeship Council for eventual adoption by the authorities of the United Nations Organisation for the care and responsibility over the Holy Places. During the British Mandate over Palestine this principle was judiciously maintained, and all the interested communities enjoyed their rights and privileges peacefully to the benefit of all concerned. Any new and radical disposition concerning the maintenance and the use of the Holy Places would undoubtedly re-create among the Christian communities of the Holy Land dissensions and disputes, which for many years have been gradually eliminated by the continued application of the Status Quo, resulting in harmonious agreements and accord. We believe that rights and privileges which have prevailed for over a thousand years should be respected to the extent to which they are exercised at present. Countless generations of members of the Churches sharing the use and the responsibilities in the Holy Places have made heavy sacrifices in order to be able to worship their Lord in accordance with their own religious rite on the very places which have been hallowed by the acts of His earthly life; any disregard of this fact would result in grave injustice. Therefore we believe that the centuries-old principle of the Status Quo is, and should continue to be, *the sole legal basis* for the disposition of the Holy Places provided in the future status of Jerusalem.

In addition to the demand for the maintenance of the status quo, the Greek Orthodox Patriarch submitted a number of other suggestions of which the most interesting concerned the impartiality of the Governor and the administrators. Already the Resolution of the General Assembly of the UN of November 1947 had laid down that the Governor of the City of Jerusalem should not be a citizen of either the Arab or the Jewish State in Palestine. The Patriarch added a religious qualification and demanded that the Governor should not belong to any community which had rights in the Holy Places; and extended this qualification even to the members of any Committee which may have jurisdiction over the Sanctuaries:

With regard to the person or persons to whom the administration of the Holy City will be entrusted, provision will be made, no doubt, to ensure that they will be selected or appointed from among persons whose impartiality is beyond question. An additional guarantee, however, which the Orthodox Patriarchate is ready to suggest, is that these persons should not belong to any of the denominations having direct interest in the keeping of the Holy Places. The same consideration would apply to any judicial body eventually to be established with jurisdiction over disputes involving the Holy Places.

Both the Latin and the Orthodox Churches throughout their history have always attached the greatest importance to charity towards the poor, the sick and the homeless. But none of their statements to the United Nations concerning Jerusalem and the Holy Places refers with a single word to the fundamental rights of the local populations, the principles of democracy and self-government or even the most elementary human freedoms; and the representative of the Custos of the Holy Land – testifying in 1947 before the United Nations Special Committee on Palestine – at the eve of the tragic war between Israel and the Arab States even went so far as to declare:[9]

83

We are *indifferent* to the political tug-of-war that is now raging in Palestine and which has riveted world-wide attention. *However*, it is of paramount *importance* that solid international guarantees embodying effective protective measures for the safe-guarding and preservation of these *Christian shrines* be assured.

Those Churches which have no direct rights to the Holy Places expressed more concern for the local inhabitants. Thus the Commission of the Churches on International Affairs, a joint agency of the World Council of Churches and the International Missionary Council, proclaimed as the first basic condition for any solution the recognition of human rights and fundamental freedoms:

Human rights and fundamental freedoms, and particularly, full religious liberty, must be safeguarded for all without distinction as to race, sex, language or religion.

This no doubt included the right of self-government.

The second condition in their view was the protection of the Holy Places and free access thereto.

Our primary concern [their statement reads] is with *people*, not *places*, and therefore we have stressed first of all the rights and freedoms of all men. Nevertheless we cannot ignore buildings and sites which are monuments of sacred events in the past and which stand indeed as Holy Places for people today, and for generations to follow. . . . Their protection and the opportunity of free access to them should be accepted as an international responsibility.

They felt that a combination of both principles should be aimed at.

This will require, we believe, political arrangements wherein measures for the protection and world-wide use of the Holy Places are *integrated* with the guarantee of human rights and freedoms for all inhabitants.

They did not appeal for internationalisation of the Holy City.

The American Christian Palestine Committee went even further:

We believe that the plan to internationalise the Jerusalem area is dangerous and unnecessary. The overwhelming majority of leaders of religious groups we interviewed expressed the belief it would not work. Many held it was impractical and certain to add confusion and impede peace negotiations now in progress. Total internationalisation is not necessary for the protection of the Holy Places. Neither the Arabs nor Israelis have any other plan or purpose than to protect and preserve them. Moslems have kept these places inviolate for many centuries, and virtually all of them are now in Arab hands. There is not the slightest evidence that Israel will molest or limit the use of any religious institution or shrine. . . .

On the basic issue of internationalisation, we would caution against the drafting of a Jerusalem Statute by the United Nations that would interfere with the just territorial sovereignty of any nation, in this case the territory of Israel and Jordan. Both of these nations properly object to the United Nations plan on this ground. Freedom of access and protection of the Holy Places can easily be secured without the internationalisation of territory or people. . . .

The greatest criticism advanced against all plans outlined to date is that they were drafted without regard to the wishes of the citizens of the Old and New Jerusalem, but rather from the political considerations of the various Member Governments of the United Nations and by outside interests. The plan we, as fact-finders, now propose is the setting up of a United Nations Commission, with no territorial sovereignty, but with full right to seek the removal of existing limitations of access to the Old City of Jerusalem and the Holy Places, all of which are in Arab territory. Guarantees should be given to such a Commission by both Jordan and Israel assuring the freedom and sanctity of the sacred places within their territories. This is all that the Christian world has a right to require of two sovereign States, which we believe will in time compose their differences. This making of the peace will be accomplished all the more speedily if Israel and Jordan are encouraged in their negotiations by the Western Powers.

Accordingly, we call upon our Government to press for a reconsideration of the United Nations Assembly decision and to urge the adoption of a plan such as outlined above. We would point out to all who are justifiably interested in the prestige and power of the United Nations that the reconsideration of its decision is within the prerogatives of the international Organisation, and that the formulation of a just and workable plan for guaranteeing the sanctity of the Holy Places will enhance its prestige and power.

In the political debate Jordan reiterated that it was not prepared to discuss any plan for the internationalisation of Jerusalem, and the representative of Israel likewise repeated his opposition to the plan. The representative of China on the other hand expressed the view that the proposal of the President of the Trusteeship Council to divide Jerusalem was not in accordance with the resolutions of the General Assembly and called for the completion of the Statute for the City of Jerusalem on the basis of full internationalisation. The Council adopted this resolution and on 4 April 1950 passed the Statute on this basis. Accordingly the City of Jerusalem was to be constituted as a *corpus separatum* under the administration of the United Nations.

The report was considered finally by the General Assembly in December of that year. Support for internationalisation had begun to wane. Sweden submitted a plan for a functional rather than territorial internationalisation by which the jurisdiction over and the control of each part of the Jerusalem area was to be exercised by the States concerned but a Commissioner of the United Nations would supervise the protection and free access to the Holy Places. Belgium suggested that four persons, appointed by the Trusteeship Council should study the matter once more and report to the next General Assembly in the following year. Jordan and Israel maintained their opposition and the representative of Israel stated that the two populations of Jerusalem, however divided in other respects, were united in wishing to preserve their own ways of life and were firmly opposed to territorial internationalisation. The unanimous opinion, he added, of the people of Jerusalem together with the economic and administrative unworkability of the scheme made internationalisation impossible.

The representatives of Australia, Denmark, Guatemala, the Netherlands, New Zealand, Turkey, South Africa, the United Kingdom, the United States, Uruguay and Yugoslavia, most of whom had opposed the scheme already at the session of December 1949, expressed the view that an international regime for Jerusalem would be unacceptable to the inhabitants and would thus be undemocratic. Lastly the representative of the Soviet Union, who in the preceding year had still supported the scheme, stated that 'a just solution must take into account the interests of the Jewish and Arab inhabitants of the City of Jerusalem'. It now appeared, he said, that the solution was satisfactory neither to the Arab nor to the Jewish inhabitants. The Soviet Union therefore could not continue to support the project and since both draft resolutions were unsatisfactory would abstain from voting. The report was voted upon by the General Assembly on 15 December and failed to obtain the required two-thirds majority. This brought the attempts to internationalise Jerusalem to an end – at least for the time being.

Jordan, Protector of the Christian Sanctuaries

On 5 January 1951 King Abdullah issued a *berat* by which he appointed a guardian and supreme custodian over all the Holy Places – Moslem, Christian and Jewish – whose authority was to be paramount. The guardian was therefore, as far as the administration was concerned, of higher standing than the heads of the different religious communities. The King instructed the new guardian to maintain the status quo for all, and to prepare a register of all rights and titles which would be official evidence and to which reference could be made in the case of need. The *berat* therefore combined, as it were, in its contents the 'Palestine (Holy Places) Order in Council' and Article 14 of the Mandate. But whilst these had been formulated in the terse style of English law, the *berat* was expressed with all the courtesy and beauty of the East.

We Abdullah ibn Al-Hussein, King of the Hashemite Jordan, by the grace of God, address ourselves to the example of a right-thinking man, a paragon of dignity, to the designated arbiter of the religious affairs and religious communities, in view of his penetrating thought and his wise understanding, to the man invested with glory and generosity, to our well beloved minister H.E. Raghib Pasha Al-Nashashibi, holder of the first class order of the Nahda.

Having ascertained that you possess eminent qualities and that your past was an example of wisdom, We have expressed our Royal wish to appoint you Guardian of the Haram Al-Sharif and supreme Custodian of the Holy Places. We hope that you will devote your knowledge and your efforts to protect the Mosque El-Aksa, which is blessed by God who has helped our soldiers and partisans to rededicate it to its original destiny; that you will extend your benevolence and your protection to all communities and the pilgrims of all nations; that you will safeguard with extreme diligence their rights, their beliefs, their cults and the places of their prayers; that within the limits of the Status Quo order will be respected, that the communities, the mosques and the churches will be assured in their respective rights, in order that peace and love – following the example of the great prophets – will here prevail; that between

87

brethren within the community of men – and in an Arab country which is sanctified by all the faiths – the divine beliefs will manifest themselves so that the prayers can be performed and the invocations of the godhead can ascend; that the guarantees will be maintained, reviving under your leadership the reign of Omar and the tradition handed down from generation to generation through all the reigns of Islam; that all the firmans of the sultans and the traditional rights, of which the patriarchs are the depositaries will be checked and recorded *'ne varietur'* in a special register for evidence to which one can refer in case of need; that faithful to a glorious past you will accomplish noble deeds, avoid mistakes and will make end to oppression; that you will observe the word of the Koran: O you humans we have created you male and female, we have divided you into nations and tribes in order that you knowest that the noblest among you is before God the most pious. May God forgive your faults and give you with his blessing courage, strength, happiness and success.[10]

Catholics everywhere saw in this measure a violation of the status quo of the Holy Places,[11] and when on 15 January Raghib Pasha Al-Nashashibi was inducted into his new office in the presence of the highest dignitaries, including the Consuls of the United States, Great Britain, Holland, Turkey and Greece, the representatives of France, Italy, Belgium and Spain signified their protest by not attending.

To the Jordanians the solemn investiture of the supreme Guardian of the Holy Places had been a major event, the assertion of sovereign power by the state, a significant fulfilment of national aspirations. The abstention of the Catholic Consuls, therefore, was felt as a studied rebuff if not a deliberate insult.

This appointment, [the Arab weekly *As Sirih* wrote] the political consequences of which have made themselves felt at the United Nations and in the different foreign capitals, has buried all hope for internationalisation as well as the realisation of the political aims which are hidden behind this project. There is nothing in this appointment which could justify the absence of the representatives of France, Belgium and Italy, and we would proclaim to the face of the world their very clear intentions if we were free to do so. By this appointment we have wished to affirm nothing other than our possession of the Holy City and our determination to see it remains Arab; and for this she can count always on the protection by our army.[12]

This was not a reaction of Islam to Christianity, but the assertion of national sovereignty in the face of religion. In fact, Moslem and Christian Arabs were united and proclaimed their solidarity in the national conflict with Israel. Thus during the Islamic Conference of December 1953, held in Jerusalem, the Moslem delegates visited the Church of the Holy Sepulchre and the Basilica of the Nativity, to show their interest in the Sanctuaries of their Christian brethren and 'to testify that the Moslems are resolved to defend these Holy Places with the same determination which is brought to bear to the defence of the Holy Places of Islam'. Likewise, Sheik Assad El-Iman, secretary of the Council of Ulemas in Jerusalem, assured his Islamic brethren that 'the Christians of this country stand side by side with the Moslems'.

The Moslems [he said] aim at a real Christian brotherhood and stretch out their hands towards their Christian brothers. The Christian sages are pledged to an Islamic – Christian unity in order to propagate the messages of Christ and Mohammed and to save the first Christian sanctuary, the Holy Sepulchre, which Omar handed over to them and the Mosque El-Aksa.[13]

In 1958 the Jordanian Government promulgated a new statute for the Greek Orthodox Patriarchate of Jerusalem.[14] Among other items it dealt with the relationship between the Arab Orthodox laity and the Greek clergy which since the nineteenth century had occupied the attention of successive governments and indeed of the Russian Church. The new statute strengthened the position of the Arabic-speaking members of the Church. It laid down that the Patriarch and his Suffragan Bishops must be citizens of Jordan and must be able to speak and write Arabic; in addition, it increased the rights of the Arab Christians in the administration of finance, schools and charitable institutions.

As far as the relationship between the Latin and the Orthodox Churches is concerned, no change took place under Jordanian rule, and the status quo in this respect was preserved. The ultimate responsibility for the Christian Holy Places remained, as in the Turkish days, with the state.

D

5 New Developments in the Churches

The Return of the Russian Church – Meeting of Rome and Byzantium

While the formal position of the Holy Places remained unchanged, far-reaching developments took place in the world of the Churches which are bound to affect profoundly the relations of the Christian communities to each other in the Holy Places. The first of these developments concerned the return of the Russian Church – and indeed of Russia herself – to the Middle East. It has been described above how deeply since the nineteenth century Russia had penetrated into Palestine. This expansion had strengthened the Orthodox Churches as a whole in relation to the West and in particular to Rome; it had increased the influence of Moscow compared with Constantinople; and lastly within the Arab world – especially in the Patriarchates Antioch and Jerusalem – it had supported the Arab laity against the Greek clergy. All these developments had come to a standstill with the October Revolution, and for nearly thirty years the interest of the Russian Church in the Middle East had been dormant. The Second World War changed this situation. The Russian Church which had persevered under most difficult conditions, became a powerful factor in the defence of the country against the Germans, and already during the war Stalin had allowed the election of a Patriarch. In 1945, the Moscow Patriarch visited the Middle East to return the visits he had received on the occasion of his election. While in Jerusalem – at that time still under British mandatory rule – he tried to win the White Russian emigrés there with their churches, convents and monasteries back to the authority of Moscow; but the attempt failed. A few years later, in 1948, Moscow celebrated the five hundredth anniversary of the emancipation of the Russian Church from the Ecumenical

Patriarchate of Constantinople. The Patriarch of Antioch attended, representing also the Patriarch of Alexandria. But owing to the tensions between the Greek and Slavonic elements in the Orthodox Church, the Patriarch of Jerusalem – following the example of Athens and Cyprus – did not accept the invitation.

When in 1948 Palestine was divided, most of the Russian monasteries, convents and churches came under Jordanian rule. But the Cathedral and the buildings of the Russian Church Mission were in the part of Jerusalem held by Israel. They were taken over by the Moscow Patriarchate and it soon became customary for the Soviet Diplomatic Mission in Israel and for the Soviet Ambassador himself to attend the services in the Russian Cathedral – particularly at Holy Trinity and St Alexius Day – and to take part in the subsequent receptions.

The Soviet Consulate in Tel Aviv established a special Department for Ecclesiastical Affairs and efforts were made to build new Russian Churches in Israel. According to canonical rules, this requires the permission of the Greek Orthodox Patriarch in Jerusalem and such permission was not easily forthcoming. In fact, voices were raised in Greek circles against the expansion of Russian influence, and conversely among Slavonic Churches it was suggested that the seat of the Ecumenical Patriarchate should be transferred from Constantinople to Moscow. In 1952 the Greek Patriarch of Jerusalem acceded to Moscow's request to break off ecclesiastical relations with the 'dissident communities' of White Russian emigrés and assured the Moscow Patriarch that there would be no longer any communion between his Church and the Russian bishops and ecclesiastics who were separated from the Mother Church in Russia.

From 1955 till 1959 Archbishop Nikodeme, now Metropolitan of Leningrad and Director of the Office of Foreign Relations of the Moscow Patriarchate, was in Jerusalem, first as a member and, from 1957 onwards, as Head of the Moscow Patriarchal Mission, and since then he has returned repeatedly. In 1960 the Patriarch of Moscow visited the Middle East again and went for the first time to Athens and Constantinople. In Syria, Lebanon and Jerusalem the Catholics did not participate in the receptions which were organised in his honour, and there were also certain difficulties in Greece. But the visit strengthened the position of the Russian Church Mission in Jerusalem, and Metropolitan Nikodeme, who accompanied the Patriarch, announced that in view of the outstanding services which the Mission had rendered, the Patriarch had conferred on its head liturgical privileges which are normally reserved for ecclesiastics with episcopal rank.

In 1963, the newly built Russian Chapel of Mary Magdalen on the shore of the Lake of Tiberias was dedicated; and in 1966 Metropolitan Nikodeme visited Jerusalem with a group of pilgrims from Mount Athos. He declared that 'large numbers of Russian Orthodox would like to see the Holy Land', and expressed the hope that 'the movement of such pilgrims in future would considerably increase'.[1]

The second development began in Rome when in 1959 Pope John XXIII announced his intention of calling an Ecumenical Council to promote the restoration of unity among all Christians. This Council – Vatican II – indeed became a turning point in the history of the Churches.

There had been, of course, throughout the years, many serious and important attempts towards reunion, and in certain fields – as for instance between the Anglican and Orthodox Churches, or the latter and the Old Catholics – progress had been made. But as far as the Holy Places were concerned what mattered most was the schism between Rome and Byzantium, the Latins and the Greeks: and in this sphere no real movement towards unity had taken place. The positions seemed to be petrified in their rigidity and the division of the Church appeared almost as a permanent unshakeable foundation of mutual relationship. Now a profound change began to reveal itself, and the schism itself was attacked. Whilst in the past Catholics had conceived Reunion as the return of the separated communities to the authority of Rome, Reunion was now visualised as a movement by all towards a common aim. Moreover, the Council in the Schema on Ecumenism admitted that the disagreements in the past had been due to developments for which 'at times men of both sides were to blame' (Article 3) and called for study and ecumenical dialogue 'on equal footing' (Article 9) in a spirit of charity. This approach opened unprecedented opportunities.

It was during the Council, in January 1964, that Pope Paul VI, who by then had succeeded to the Papal See, made his historic pilgrimage to the Holy Land. Never in the whole history of Christendom had a pope visited the Holy Places. It was the first return to the sources of the faith. In addition the pilgrimage led after centuries of separation to a new meeting between Rome and the highest representatives of the Orthodox Churches; and was hailed for this reason as 'the greatest and most important event in the history of contemporary Christendom'.[2]

On his pilgrimage Pope Paul VI met three of the Eastern Patriarchs: Benedictos I, the Greek Orthodox Patriarch of Jerusalem; Yeghishe Derdérian, the Armenian Patriarch of Jerusalem; and Athenagoras I, the Ecumenical Patriarch who had come from Constantinople. In a 'Sacred Encounter' they met in Jerusalem, 'the centre of Christianity, the centre of the world'. And the words they addressed to each other – after a separation of the Churches lasting nearly a thousand years which had often been poisoned by bitterness – point to a new era in the history of Christendom.[3]

'Very Holy Pope, who presides over the Roman Catholic Church,' the Greek Patriarch of Jerusalem addressed the distinguished pilgrim, 'Zion, the venerable Mother of the Churches, joyfully salutes your happy arrival.'

'It is our most cherished wish,' said Pope Paul in his reply, 'that charity may reign more and more between all . . .'

'Great is our emotion,' said the Pope to Archbishop Athenagoras, 'profound is our joy in this truly historic hour when after centuries of silence and waiting the Catholic Church and the Patriarchate of Constantinople meet again in the presence of their highest representatives. . . . An ancient Christian tradition likes to see "the centre of the world" in the place where the Cross was erected and it was appropriate that we pilgrims from Rome and Constantinople could meet in this place – blessed and sacred for ever – and unite in common prayer. . . .'

'For centuries,' Athenagoras replied, 'the Christian world lived in the night of separation. Their eyes became tired by staring into the darkness. May this meeting be the dawn of a bright and blessed day.'

And the two pilgrims jointly prayed to God

that this meeting may be the sign and prelude of things to come for the glory of God and the illumination of his faithful people. After so many centuries of silence they now have met each other in the wish to fulfil the will of the Lord and to proclaim the ancient truth of his Gospel entrusted to his Church.

There was an exchange of symbolic presents. The Pope gave to each Patriarch a chalice, signifying the sacramental character of the Eastern Church, whilst the Ecumenical Patriarch presented the Pope with an '*engolpion*' stressing the hierarchical aspect of the Church of Rome.

No attempt of course was made to deal with dogmatic or liturgical questions. 'Differences in field of Doctrine, Liturgy and Discipline must be examined at the right time and place.'[3] But the way was opened for a new approach of the separated Churches to each other in the spirit of Charity.

Whilst the Pope had been able to speak on behalf of the Catholic Church, the Ecumenical Patriarch does not enjoy equal authority, and decisions have to be made by the individual Orthodox Churches themselves.

In November 1964, the third Pan-Orthodox Conference met in Rhodes to consider the issue. 'It is just to recognise,' said the president in his opening address, 'that the venerable Roman Catholic Church has done much to promote unity with our Orthodox Church by creating a favourable climate for the development – faster than could be expected – of a *rapprochement* between the Churches of the Ancient and the New Rome towards Christian unity. Particularly the visit of Pope Paul VI to the Holy Places of the East and his meeting at Jerusalem with Patriarch Athenagoras I is an historic event and a milestone on the way towards new relationships between the Orthodox and the Roman Catholic Churches.'[4]

He warned that the way to reunion would be long and difficult, that it would be necessary to overcome 'the obscurity of prejudices and intolerance, conceit and presumption, exclusiveness and narrowness'.

We must equally take into consideration the Platonic structure of Eastern theology and the Aristotelian inspiration of the theology of the West . . . and we must recognise on both sides that propaganda, proselytism, the tendency to absorb one Church by the other, and the invitations to return, are methods of the past, rejected by the Christian conscience which will but aggravate the breach, increase the suspicions and perpetuate the separation. The Churches, therefore, are called to repent, and to ask mutual forgiveness. . . .

The Pope himself had sent to the conference a message of goodwill – in itself an unprecedented act – which was read to the assembly in the three official languages of the Conference, Greek, Russian and Arabic.

Concerning the proposed dialogue with the Roman Church different tendencies came to light. The representatives of Constantinople felt that contacts should be taken up as soon as possible; others were of the opinion that conversations should be postponed until the end of the Vatican Council; and a third group consisting of the Slavonic Churches, the Rumanian Church, and the Patriarchate of Antioch wished to move even more cautiously. This latter attitude ultimately prevailed, and the Conference decided unanimously that the time for a true theological dialogue with Rome had not yet come, that further preparations were required, and that the individual Orthodox Churches should study the issues and exchange their views on the result of their studies. It was, however, left to each of the Orthodox Churches to continue its fraternal relations with the Roman Catholic Church on its own account – but not on behalf of the totality of the Orthodox Churches.

Metropolitan Meliton, the President of the conference, summed up the situation as follows:

The Conference has decided that the Orthodox Church will prepare itself by the work of the local Churches, work conducted in depth and systematically for an official theological dialogue, on equal level with the Church of Rome. But at the same time and on the same subject, the conference has decided to begin here and now the Dialogue of Charity in cultivating fraternal relations between the local Orthodox Churches and the venerable Roman Catholic Church. We shall ourselves begin to exercise charity. A dialogue requires studies. Charity has no need for studies. It needs practice, initiative, generosity and the spirit of sacrifice. The Dialogue of Charity precedes the Dialogue of the Churches.[5]

In the spirit of these words a remarkable adventure in charity, imagination and forgiveness was performed jointly by Rome and Constantinople. The symbol of the schism between East and West had been throughout the centuries the mutual excommunications of 1054, when Humbert, the ambassador of Pope Leo IX, had placed on the altar of the Hagia Sophia the bull of excommunication of the Patriarch Michael Cerularius, and the latter condemned the ambassador and those who had conceived it. In an unprecedented act Rome and Constantinople decided – after 911 years – to eradicate these events from the memory of the Church. In two ceremonies, held simultaneously on 7 December 1965, in St Peter's Church in Rome before an assembly of Council members and in the presence of a delegation of the Patriarchate of Constantinople, presided over by the Metropolitan Meliton, and in the Patriarchal Church of Istanbul during a solemn liturgy in the presence of a pontifical mission under the presidency of Cardinal Shean, a joint declaration was read which, referring to the deplorable events of 1054, contained the following statements:

Pope Paul VI and the Patriarch Athenagoras I in synod declare in full agreement:

They regret the offensive words, the reproaches without foundation, the condemnable actions which have marked or accompanied the sad events of this epoch: they regret equally and remove from the memory and the world of the Church the sentences of excommunication, the memory of which up to our days has been an obstacle of a reconciliation in charity, and they vow to forget them: they deplore, finally, the unfortunate precedents, and the subsequent events which under the influence of different factors, including lack of understanding and mutual suspicion, led ultimately to an effective rupture of ecclesiastical communion.

They fully realise that this gesture of justice and mutual forgiveness cannot be sufficient to make an end to the differences, ancient and more recent, which subsist between the Roman Catholic Church and the Orthodox Church and which will be overcome by the action of the Holy Spirit through a purification of the hearts, through regrets over the historic injustices and by an effective will to reach understanding and a common expression of the apostolic faith and its requirements.[6]

The reading of this common statement was followed by a final and formal confirmation of the decisions by the Pope and the Patriarch. Before Metropolitan Meliton left Rome, he placed a bunch of flowers in St Peter's Church on the tomb of Leo IX who, nearly a thousand years ago, had sent Cardinal Humbert to Constantinople. He thus concluded the episode of mutual excommunications with a gesture of *'profonde délicatesse'*.

Such were the developments within the Roman and the Orthodox Churches when in June 1967 a new campaign opened in the long-drawn-out war between Israel and the Arab States.

6 We Came to Jerusalem Not to Possess Ourselves of the Holy Places of Others

On 7 June 1967, the Israel Minister of Defence, General Moshe Dayan, broadcast the following proclamation:

This morning the Israel Defence Forces liberated Jerusalem. We have united Jerusalem, the divided capital of Israel. We have returned to the most sacred of our Holy Places, never to part from it again.

To our Arab neighbours we stretch out, again at this hour – and with added emphasis – the hand of peace. And to our Christian and Moslem fellow-citizens we solemnly promise religious freedom and rights.

We came to Jerusalem not to possess ourselves of the Holy Places of others, or to interfere with the members of other faiths, but to safeguard the City's integrity and to live in it with others in unity.

This message, delivered under the immediate impact of a battle, is reverberating still, with the emotions of the fighting certainly expressed with clarity and precision the feelings, the hopes and the intentions of the overwhelming majority of the people of Israel at this historic moment.

As far as the Christian Holy Places are concerned, the most relevant part of the proclamation is the statement: 'We came to Jerusalem not to possess ourselves of the Holy Places of others. . . .' Nobody can doubt the truth of these words. There must have been large numbers of Israelis who had hardly ever heard of the Christian Sanctuaries, and many more who had but the vaguest notion of their significance. No one, certainly, could have seen the purpose of the war in the conquest of the Holy Grave or the Basilica of the Nativity. For the Israelis the issue was their national existence; and their enemy was not the Christian but the Arab, whatever his religion might be. Moreover, the sites of the Christian Sanctuaries have no particular religious significance for Jews. Golgotha was outside the walls, let alone outside the Temple area. Judaism does not lay any special claim to the sites of the Holy Sepulchre or the Basilica of the Nativity.

Concerning the Sanctuaries of Islam, the situation is more complex. Both the Mosques of Omar (Dome of the Rock) and El Aksa stand in the Temple ground. No doubt here too the assurance of inviolability was sincere and valid – but there are complicated questions.

The Temple ground is holy to Moslems and to Jews. It contains the Holiest of the Holies of Jewish memories. Moreover Jewish Orthodoxy has always maintained that ultimately – in the days of the Messiah – the Temple will be rebuilt and the sacrifices be restored. What will happen then to the mosques? These questions were raised most forcefully when the Chief Rabbi of the Israel Army, Brigadier Goren, with some of his followers – within hours after the conquest – entered the Temple area and conducted Jewish prayers on ground that the Moslems consider holy to Islam. The Israel government intervened and the status quo in this respect was re-established.[1] But the suspicions and the fears of the Moslem world have not been allayed, and the ultimate issue is still unsolved.

No such difficulties exist in regard to the Christian Holy Places, and no tensions between Jews and Christians threaten the maintenance of the present state. How then does the new situation compare with the position of the Christian Sanctuaries under Moslem rule? When, in 638, Caliph Omar accepted the surrender of Jerusalem by the Patriarch Sophronius, and the conquered undertook to pay the '*jiza*' (a poll tax or tribute) in accordance with the laws of Islam, he left the Church of the Holy Sepulchre to the Christians. The treaty which was signed reads as follows:

In the name of Allah, the Compassionate, the Merciful: This is what Abdullah Omar, Prince of the Believers has guaranteed to the people of Jerusalem: He has guaranteed their lives, property, churches and crosses ... their churches will not be dwelt in [by foreigners], nor will they be destroyed or ruined in any part. Nor will their crosses or property [be destroyed]; They will not be persecuted for their religion, nor will they be molested. . . . The inhabitants of Jerusalem shall pay the jiza as much as that of the inhabitants of Mada'in. . . .

This document is guaranteed by the assurance of Allah, of His Apostle, of the Caliphs, and of the believers, if [the inhabitants] paid their duties of the jiza.[2]

Similarly Saladin, who in 1187 reconquered the city from the Crusaders, abstained against the suggestions of his advisers, from touching the Holy Grave, and the Church was again left to the Christians.

When in May 1948, Abdullah took the city in the aftermath of the British Mandate, it was no longer a conflict between Islam and Christianity. In fact, his own army contained many Christian soldiers and especially officers. He proclaimed the sovereignty of Jordan over the Old City, but he did not touch the status of the Christian Holy Places, and assured the Pope of their security. Now the Israel government had declared Jerusalem the united capital of Israel. The Christian Sanctuaries are not more affected by this change than by the proclamation of Abdullah. The Church of the Holy Sepulchre and the Basilica of the Nativity remain unchanged in Christian hands as they had been before.

Fundamentally therefore the position of the Christian Holy Places is the same under the rule of Israel as under the Arabs. Yet there are some differences which are not without significance.

Moslem rule over the Christian Sanctuaries had in practice lasted for nearly thirteen hundred years; and thus established a long and living tradition both in the minds of the rulers and the ruled and even of the world at large. Moreover, Arab nationalism – although rooted as much in Islam as Zionism is in Judaism – comprises an active Christian minority. Indeed many of its leading spokesmen and writers are or have been Christians. For them religious and national interests in the Christian Holy Places are one and strengthen each other. Lastly, and perhaps most importantly, Islam has incorporated and absorbed some Christian elements. The firmans of the Sultans pronounce the blessings of God over Jesus and the Virgin Mary, whenever their names are mentioned. All this is different regarding Israel. There never was – prior to 1948 – a time when Jews ruled over Moslems and Christians. Accordingly neither the ruled nor the rulers can look back on any tradition of such a state of affairs. It is a fact never heard of before, and to some even a scandal or a stumbling block. Furthermore, there is no Christian sector in the Jewish National Movement which would create a special link with the Christian Sanctuaries; and lastly, there is no bridge from Judaism to Christianity comparable to that from Islam to the Christian world, and no Jewish blessing is pronounced over Jesus of Nazareth. All these factors may create some challenges for the future. But meanwhile Israel had to proceed with the immediate issues, and this she did.

Immediate Actions

On the same day on which General Dayan broadcast his message to the nation, the Prime Minister, Mr Eshkol, invited the leaders of all religious communities, and having described the events of the preceding days, addressed them as follows:

Order has now been restored with our forces in control of the City and its surroundings. Be assured that no harm of any kind will be allowed to befall the Holy Places. I have asked the Minister of Religious Affairs to contact spiritual leaders in the Old City to ensure orderly relations between them and our forces so that they may pursue their religious and communal activities unhindered. At my instance, he has given instructions that arrangements at the Western Wall shall be determined by the Chief Rabbis of Israel, those in places sacred to Moslems by a Council of Moslem ecclesiastics, and those in places sacred to Christians by a Council of Christian religious dignitaries.[3]

According to these instructions by the Prime Minister, the Minister for Religious Affairs, Dr Z. Wahrhaftig, issued on 8 June the following declaration:

The Proclamation of Israel's Independence of 14 May 1948, vouchsafed equality of rights to citizens of Israel for all faiths and the scrupulous safeguarding of their Holy Places. For the past nineteen years, the State has adhered painstakingly to these principles, ensured full freedom of religious worship to adherents of all faiths, whether citizens of Israel or pilgrims coming to worship at their Holy Places. This has been confirmed more than once by the Heads of religious communities in Israel and by overseas visitors.
Now that further areas have come under Israel control, Holy

Places of supreme importance, sacred to Jews, and foremost among them the Western Wall, as well as to Moslems and Christians, are brought under the jurisdiction of Israel. Immediately after the entry of Israel Defence Forces into the Old City and Bethlehem, the Prime Minister proclaimed, in the presence of the Heads of all the religious communities, that the arrangements for safeguarding the Holy Places would be determined by the respective Heads of the three religions – each for the place sacred to his faith.

I have accordingly appointed a temporary Authority and issued detailed instructions for the faithful observance of the principles enshrined in the Proclamation of Independence. The necessary ordinances are being prepared and within the next few days I will set up responsible councils of religious leaders to implement the legislation.[4]

On 27 June the Knesset (the Parliament of Israel) passed the following law:

PROTECTION OF HOLY PLACES LAW 1967

1 The Holy Places shall be protected from desecration and any other violation and from anything likely to violate the freedom of access of the members of the different religions to the places sacred to them or their feelings with regard to those places.

2 (a) Whoever desecrates or otherwise violates a Holy Place shall be liable to imprisonment for a term of seven years.

  (b) Any person who does anything likely to impair freedom of access to a Holy Place or to hurt the feelings of anyone to whom the place is sacred, shall be liable to imprisonment for a term of five years.

3 This Law shall add to and not derogate from any other law.

4 The Minister of Religious Affairs is charged with the implementation of the Law, and he may, after consultation with, or upon the proposal of, representatives of the religions concerned and with the consent of the Minister of Justice, make regulations as to any matter relating to such implementation.

5 This Law shall come into force on the date of its adoption by the Knesset.[5]

Lastly, the Prime Minister assembled in his office on the same day more than forty religious leaders of the country, including the two Chief Rabbis of Israel, the Greek Orthodox, Latin and Armenian Patriarchs and the Grand Mufti of Jerusalem and addressed them as follows:

It is my pleasure to inform you that the Holy Places in Jerusalem are now open to all who wish to worship at them – members of all faiths, without discrimination. The Government of Israel has made it a cardinal principle of its policy to preserve the Holy Places, to ensure their religious and universal character, and to guarantee free access. Through regular consultation with you, heads of the communities, and with those designated by you, at the appropriate levels, for this purpose, we will continue to maintain this policy and see that it is most faithfully carried out. In these consultations I hope that you will feel free to put forward your proposals, since the aims that I have mentioned are, I am certain, aims that we share in common. Every such proposal will be given full and sympathetic consideration.

It is our intention to entrust the *internal* administration and arrangements of the Holy Places to the religious leaders of the communities to which they respectively belong: the task of carrying out all necessary procedures is in the hands of the Minister of Religious Affairs.

From the horrors of a war openly launched to obliterate the State of Israel a situation has emerged that is full of hope and of almost unlimited possibilities for the people of our region – given the will on all sides to cast away the rancours of the past and start building together for a better future.

The God-sent opportunity thus given us must not be forfeited. Many of us, in different walks of life, will feel called upon to do our part in attaining that harmony and brotherhood which are so essential to a peaceful settlement of Israel-Arab differences. Surely the desire for peace and a better life for humanity is common to the spirit of all the great religions represented here.

To this address the Greek-Orthodox Patriarch of Jerusalem, Benedictos, replied:

We have heard with pleasure of the free access to all holy sites and we deeply appreciate your kind words. . . . I believe that I speak on behalf of all my brothers and fellow-leaders here tonight if I say that we are all pleased with the behaviour of the Israel Army. All of its men have shown us kindness and a willingness to serve us. Everybody has displayed respect for the Holy Places and churches. . . . As religious leaders it is our duty to beseech God Almighty to grant us peace, justice and freedom to worship. . . . We are happy and grateful that the Israel Army has respected the Holy City, our convents, churches and our religious institutions. Let us hope and pray that God will bestow His peace and goodwill upon all of us.

As a result of care and moderation on both sides, fortunately neither the Church of the Holy Sepulchre nor the Basilica of the Nativity had been seriously damaged in the fighting. The task now, therefore, was to protect the Sanctuaries from any desecration, maintain their dignity, and to avoid any molestation of the faithful. The Government set to work on all three counts. As far as is known, there was only one case in which the integrity of a Holy Place was violated. On 2 August a golden tiara, a gift of a queen of Portugal in the seventeenth century to the Church of the Holy Sepulchre, was stolen from the Chapel of the Crucifixion, but it was traced by the police and restored to the Church seven weeks later. Shortly afterwards, two youths who had stolen the tiara (from the Madonna's head) were sentenced to five and four years' imprisonment respectively. No other damage, fortunately, seems to have taken place.

The task of maintaining the dignity of the Churches was of a different kind. It was not so much to prevent any deliberate or wilful desecration but to protect the Sanctuaries against acts of carelessness and ignorance. Besides posting police and military guards outside the Sanctuaries, the Government fixed at the entry of all Holy Places plaques or posters in three languages, containing directions for appropriate behaviour both in the Sanctuaries themselves and – equally important but not always clear to the inexperienced visitor – in the whole area of the Sanctuary, such as courtyards, gardens, cloisters, and so on. The poster fixed at the entry to the area of the Church of the Holy Sepulchre (not to the Church itself) read as follows:

ISRAEL POLICE
INSTRUCTIONS TO THE VISITING PUBLIC

1 The visitor should dress and act in a manner appropriate to the holiness of the site.
2 Eating, drinking, smoking, bringing in animals, bearing arms, and creating a disturbance are forbidden.
3 It is forbidden to enter with babies.
4 The use of radio-transistors, loud conversation and creation of a disturbance are forbidden.
5 Strict attention to local authorities, in all that relates to proper behaviour is obligatory.
6 Those who do not abide by these instructions will be asked to leave the premises.

In addition the Ministry of Religious Affairs fixed similar, although not as detailed, notices at the entrance of every Christian Church.

First Negotiations with the Vatican

At the beginning of July the Under-Secretary of State in the Vatican, Mgr Angelo Felici arrived in Jerusalem to form an opinion of the situation and to discuss it with the Israel Prime Minister; and on 11 July the following joint statement was issued:

In a meeting between Mgr Felici and the Prime Minister which was held in an atmosphere of cordiality and mutual understanding, there were discussed a number of possible formulae that might be taken into consideration for the purposes of an acceptable solution of the important issue connected with the Holy Places. The conversations will continue.[6]

On the next day in the General Assembly of the United Nations the Israel Foreign Minister referred to the issue of the Holy Places. The Israel Government had submitted a statement in accordance with the principles which had been proclaimed earlier by the Prime Minister, confirming 'that the Holy Places of all faiths shall be placed under the responsibility of the religious interests which hold them sacred'. The minister added that in future – and he considered the suggestion as historic – exclusive and unilateral control by the government should be replaced by negotiated agreements. 'Never in human memory has there been any disposition by any government in the region to exclude the Holy Places from its exclusive and unilateral control', and he referred especially to the negotiations between the Israel Prime Minister and Mgr Felici, adding 'that other conversations in a similar sense are being conducted with the representatives of other great world religions'.[7]

The claim that 'never in human memory' had a similar attempt been made did perhaps give scant justice to the persistent, year-long efforts of Great Britain and in particular, Lord Balfour in the twenties, to reach general consent on the question of the Holy Places which have been described above. But the statement certainly showed the importance which the Israel Government attached to an agreed solution. In September

1967, Mr Eban at the Council of Europe's Consultative Assembly in Strasbourg reiterated 'that the Israel Government was willing to grant to the Holy Places of the three universal religions special status of a diplomatic nature, and would not exert unilateral authority'; and in October 1968, in his offer of a nine-point plan for permanent peace submitted to the General Assembly of the United Nations, Mr Eban asserted again that

Israel does not seek to exercise unilateral jurisdiction in Christian and Islamic Holy Places; it is willing to define a status giving effect to their universal character. We would like to discuss appropriate agreements with those traditionally concerned. Our policy is that Christian and Islam Holy Places should come under the responsibility of those who between themselves hold them in reverence. [8]

Christmas in Israel

The first test for Israel's administration of the Holy Places came at Christmas 1967. It was a formidable task. Security, order and decorum had to be preserved. This was not a local affair. It was enacted under the eyes of the world, which were directed to the 'little town of Bethlehem'; and watched every step with the utmost scrutiny; and there was the awareness of an unprecedented religious situation.

In Ottoman days the problem had been how to deal with the tensions between Latins and Greeks. This was not the problem now. Instead two other issues had arisen and demanded the attention of the authorities. The first was the task of protecting the faithful from sightseers. Already in Mandatory times many Jews, particularly students and other intellectuals, had been attracted by the services in the Holy Places at the Christian High Holidays; and since 1948 on these occasions many Jews had crowded into churches in the Israel sector of Jerusalem, leaving insufficient room for Christian worshippers. This time it was to be expected that in addition, many might be attracted by sheer curiosity. The government therefore, decided to take the necessary steps. Already on 7 November 1967, *The Times* reported that on Christmas Eve Jews would be barred from Bethlehem by the Israel Government; that the Church authorities would themselves control admission to the traditional Midnight Mass and that non-Christians would be excluded by the Israelis from the entire city. On 24 December the *Observer* gave further details of the arrangements:

The Army has set up check-points around the City of David through which only passholders are allowed to go. Passes have been issued in elaborate order of priorities: first Israeli Christians; second organised Pilgrims' Parties; third Christian Tourists; fourth non-Christian Tourists, with the aim to prevent genuine worshippers from being hemmed in by sightseers.

The second problem concerned security. The Christmas celebrations took place in a state of war, almost on a battlefield. Israel had issued an invitation to the Arab Christians in Jordan, to come for Christmas to Bethlehem, but strong warnings were given in Jordan against accepting the invitation. It was therefore to be feared that violence might break out during the procession – not for religious but for political-national reasons – and the Israel Government took most elaborate measures of military and police protection to avoid any incident.

Le Monde, after the event, reported that nothing had been omitted to assure the security of those who came to pray. 'There was an enormous deployment of forces, jeeps with machine guns, frontier-guards, armed police with Bren guns, and a great number of detectives'; and no untoward incident occurred. On 24 December at noon, the Latin Patriarch of Jerusalem, Mgr Alberto Gori, accompanied by high church dignitaries, set out from the Old City. According to custom he was received on his way at the Monastery of Mar Elias and the Tomb of Rachel. His car, escorted by a detachment of Israel mounted police, was preceded by a platoon of Christian boy-scouts on bicycles, and followed by a motorcade of dignitaries who had welcomed him along the road. At Manger Square the Patriarch was greeted by the Mayor of Bethlehem, and then led the procession into the Basilica of the Nativity to the pealing of church bells, making the entry into the Basilica through the 'Small Door', and turned then through the outer Cloister to the Church of St Catherine where solemn Vespers were chanted. At night the Patriarch celebrated Pontifical Mass, assisted by local and visiting clergy. The church was full to capacity. According to custom, the Catholic consuls (of France, Belgium and Spain) in formal dress were seated in the first row on the right; and there was certainly an awareness of an historic situation, when General Uzi Narkiss, the Commanding Officer of the Central Front, took his seat of honour as representative of the Government of Israel, 'the first Jew since the days of Herod the Great to rule in Bethlehem' (*Observer*, 24 December 1967).

Shortly afterwards, according to their calendars, analogous Christian ceremonies took place in Bethlehem for the Greek-Orthodox, Coptic, Syrian and Armenian communities. In all cases the rules of the status quo and the established customs and traditions were strictly and faithfully observed.

On 29 December the President of Israel held the traditional New Year's reception for the heads of Israel's Christian communities.

Let me remind you [he said in his address] that in their grimmest ordeal our defenders in Jerusalem displayed supreme veneration for all the sites sacred to the several faiths, safeguarding, with their very lives, the integrity and inviolability of those places. From now on, every devout person, whether resident or a pilgrim coming from some other land, is guaranteed free access to the shrines revered by him. For all the churches in the land, freedom of religious worship and of religious education is preserved with neither discrimination or interferences. Wherever holy edifices were damaged during the days of severance or fighting, it is our firm intention to embark with all possible speed on due rehabilitation. As always, so now no less, we earnestly wish to ensure a life of tranquillity, security and dignity throughout the length and breadth of our land, without distinction of creed or race. I welcome you, those whose visits we have rejoiced to receive year after year, as well as those for whom this is the first time to foregather with us.

The reply was given on behalf of the Church leaders by the Greek-Orthodox Patriarch. He thanked the President for his good wishes, and as if he had feared that behind the scenes some changes concerning the Holy Places had been considered during the year, he reminded the assembly that the status quo had to be maintained without any alteration.

As Heads of our Churches we will not cease to recite prayers in the Holy Shrines to the Prince of Peace. We will direct all our endeavours towards that end, so that tranquillity, security and peace, righteousness, mutual love and understanding may prevail in this Holy Land, wherein we have been living for centuries and are responsible for, and guardians of, the Holy Places, which constitute the focus of the world interest and whose status quo, therefore, has to be safeguarded, and where the privileges and rights of our institutes have to be respected and maintained, unaltered for ever. We greet the New Year 1968.

The celebrations at Easter were equally conducted according to tradition. In the days of Jordanian rule the Government had been represented by the Governor of Jerusalem. The Prime Minister now appointed his Adviser on Arab Affairs to represent the Government of Israel in the celebrations in the Old City, and the Church leaders agreed. The Latin Easter Week began on Palm Sunday, 7 April, and thousands of pilgrims, Catholic and Anglican, according to ancient custom, followed the route of Jesus when he entered Jerusalem. On Good Friday the procession followed the Via Dolorosa, and in the evening the solemn service in the Church of the Holy Sepulchre was conducted by the Franciscan Custos of the Holy Land. The congregation, holding lit candles in their hands, made a circuit inside the Basilica which ended at Calvary, the place where the Cross had stood. A special place at Calvary had been kept for the representative of the Israel Government but owing to a strange religious coincidence, he could not attend the service on that evening. It was Passover Night, and the holiness of the Jewish Passover made it impossible for him to be present at the Christian Easter. It is Jewish tradition at the Passover Night to keep a place empty at the table for the Prophet Elijah, and it may well be imagined that on that night he, the representative of the Israel Government, kept a place in his home for the Prophet, whilst in Calvary the Custos of the Holy Land kept at the same time a place for him at the memorial service of the Deposition from the Cross.

On Easter Sunday High Mass was held in the Church of the Holy Sepulchre by the Latin Patriarch in the presence of a large congregation of diplomats in their colourful uniforms. This time the representative of the Israel Government was present, with senior police officers and many dignitaries.

On the same day Holy Week began for the Orthodox churches and was celebrated with all the customary dignity and beauty. On Friday, the Holy Sepulchre was sealed for two hours according to tradition to commemorate the advice of Pontius

Pilate before the Resurrection, and the ceremony was witnessed officially by the representative of the Government of Israel. Solemn circuits were held in the Church, first by the Greek – Orthodox, then by the Armenians, who were joined by the Copts and Syrians. The Greek ceremony was led by Archbishop Germanos, who emerged from the Sepulchre with burning candles held high in his outstretched arms. The ceremonies concluded on Sunday with a splendid and colourful procession, headed by the Patriarch who was flanked by the Greek Consul General and the representatives of Israel. The bells were tolling and the marchers were splashed with perfume and showered with rose petals by spectators on the roofs of the buildings lining the alleys. After the ceremony was over, the Commander of the Jerusalem Police emphasised the assistance he had received from the leaders of the Churches and, according to press reports, the latter expressed their satisfaction with the arrangements. No serious incidents disturbed the celebrations. But some of those who had witnessed the Christian festivals in the preceding years commented on the sadness which now had overshadowed the events. Partly this sadness was certainly caused by the war and all its tragic consequences of destruction, dislocation and separation, but it is well possible, and indeed likely, that, apart from the Arab-Israel war, many were uneasy or bewildered because the power over the Holy Places of Christendom had passed into the hands of the Jews.

7 'An Oasis of Peace and Prayer': A New Appeal for Internationalisation

Whilst Israel endeavoured to administer the Christian Holy Places according to tradition, following the example of her predecessors Jordan, Britain and Turkey, there was naturally deep concern in the Christian world about the situation and its significance, particularly in those Churches which are specially connected with the Sanctuaries. Already before the outbreak of the fighting and during the campaign itself all Churches showed profound interest in the fate of the Holy Places, and on 7 June Pope Paul VI addressing a group of pilgrims in the Basilica of St Peter's made a fervent appeal for their safety:

It is indeed of the utmost importance for all descendants of the spiritual race of Abraham – Jews, Moslems and Christians – that Jerusalem should be declared an open city, that it should be outside all military operations and be spared every act of war.... We address a most urgent appeal in the name of the whole anxious Christian world and even of all civilized humanity to the governments of the nations in conflict and the commanders of the armies in the field, that Jerusalem may be spared the rule of war, that the Holy City may remain a refuge for the defenceless and the wounded, a symbol of hope and peace for all.[1]

For twenty years – if not longer – the policy of the Holy See concerning Jerusalem and its surroundings, to which also Nazareth was sometimes added, had aimed at internationalisation. These plans now came to the forefront again. On 13 June the Minister General of the Order of the Franciscans declared in the Vatican that the internationalisation of the Holy Places remained in the eyes of the Pope the best solution[2] and on 26 June the Pope himself proclaimed to the Secret Consistory:

111

The Holy City of Jerusalem must remain for ever what it represents: a city of God, a free oasis of peace and prayer, a place of meeting, of inspiration and harmony for all, with a statute of its own, internationally guaranteed.[3]

On 1 July, Mgr Giovannetti, observer of the Vatican at the United Nations, handed to the delegations an aide-memoire which reminded them of the various resolutions of the General Assembly about the internationalisation of Jerusalem, and ended with the following words:

The only solution which offers a sufficient guarantee for the protection of Jerusalem and its Holy Places is to place the City and its surroundings under an international regime.[4]

All these pronouncements were in accordance with the established policy of the Holy See and the decisions of the United Nations of 1947–8 and 1949. But difficulties soon began to reveal themselves, which sprang not from the fact that Jerusalem was in the hands of the Jews, but from the ancient dissensions between the Christian communities. In the beginning of July the activities of the Vatican concerning Jerusalem greatly increased. As described earlier, Mgr Felici was sent to Israel to negotiate with the Prime Minister, Mr Levi Eshkol. The Pope himself received in Rome the Israel Ambassador to Italy for a long interview. He also saw King Hussein of Jordan. No agreement, however, was announced. Instead the Vatican published shortly after Mgr Felici's return an aide-memoire which reported that

the information gathered by the Ambassador of the Holy See has enabled him to gain a deeper understanding of the complexity of the problems concerning the Holy Places in the present situation and the great difficulty of finding a solution which could reconcile and satisfy all points of view.[5]

The aide-memoire did not refer to the internationalisation of Jerusalem as a whole, but limited itself to the issue of the Holy Places:

The Holy See, considering this its right and duty, will continue to take an active interest in the Holy Places, whose character is sacred not only for the Christian world, but for the whole human family. He will not fail in particular to intervene with a view to

assure for the Holy Places a special Statute including guarantees
which will free the Holy Places from all vicissitudes of the political
situation.

According to the *Cahiers De L'Orient Contemporain*[6] the
government of Israel had proposed to Mgr Felici the transfer-
ence of the Christian Holy Places of Jerusalem and Bethlehem
to a committee, composed of the representatives of the different
Christian communities. Whether such an offer actually was
made has not been officially announced. Judging from the
experiences of the League of Nations in the early twenties the
composition of this committee would probably have presented
considerable difficulties. At that time Cardinal Gasparri had
warned that a committee on the Holy Places 'consisting of
representatives of the different Christian denominations would
without fail lead to a bitter struggle among them, and would
make it impossible to reach any impartial decision',[7] and more
than thirty years later Mgr B.Collin had declared that the
establishment of an international regime for Jerusalem must be
dependent on the prior solution of the 'thorny question'
(*l'épineuse question*') of the internal Christian rivalries in the
Sanctuaries.[8]

On 15 July Pope Paul VI announced to the Cardinals his
intention to visit the Ecumenical Patriarch Athenagoras I in
Constantinople in a continuation of their efforts to further the
reunion of their Churches. The discussion of the Holy Places
was included in the programme.

We wish to examine together [said the Pope] in which form and by
which means it is possible, in a common approach at the present
juncture to protect not only the integrity, but also the sacred and
unique character of the Holy Places in the country which was the
fatherland of Christ, the scene of the Gospels, the cradle of the
Church, and which is the inspiration of every Christian heart.[9]

The *Tablet* commented on this point of the programme as
follows:

The Pope and the Patriarch exchanged the kiss of peace on the
Mount of Olives during his pilgrimage to the Holy Land in 1964.
Now it will be exchanged again, we hope, to symbolise some lasting
solution for the Holy Places, and some promise of the ultimate
reunion of East and West. The Pope has made it clear that he

expects to discuss with Patriarch Athenagoras and other Orthodox leaders an Israeli Government proposal for the future state of the Holy Places which was brought back to Rome by Mgr Felici after ten days of discussion in Israel. The official Vatican policy on the internationalisation of Jerusalem, unacceptable as it is to both Israel and Jordan, may give way now to a common policy about the Holy Places, at once safeguarding them and satisfying all the faiths which hold them in veneration. The reconciliation between warring nations and quarrelling sects that such an agreement could bring, would indeed be a blessing and in itself amply justify this journey.[10]

Voices of a very different character, however, were heard from the East. On 19 July the Patriarch of Moscow utterly rejected the idea of internationalisation and warned the Heads of the Eastern Churches against 'the vile colonialist conspiracy which the states of the tripartite aggression were hatching in order to bring the Western Churches to accept the project of the internationalisation of Jerusalem, treating it in practice as if it was part of Israel.[11] On 23 July the Lebanese paper *Lisan el Hal* reported that two Orthodox bishops had been sent to Constantinople by the Patriarch of Antioch to oppose any plan of internationalisation of Jerusalem:

Any project other than the arabisation of the city of Jerusalem has already been rejected by the Church of Moscow, the Third Rome. Moreover there is another fundamental point which has to be recognised: The Church, which is first and foremost interested in this question – besides the Catholic Church – is the Orthodox Church of Jerusalem, and this Church cannot express its thoughts freely until the occupation of its territory has come to an end. It is not to be expected that Athenagoras will take a decision which differs from that of the other Eastern Patriarchs, and that he will adopt the project proposed by Pope Paul VI. That would be the way to weaken the position of Constantinople in the Orthodox world. Athenagoras is not unaware of this. It is also a point which should engage the attention of Paul VI because the unity of the Orthodox is a precondition of their unity with Rome.[12]

The Pope arrived in Constantinople on 25 July for a visit of three days, which included a pilgrimage to Ephesus. In October Patriarch Athenagoras returned the visit for a similar period. These were great events in the history of the Church which may well be steps on the long and difficult road to the ultimate reunion between Rome and Byzantium. Many issues were discussed: the question of mixed marriages, joint scholarly study of such subjects as Church history, tradition, patristics and liturgy – but Jerusalem and the Holy Places in spite of the special announcement made before the departure, were not mentioned in the final joint declaration.

The Protestant Churches as such took no position on the issue of Jerusalem. But a number of leading theologians including Dr Reinhold Niebuhr and Professor Krister Stendhal in a manifesto published in the *New York Times* identified themselves with the unification of Jerusalem.

We see no justification [the manifesto read] in proposals which seek once again to destroy the unity which has been restored to Jerusalem. This unity is the natural condition of the Holy City, and now once again assures the world's religious peoples the freedom or worship at the shrines which remain the spiritual centres of their faith.

We are gratified that the sanctity and protection of the Holy Places of all denominations have been assured by the Government of Israel, whose record over the last twenty years in providing free access to Christian shrines within its jurisdiction inspires confidence that the interests of all religions will be faithfully honoured. This confidence is further strengthened by Israel's offer to place the Holy Places under independent denominational supervision.[13]

Meanwhile, on 12 September 1967, the Secretary General of the United Nations submitted his report on the situation in Jerusalem.[14] Concerning the Holy Places he wrote that the statements and statutory measures taken by the Israeli government had been very favourably received and that 'various religious representatives in fact spontaneously told his Personal Representative that so far the Israel authorities had conformed to the principles which had been laid down and that there was therefore no ground of complaint' (para. 141).

'It was essentially only the Catholic Church which adopted a systematically divergent attitude. As is well known,' he added, 'the Holy See remains convinced that the only solution which offers a sufficient guarantee for the protection of Jerusalem and its Holy Places is to place that city and its vicinity under an international regime in the form of a *corpus separatum*' (para. 143).

In his Christmas message of 1967 to the Cardinals the Pope did not deal with the political status of Jerusalem, but limited himself to the issues of the Holy Places themselves and the religious and civil rights 'which legitimately belong to all present in the territory of Palestine'.

A number of newspapers saw in this a change of the Holy See's attitude to the question of Jerusalem. But in May 1968, it was announced that the Vatican still supported the internationalisation of the city and 'neither proposed nor contemplated any alternatives up to the present time'. A spokesman of the Vatican added that the scheme involved the 'creation of a *corpus separatum* consisting of Jerusalem and surroundings under international administration in accordance with the resolution of the United Nations which in 1947 decreed the partition of Palestine'.[15]

The Christmas message to the Cardinals of that year declared:

Once again, on this occasion, We call attention to the requests publicly made by Us to obtain an internationally guaranteed agreement on the question of Jerusalem and the Holy Places, in which, through the three monotheistic religions witnessed there, a great part of humanity is vitally interested.[16]

On 6 October 1969, Pope Paul VI received Mr Abba Eban, the Israel Minister of Foreign Affairs. The communiqué which was issued afterwards by the press office of the Vatican announced that the Holy Father and the Minister had reviewed the different problems connected with the present situation in the Middle East, and mentioned particularly the questions of the Holy Places and the sacred and unique character of Jerusalem.

The communiqué did not refer to the internationalisation of Jerusalem, and this attracted considerable attention. The Greek Catholic Review *Proche-Orient Chrétien*, which is published by the White Fathers of St Anne in Old Jerusalem, wrote:

There is no doubt that the Vatican is opening its mind more and more to the reality of Israel. Since Vatican II, the Holy See has decided to leave aside more and more the political problems and to devote itself fully to a mission of peace and understanding between the peoples. Concerning the Holy Land, the Holy See no longer considers the problems exclusively or even principally in relation to the Holy Places, but aims at assuring a state of peace in the whole region for the benefit of both the local inhabitants and the pilgrims. There is, therefore, a clear change of policy: it is not so much a political force trying to impose a solution but rather a moral authority which offers its good offices, so that those who are most interested in the re-establishment of peace – the different groups of the local population – can find a *modus vivendi*.[17]

Le Monde on the other hand reached different conclusions. Commenting on 'this very carefully worded communiqué' it thought that the reference to 'the sacred and unique character of Jerusalem' was the confirmation of the Vatican's thesis about the necessity of an international control of the Holy City. 'It follows therefore,' the commentary concluded 'that the position of the Holy See concerning the question of the Middle East has not changed.'[18] This interpretation is supported by the fact that immediately after the interview the Vatican made known that no change in the attitude of Rome towards Israel had taken place, and that in view of the feelings of the Arab world these assurances had been repeated on behalf of the Holy See in Syria, Jordan and Egypt. In fact the Apostolic Nuntiatur in Damascus announced that the audience granted by the Supreme Pontiff to Mr Eban in no way implied any change of the attitude of the Holy See towards the question of Jerusalem and the Holy Places; and analogous assurances were given by the Apostolic Delegate in Jerusalem and the Apostolic pro-Nuntio in Cairo.

Whatever the correct interpretations of the different statements may be, the proposal to internationalise Jerusalem for the sake of the Holy Places, has been official policy of the Holy See for more than twenty years. It has been frequently repeated, never been withdrawn and thus remains, in principle, unchanged on record. The question whether the realisation of the scheme is practicable at the moment, is of small importance since conditions may change. Nor does it matter that at present the Holy See stands alone in advocating the proposal. Every suggestion of the Supreme Pontiff of the Roman Catholic Church commands respect and the most careful attention, particularly in a matter of such importance. Moreover the idea – however vague and undefined – of an internationalised Holy City attracts in many minds sympathy and hope; and above all there is the vision of Jerusalem as an 'Oasis of Peace and Prayer'.

It is appropriate, therefore, to examine whether in fact the internationalisation of Jerusalem is required – or even able – to safeguard the universal interest in the Christian Holy Places.

The practical aims which internationalisation is to achieve have been formulated on many occasions and can be summarised as follows: free access to the Sanctuaries for all who wish to pray there; freedom of worship without interference; preservation of the Holy Places, religious buildings and sites; and general protection of the Sanctuaries. All these requirements have to be examined both in relation to any possible hindrance by the government of the country and in view of the problems which for many centuries have arisen out of the division of the Christian communities themselves.

A Special Situation

When in November 1947 the United Nations passed the resolution about the partition of Palestine, a special situation existed which – independent from the general merits of the case – could have justified an international regime. The two new states which were to be created, naturally lacked experience in government. It was doubtful, therefore, whether they would be technically capable of coping with so intricate a task as the administration of the Holy Places with all its international implications. Prudence in these circumstances could suggest that this task be taken out of their hands. Today the situation is different. Both Jordan and Israel have proved that they are able to deal with all technical aspects of the matter. Already in 1949, the representative of Jordan maintained that the internationalisation of Jerusalem was a 'measure without purpose' since the Holy Places under the guard of his government were intact and in perfect security; and as far as the Christian Sanctuaries are concerned nobody can deny the truth of this statement. Likewise Israel in the short period since she has been responsible for the administration has proved herself equal to the task. The case for internationalisation, therefore, can no longer be based on the alleged incapability of the states concerned, but must be justified by the intrinsic value of the scheme and its superiority over other solutions. What then is the situation?

Free Access

Concerning free access it is necessary to begin with a technical remark. Access to the Sanctuaries is dependent not only on the arrangements at the doors of the Churches or at the gates of the City, but first and foremost on the admission to the country. A government unfriendly or hostile to the influx of pilgrims could interfere at the frontier, and even the best arrangements at the gates of the city would become ineffective. To meet such a threat there exist two possibilities: either the international authority extends its control to the borders of the territory, or it relies for the admission of pilgrims on treaties with the governments concerned. The former is obviously impracticable. No one would suggest today, as the Peel Commission did, the establishment of an 'international corridor from Jerusalem to Jaffa including Lydda and Ramle'. The second alternative on the other hand is certainly feasible, and has been suggested on different occasions. But this raises the question: if treaties are sufficient to safeguard the entry into the country, why should they be ineffective to safeguard the entry at the city gates? Why, therefore, should it be necessary to internationalise the city, in order to secure free access, if a treaty can have the same effect at the frontiers of the land?

Secondly, it is submitted that the issue of free access in fact hardly exists any longer; it has become almost an anachronism. There were, of course, in the Middle Ages periods when Christian pilgrimages to the Holy Land had become impossible or very difficult, although in principle Islam showed considerable tolerance to both Christianity and Judaism. But opposition to Christian pilgrimages as far as it ever existed, came to an end during the Ottoman Empire either for reasons of policy or because of the financial benefits derived from the pilgrims. The problem was that in the Western world very few were willing to undertake a pilgrimage, and it has been described above to what extent the number of Western pilgrims in the eighteenth and nineteenth centuries had dwindled. This had not been the fault of the Turks.

On the other hand, access to the Holy Places had frequently been denied to Christians by Christians themselves during their centuries-old internal conflict, from the days when Godfrey of

119

Bouillon after the first Crusade banished the priests of the Eastern rites from the Church of the Holy Sepulchre, or the Greek Patriarch of Jerusalem excluded all those from pilgrimages who had not obtained his permission; and the Dutch at one time even had to stipulate to the Turkish authorities that the monks in the Christian Holy Places – Latins and Greeks alike – should not be allowed to refuse them admission because they were Protestants. All this, however, now belongs to the past, and the right of free access is uncontested.

'No government,' writes a modern Christian commentator[19] 'whether Christian, Moslem or Jewish, would think of putting any obstacle whatsoever to the flow of pilgrims who not only pour out their devotions to the Holy Places, but also supply the state under whose control these places are with much appreciated foreign currency.' He even adds sarcastically: 'one does not kill the goose which lays the golden eggs.' Whatever the motives may be – policy hope for financial gain, indifference, tolerance, wisdom or even charity – no government today will in times of peace bar bona fide pilgrims from the Holy Places of Christendom.

Israel – as Jordan before her – is making great efforts to facilitate the influx of pilgrims from everywhere. The Ministry of Tourism has a special department for pilgrimages. Visits by groups of pilgrims are organised and freely advertised in many lands. The doors and gates are open and no-one – neither Jew nor Arab – would deny true pilgrims free access to the Christian Sanctuaries. True pilgrims are welcome to all, and certainly no international action is required to secure their admission, which is in full accordance with the interest and wishes of the country in control. To secure free access to the Christian Holy Places internationalisation is unnecessary and superfluous, and in the words of the Jordanian Government in 1949 'a measure without purpose'.

Freedom of Religious Worship

As far as the freedom of religious worship is concerned the situation is not dissimilar. There were, it is true, at times certain restrictions of Christian worship under Moslem rule concerning the ringing of Church bells, the 'undue raising of voices' and similar issues. But interference with the religious services themselves must have been very rare, if not unheard of. The great Christian controversies about dogma, liturgy, the form of the eucharist, which have split the Christian world to its foundations, would hardly have been known to the non-Christian rulers of the country and, if explained to them would have appeared remote subtleties of a strange and alien world unlikely to rouse their interest and passion. It can hardly be imagined that these rulers, having admitted Christian pilgrims, should have interfered with their worship in the Sanctuaries, insisting for instance that the creed should contain the *'Filioque clause'* or the Mass be celebrated with unleavened bread. In any case no such complaints appear to have been recorded. Again, the main interference with free exercise of worship came from internal opponents, i.e. 'dissident Christian sects' profoundly involved in the theological controversies. In fact, the conflict between the Western and Eastern Churches in the Sanctuaries has interfered more with the freedom of worship than any action by outside forces.

Its history has lasted for hundreds of years and as late as 1970 fighting broke out in the Church of the Holy Sepulchre between Copts and Abyssinians at the Easter celebrations, and Israeli riot police had to be called to restore order.[20] In modern times no complaints have been recorded against any interference by a non-Christian authority with the freedom of worship in the Christian Holy Places. No reason can therefore be adduced why on this account the government of the country should be replaced by an international regime. The internationalisation of a whole city would be an extraordinary measure to prevent actions which have, in fact, not happened. Thus, neither the requirement of free access to the Sanctuaries nor that of freedom of worship in the Christian Holy Places can establish a case for the internationalisation of the City of Jerusalem.

Preservation of the Sanctuaries

The first task in preserving the Holy Places is the maintenance of their religious character for the purpose to which they were dedicated. The Crusaders whilst in control of Jerusalem had converted the Mosque of Omar into a church – the *Templum Domini* – but when Saladin reconquered the city he did not take revenge and left the Church of the Holy Sepulchre unscathed in the hands of the Christians. Likewise the Ottoman Sultan Selim I, when he in turn occupied Jerusalem in 1517, preserved the Christian character of the Sanctuaries; and although the Church of the Holy Sepulchre was closed for some time, it remained a Christian Holy Place. Throughout the successive rules of the Ottoman Turks, the United Kingdom and Jordan, no changes ever took place, and there is no shadow of suspicion that Israel might follow any other policy. The preservation of the Christian Holy Places therefore is in no way endangered.

Repairs

The second task in preserving the Holy Places is to keep the buildings in a state of good repair. The right to repair the shrines has always been vested in the Christian communities themselves and was no responsibility of the government of the country. According to Islamic Law the authority to repair a part of a building such as a roof or a floor implies the right to an exclusive possession on the part of the restorer; and in view of the many controversies between the Christian communities about their rights in the Sanctuaries, necessary repairs have often been delayed for years. In many cases the governments of the day even undertook urgent work at their own expense to overcome the deadlock between the interested parties. It was therefore a major achievement when in 1958 after long negotiations Greek Orthodox, Roman Catholics and Armenians agreed on certain urgent repairs in the Church of the Holy Sepulchre. Although the work was interrupted, it started again in 1963, and Pope Paul VI during his visit to Jerusalem saw in this co-operation a symbolic significance. The issue of repairs is a matter for the different Christian communities and can give no cause for an international intervention.

Protection – An Ambiguous Notion

Few words have a more multifarious meaning and have been more misused than the word protection. It may describe the interests of the protected or that of the protectors. In International Law, Protectorates meant in theory 'institutions by which a great state gave "protection" to the ruler of a small and weak one'. But in fact 'it became in the nineteenth century almost a mode of acquisition of territory and the first step towards colonialisation'.[21] As far as the Holy Places in Palestine are concerned 'protection' very often was a means to exert foreign influence. France became the 'protectress' of the Catholics, whilst Russia claimed the same position for the Orthodox; and the national interests of the respective protectors clashed in the Crimean war. Protections of this kind came to an end with the First World War, and today the word can be used free from its imperial or colonial associations.

PROTECTION IN PEACETIME

The claim that internationalisation might be necessary to achieve the protection of the Holy Places, can in peacetime only be based on the assumption that the national government of the country is either unwilling or unable to fulfil this task. No government of Palestine since the days of the 'mad Caliph Hakim' in the eleventh century, has lacked the will to protect the Christian Holy Places, and in fact no government since those days has ever laid hands on the Christian Sanctuaries.

On the other hand, no government, whatever its composition, is able to prevent under all conditions damage by individual malefactors or by accidents. Thus in 1808, a great fire raged in the Church of the Holy Sepulchre which destroyed the dome and created severe damage. Whether this fire was caused accidentally or was the result of arson has never been fully established. The Orthodox authorities in Jerusalem at that time maintained that the fire had been deliberately started by the Armenians and some Orthodox writers up to the present day take the same view.

Again, other fires in the Sanctuaries occurred under Jordanian rule, one in the same Church, another in the El Aksa Mosque, but no-one has claimed that the government of the country was responsible for these misfortunes and no demand was made to replace it by an international regime. Moreover, there is no reason why in cases of this kind an international police force should be more efficient than the police of the government which carries the full responsibility for the fate of the country.

The security of the Christian Holy Places was respected by the Moslem rulers for about a thousand years. But there were many cases where the Sanctuaries were violated and damaged in the course of internal Christian struggles. Thus the Latin tapestries on the main wall in the Grotto of Bethlehem were repeatedly burned by dissident Christians and are now made of asbestos to avoid a repetition; and the famous silver star in the Basilica of the Nativity was wrenched from its foundations in October 1847, not by Moslems or other 'unbelievers', but in a bitter struggle between Latin and Orthodox monks.[22] No government of Palestine has been responsible for such acts of destruction.

At this point it may be right to mention an event which although it did not attract much international attention, may be the first rumbling of an approaching storm. On 13 March 1968, Metropolitan Nikodeme, on behalf of the Moscow Patriarchate cabled to the President of Israel protesting strongly against alleged attacks on Russian Church property in Israel which, he said, had been accompanied by 'looting and banditry'. He described the incidents as an interference with the inviolability and safety of the Holy Places, and urged the President to take all necessary steps to protect the Russian Orthodox Church so that 'the sons and daughters of the Holy Church can live in tranquillity and security and perform their Christian service'.

From the correspondence published in the Israeli Press and in the Monthly Bulletin of the Moscow Patriarchate,[23] it appears that the complaint referred mainly to some minor misdeeds of adolescent offenders, committed in the years 1964 to 1966, i.e. before Israel occupied the Old City, and before the promulgation of the Protection of the Holy Places Law. It can be hoped therefore that no reason for complaint will be given again on this account. Moreover, the incidents concerned the Gorny Monastery in Ein Karim near Jerusalem and the Russian Garden of Abu Kadir near Jaffa, but did not touch the Holy Places themselves. The only act of real desecration of a Christian Sanctuary which has become known since June 1967, was the theft of the tiara from the head of a madonna in a chapel of the Church of the Holy Sepulchre in 1967. As described above, two youths were severely punished by the courts for the misdeed, and the tiara was restored to the Church authorities.

Such incidents can happen in every country, and no nation has ever been deprived of its sovereignty for such a reason.

PROTECTION IN TIME OF WAR

In time of war, of course, the situation is completely different. 'Free access to the Sanctuaries' becomes meaningless when the country itself is under blockade or cut off by fighting. In war no nation will admit its enemies as pilgrims; and even if Jerusalem was internationalised, the war may set its guards against each other.

As far as the protection of the Holy Places is concerned, it would hardly serve a useful purpose to consider the case of a global conflagration, since after such catastrophe few may be left to pray at any Sanctuary. The question is, however, relevant with regard to the more limited confines of the Arab-Israel war even if this should increase again in intensity; and it would indeed be tempting to imagine that the internationalisation of Jerusalem could in this conflict 'extricate the Christian Holy Places from the vicissitudes of the political situation' and make Jerusalem 'an oasis of peace and prayer'. This hope, however, cannot be maintained. For no neutralisation is possible unless it is desired by the population concerned. Neutralisation cannot be imposed from outside. It depends not only on the readiness of the armies outside to respect the protected area, but much more on the willingness of the inhabitants inside to keep out of the conflict and they will only be ready to do so if – like in Switzerland – their loyalty to a common ideal of neutrality is greater than their involvement in the struggle. No such conditions exist today in Jerusalem, or indeed in the Middle East. Even if the internationalisation of Jerusalem were decided upon by the United Nations and could be enforced – two assumptions which are very unlikely to materialise – the citizens of Jerusalem, Jew and Arab alike, would not remain disinterested in the conflict, keep outside as neutrals and enjoy 'an oasis of peace and prayer' whilst the battle which decides their fate is raging around them. Only if the total population of Jerusalem – both Jews and Arabs – were removed from the area, and if Jerusalem were turned into a museum or grave-yard could there be an oasis of peace; and this will hold true until the conflict between Israel and the Arabs has been brought to an end, and peace has been established, as a result of reconciliation between the warring parties.

Up till now common sense and wisdom of the local commanders on both sides has prevented any major damage to the Sanctuaries, and it is to be hoped that this spirit will prevail. There would probably be no difficulty in exchanging mutual promises to this effect or even in giving unilaterally binding declarations. A distinguished Italian scholar, Professor Pio Ciprotti,[24] recently suggested that the Holy Places be registered as Monuments of Art. No Jew or Arab would object to such a scheme, and concrete measures undertaken by the people on the spot with the intention of keeping the Sanctuaries as far as possible out of danger are more likely to succeed than international arrangements imposed from without.

Internationalisation and Self-Government

In order to put the scheme of internationalisation into practice the local populations of Jews and Arabs were asked to renounce their right to self-government. Both nations time and again expressed in the strongest terms their opposition to the proposal; and the Government of Israel in a memorandum to the United Nations on 26 May 1950, besides stressing the Jewish character of Jerusalem, presented the general and fundamental reasons against internationalisation. They apply to Jews and Arabs alike, and in principle are not affected by the present situation in Jerusalem, created by the war.

The consent of the people of Jerusalem is indispensable to the effective functioning of the City's institutions. The right of a mature population to select and maintain its own government cannot be challenged by any consistent adherent of democratic principles. Moreover, the preservation in Jerusalem of a regime based on the initiative and consent of its own population is not only an unassailable political ideal; it is also a dictate of practical statesmanship with a direct bearing on the issue of implementation. The idea that any regime for the protection of religious interests can endure amidst a discontented, aggrieved and turbulent population will be instantly rejected by any serious mind. Religious peace cannot be secured by political suppression. Thus considerations of justice and of practicability combine to make the will of Jerusalem's population the essential basis for the City's political institutions.

It has been shown above, how many governments and religious communities during the deliberations of the United Nations in 1950 and 1951 expressed the same view. But among those who advocate internationalisation no-one up to the present day has considered it necessary to explain how the project can be reconciled with the elementary right of every nation to govern itself.

Concerning the proposed constitution of the City the memorandum pointed out that:

The Statute, with its omnipotent Governor and its artificially constituted Legislative Council, is modelled on the absolutist forms of government which used to be applied in backward regions in the days before the elementary principles of self-government began to secure a foothold even in the dependent areas of the world. It is a patent fact that the population of Jerusalem is opposed to the scheme – as would be the people of any other city. . . . This fact alone destroys the moral validity and the practical relevance of the Statute.

The memorandum added a warning that the scheme could not be enforced by the police:

A police force can only function in civilised societies as the agent of the entire community against a few individuals who defy its recognised law. No police force can ever be effective if it stands in isolation from, or in opposition to, the majority will of the community. Thus the political regime of the State, lacking any local support, can neither be implemented nor be enforced by any available means.

Economic Impossibility

In the economic sphere the scheme meets with almost insurmountable difficulties which were described in the Israel memorandum as follows:

The life of the City depends upon the surrounding country for its food and water, its communications, its educational, health and social services, its development budget, its subsidies, its foreign

127

currency assets, in short for all the sources of its subsistence and employment. The City is not even remotely self-supporting either agriculturally or industrially, and would never in all its history have been able to maintain its population except as part of a wider and more productive political unit. . . . All the arteries which bring the lifeblood to the heart of Jerusalem would be severed by the creation of a *corpus separatum*. The City would become like a diver whose airline is cut. Yet the Statute is completely devoid of a single provision for replacing its source of livelihood. The Statute legislates for Jerusalem economic and financial isolation without even beginning to consider how an area with a population of several hundred thousand can subsist for a single day in a state of landlocked economic isolation. . . . The Statute would involve economic strangulation as well as political disintegration.

This aspect alone would make the implementation of the scheme utterly impossible.

Thus, the plan to internationalise the City of Jerusalem cannot be maintained. It is unnecessary as far as free access to the Holy Places and freedom of worship are concerned and irrelevant for the protection of the Sanctuaries. It violates the fundamental rights of self-government and is economically untenable. It would create not a *'corpus separatum'* but a *'corpus amputatum'* which could not be kept alive by artificial means. Lastly, it could only be put into operation against the will of the total population; and if force were used to bring this about, it might turn Jerusalem into a new Stalingrad or a new Massada.

Internationalisation of the Walled City

Since the internationalisation of the City of Jerusalem is impossible for reasons of impracticability as well as of principle, the question has been raised whether the universal concern in the welfare of the Holy Places, their security, accessability and sanctity can be internationally satisfied by some other means. Following the end of the Mandate, a number of alternative suggestions have, therefore, been considered, including a scheme by which the territory of internationalisation would be reduced to the Walled or Old City within Jerusalem, in which in fact the main Sanctuaries of the monotheistic religions are

situated. The area in question does not comprise more than one
and a half square miles and the population living within the wall
is comparatively small. Such reduction of the project might be
relevant, at least in the economic sphere, since the maintenance
of the reduced unit by the outside world should not be impossible. But all other issues remain the same: Internationalisation
is unnecessary to achieve free access, freedom of worship and
the preservation of the Sanctuaries; the problems of protection
are hardly changed, and the principle of self-government is
independent from the size of the population involved.

Nevertheless, it is noteworthy to add that in 1950, when the
Old City was in Jordanian hands, the Government of Israel
was ready to consider its internationalisation, but pointed out
that this was impracticable in view of Jordanian opposition.
The relevant passage in the Israel memorandum of May 1950
reads as follows:

Since nearly all the Holy Places in Jerusalem are located within a
small area of one and a half square miles within the Walled City
and its immediate environs, the Government of Israel and also
many leading Christian authorities have from time to time considered
the question of an international regime confined to that limited
area, in the administration of which the three monotheistic faiths
should have acknowledged status. This project has, however,
encountered insurmountable obstacles in view of the opposition
of the Hashemite Kingdom of Jordan, which occupies the entire
area of the Old City. The Government of Israel is ready ... to
cooperate in the creation of an international regime of such limited
territorial scope, but it must point out that the practicability of such
a solution depends entirely on the Hashemite Kingdom of Jordan.

Today the government of Israel no longer holds the same
views, and Jordan has not taken up the attitude which Israel
maintained at a time when the Old City was in the hands of the
enemy. Neither of the two governments agrees to the project,
and this prevents its realisation.

But it could perhaps be imagined that one day Israel and
Jordan might consider establishing between themselves on a
democratic basis a joint – not an international – administration
of the Walled City, and agree for this limited purpose to a
condominium by the two peoples who are most intimately
involved.

Internationalisation of the Holy Places

There lastly remains one more suggestion; to reduce the area of internationalisation still further, namely to the Holy Places themselves.This possibility has been raised among others, by Mgr Collin, although in principle he advocates a *corpus separatum* by internationalisation in the widest sense. In his classic study *Le Problème Juridique des Lieux Saints* (1956), he pointed out that the administration of Jerusalem involved so many worldly issues, such as local politics, municipal affairs, etcetera, that it might be preferable in the Christian interest to limit internationalisation to the Sanctuaries only and to eliminate what he called the '*inquiètantes contigences locales*'. This limitation would free the international administration from the problems of parochial policy and other troublesome local issues. It would even – and this is more important – leave the fundamental political rights of the population untouched. But it meets with grave objections.

Firstly the Holy Places would acquire exterritoriality and become foreign enclaves under international control. The monks and other ecclesiastics living in the Holy Places would find themselves surrounded by a legal-diplomatic wall, separated from the surrounding country on which they depend for the needs of their physical existence. Those living outside the precincts would be equally separated from the Sanctuaries. The Patriarchs themselves, for the first time in history, would have to cross an international border if they wished to pray at the Holy Sepulchre or in the Basilica of the Nativity; and the ordinary local Christian communities would be legally cut off from their sacred possessions by an invisible but real barrier, internationally constructed and juridically maintained. But worse: the purpose of the whole measure – the guarantee of free access for the worshipper and the security of the Sanctuaries – would in no way be furthered, but indeed almost made impossible. To maintain order, the United Nations regime would need a police force. Where could this be established? Moreover, access and security cannot be maintained from inside the buildings but must depend on the control of the surrounding country. They must therefore be – as they always were – the responsibility of the government of the country. The Holy

Places and the religious services in them do not exist in isolation, but within a large community of local worshippers, pilgrims, sightseers, onlookers and the general public. All of them have to be included in the task of keeping order, security and dignity. A single service may affect thousands of people who throng the roads to Jerusalem and the narrow lanes within the City. At the Maundy Service of the Washing of the Feet during Easter week 1968, the Israel Government had to provide, at the request of the Church authorities, two hundred constables to control the crowd at the entrance of the Church of the Holy Sepulchre. Moreover, religious processions cover wide areas. Thus, at Christmas the Latin Patriarch proceeds solemnly with the highest dignitaries from the Old City of Jerusalem to Bethlehem, being received on his way ceremoniously at the Monastery of Mar Elias and the Tomb of Rachel. The whole procession and the reception by the Mayor of Bethlehem are held *outside* the Holy Places on the Square of the Manger, and even the solemn Vespers are chanted not in the Basilica of the Nativity, but in the neighbouring Catholic Church of St Catherine. Similarly, the procession of the Orthodox on Easter Sunday, led by the Greek Patriarch of Jerusalem, takes place among multitudes who fill the streets and line the roofs 'splashing perfumes and showering rose petals'. These expressions of joy, togetherness and participation cannot be directed or guided from inside the building of the Holy Sepulchre or the Basilica of the Nativity, and even less from an office building of the United Nations in New York. They are part of the life of the people in the country, and no barrier, artificially erected, can do justice to their needs. The answer to the problem must be found on the spot in the human relations of those who have to live there together, and this can be ultimately only brought about by Arab-Israel understanding.

Internationalisation under Rome or Moscow?

Up till fairly recently it could be expected that the internationalisation of Jerusalem would lead to an extension of Western influence both in the political and the religious sphere. The idea itself was linked to that of the Mandates, and the League of Nations in its early years represented not so much the community of nations as a whole, but the victor states of the First World War to whom some neutrals had been added. Thus, of the whole continent of Africa only Liberia and the Union of South Africa belonged to the original members. Islam was represented only by Persia, and for more than ten years the League had not a single Arab member. India was still under British rule, and the Soviet Union did not join until 1934. It was a world in which the West stood at the zenith of its power and influence, and even at the end of the Second World War when the idea of the internationalisation of Jerusalem was taken up again and further developed, the rise of the East was only in its beginning.

In the religious sphere there had been similar developments and in the West many had hoped for the emergence of a new Latin preponderance in the Holy Land. It has been described above how the Catholic world had been inspired by a nostalgia for the Crusades, strikingly expressed by Pascal Baldi who considered it providential that 'Jerusalem was held under the domination of Italy, France and England' (in this order!), 'the three nations who had played so great a part in the Holy Wars', and who looked forward to 'the renewal of the splendours of the first century of the Crusades'. Of the twin ideals which had dominated the Crusades one, the liberation of the Christian Sanctuaries from Moslem rule, had been realised by the combined efforts of the Allies, and Rome set itself to the task of fulfilling the other, the re-establishment of Latin Christianity in Palestine.

Originally Rome had hoped that the Mandate should be entrusted to France, the traditional protectress of the Catholic Church. *La Croix* in June 1919 protested passionately against the proposed arrangements:

Palestine will not be included in the zone which the authors of the future peace treaty have attributed to the suzerainty of France. An alien Power therefore will have the mandate to guarantee public order, the freedom and the security of the communications to Jerusalem, Bethlehem and Nazareth; and France will cease to be the guardian of the Holy Places, the protectress of the Latin and Catholic Sanctuaries in the august Basilicas of the Holy Sepulchre in Jerusalem and of the Nativity in Bethlehem.

and when later on the Mandate was ultimately given to Great Britain the Vatican attempted to secure a leading influence of the Catholic countries in the control of the Holy Places. In all these years Russian influence in the Middle East was weak and the new active interest of the Russian Church was only beginning.

It may well be that memories of that era are still resounding in the present appeals for the internationalisation of Jerusalem, but the scene has changed fundamentally. The control of the West over the Arab world has ceased from the Atlantic to the Persian Gulf. The United Nations – very different from the early League – comprise large and powerful groups of Asian and African nations, in addition to the communist states under the leadership of the Soviet Union. Russia's influence in the Eastern Mediterranean has become a paramount factor in the Middle East. Already in 1948 when the Security Council considered sending military observers to the Arab-Israeli battlegrounds, the Soviet Union had demanded the inclusion of Russian officers, and today no international agreement on the Middle East could be imagined without Russia's active participation. Up till now the Patriarchate of Moscow has objected to any scheme of internationalisation of Jerusalem and has insisted, in accordance with the policy of the Soviet Union, on the restoration of all occupied territories to the Arab states. But if one day this policy should change and an internationalisation of Jerusalem should be brought about by the Powers – perhaps by joint intervention of America and Russia to preserve world peace – this would not be a restoration of the Latin Kingdom, nor a revival of the capitulation of 1740, with France as the protectress of the Catholic Church, nor a reconstruction of the world of Versailles of 1919, with its Council of the League dominated by the Western Powers. Internationalisation of Jerusalem today – if ever it came true – would rather be like the occupation of Berlin by the Allies in 1945, with the establishment of new *Kommandatura* in which the Russian contingent would be a very strong partner indeed.

Parallel with such a development there would probably be a great expansion of the influence of the Russian Church, and it is possible to visualise a future in which the number of monks and nuns in the Russian monasteries and convents in the Holy

Land will multiply by new arrivals from the Soviet Union; in which pilgrimages from Russia – so strong before the First World War – are resumed, as foreshadowed by Metropolitan Nikodeme; and in which the Patriarch of Moscow will give powerful support to the Orthodox in Jerusalem, vying with Constantinople for the leadership in the Eastern Church.

In recent times Moscow has taken important steps in this direction. One concerns the field of the reunion of the Churches where Moscow took an independent initiative by resolving to offer Roman Catholics (and Old-believers) the Holy Sacraments if they applied for them.[25] Although the relevant decision of the Holy Synod seems to have had in mind in the first instance cases where the applicants have no priest or church of their own denomination at their disposal, the formulation of the decision does not contain this qualification. Metropolitan Nikodeme in a special statement[26] pointed out that the Orthodox and Roman Churches agree about the identity of the sacraments, recognising them as mutually valid, and expressed the hope that the decision of the Holy Synod would help to restore the union of the Churches. Patriarch Athenagoras himself declared that he rejoiced in the decision, although he had not been officially informed about it, and thus recognised and accepted the initiative of the Moscow Patriarchate in this important field.[27]

The other step concerns the Russian Orthodox Church in America.[28] Russian Orthodox Christians had first entered America via the Aleutian Islands at the end of the eighteenth century and the congregation had grown throughout the nineteenth century. In 1919 as a result of the revolutionary situation in Russia the Russian diocese in America proclaimed its temporary self-government. In the fifty years of its *de facto* independence it grew into a well organised Metropolitan district and the Orthodox faith had become the faith of hundreds of thousands of native Americans who naturally were anxious to establish a local Orthodox Church independent from the Mother Church in Moscow. In 1946 the 'Metropolia' had asked the Moscow Patriarchate for independence or autocephaly. But Moscow insisted on some form of subordination. Now unexpectedly, the Moscow Patriarchate declared its readiness to renounce this claim. The Ecumenical Patriarch objected that according to canonical rules Moscow could not grant independence to the Russian Orthodox in America and on 8 January 1970, addressed a formal protest to the Moscow Patriarchate. 'If the Holy Church of Russia, in spite of our brotherly entreaty should proceed with the realisation of the proposal to announce the autocephality of the Russian Orthodox Metropolia in America, then this Throne will not recognise this action . . . will label this Church as uncanonical and . . . take any other action needed to secure canonical order.'

But the Moscow Patriarchate ignored these entreaties and Metropolitan Nikodeme announced that negotiations towards independence were continuing. He even took the opportunity to proclaim at a press conference at the United Nations, addressing Christendom as a whole, that:

the alienation of the youth from the Churches and the ecclesiastical hierarchy which is characteristic of the Western world, does not exist in the Soviet Union, that the number of believers there does not decrease and that, on the contrary, more and more people beyond the age of thirty take an interest in the Church and religion.[29]

Whilst the influence of the Moscow Patriarchate is thus increasing, the position of the Ecumenical Patriarchate in Constantinople is becoming more and more precarious. At the end of the First World War the number of Orthodox Christians in Turkey had amounted to about eight million. After the great exchange of populations in 1922, only fifty thousand Orthodox Greeks remained. The Treaty of Lausanne stipulated that the Patriarchate would stay in Istanbul as long as the number of Greek Orthodox of Turkish nationality amounted to at least twenty thousand. Today their number has shrunk to thirty thousand or less and the Patriarchate finds itself under strong pressure. At the end of May 1970 right-wing Turkish students publicly burned a cross as they demonstrated in front of the Greek Orthodox Patriarchate in Istanbul and demanded its expulsion.[30] The *Greek Herald* of New York wrote that 'the hope of preserving the Patriarchate in Constantinople – a city which has lost its Greek and Christian character – is based on "romanticism" '. The future of the Ecumenical Patriarchate in Istanbul has therefore become doubtful.

Some have suggested that in case of emergency the Ecumenical Patriarchate may move to Athens, but there may be strong pressure from Orthodox Slavs, and possibly others, to choose Moscow instead of Athens. More than twenty years ago voices were raised among Orthodox Slavs in the Balkans demanding a revision of the statute of the Ecumenical Patriarchate.[31] They claimed that the Patriarchs of Constantinople had never been in the fullest sense of the word impartial, and had been 'more Greek than Ecumenic'. They insisted that in future the high office of the Patriarch should be open not only to Greeks but to all Orthodox without regard to their nationality and proposed that the seat of the Patriarch should be transferred to Moscow.

If one day the supreme Ecumenical dignity should be granted to Moscow as the greatest and most powerful city of the Orthodox world, this would indeed be the fulfilment of the vision of Moscow as the Third Rome.

Internationalisation and the Local Christians

Catholics and Moslems alike have felt the connection between the Crusades and the modern proposals for an international regime for the Holy Land. But while the former looked forward to the re-establishment of 'the splendours of the first century of the Crusades', the Moslems view such prospects with dismay. They remember the massacres of the Moslem prisoners at the fall of Jerusalem, the transformation of the Mosque of Omar into a Church and the defilement of the El Aksa Sanctuary, which was turned into living quarters for the Templars. 'The internationalisation,' proclaimed the Pan-Islamic Conference of 1953, 'is the continuation of the Crusades . . . the internationalisation of Jerusalem is a manœuvre which the whole world of Islam will resist.'[32]

Not only the Moslems, but also Christian Arabs of Palestine oppose the scheme, because it might strengthen the influence of Western Christendom and generally give too much emphasis to the Christians abroad. To them the project seems to be devised not so much for the local population but for those who come from foreign countries to pray: the pilgrims. But the pilgrim – in Latin *peregrinus* – is not only 'one who journeys to a sacred place', the word also means 'stranger'; and the stranger, having completed his pilgrimage, returns home. No nation can be happy to live under a system which is constructed mainly for visitors from abroad, even if they share the same religion.

More important still, an approach which is based on the idea of the pilgrimage is in danger of overvaluing the real importance of the Holy Places. A modern Christian Arab writer expressed these thoughts in moving words:

> Christianity, because of the number of its European adherents and its European culture, appears to many as European.... The idea of the internationalisation of Jerusalem is a fruit of this European character and an implicit affirmation that what matters at Jerusalem is the character of antiquity of its places, its stones and not its people.... To give a special statute to the city of Jerusalem independent from Palestine means, in fact, to affirm that the city of Jerusalem is more important than Palestine. But Holy Scripture says the places of worship, however precious they may be, are temples built by the hands of men, whilst men are the temples of God. In our opinion the inhabitants of Palestine are more loved by God than the Church of the Resurrection – for if the tomb of Christ is a souvenir, the Arabs are no souvenirs .... May the two great Bishops (of Rome and Constantinople) with their charity, their humility, the breadth of their vision, and the spiritual restlessness which vibrates in their heart, hear from the mouth of the faithful of Jerusalem which destiny they wish for their city.[33]

The central issue of the Middle East today is the conflict between Israel and the Arabs. On the ultimate solution of this problem everything will depend. The proposal to internationalise Jerusalem for the sake of the Christian Sanctuaries is not directed to this purpose; and this is its fundamental weakness. The profound sympathy of the Church with all who suffer is beyond doubt, but the scheme to internationalise Jerusalem does not spring from this sacred source, and cannot be considered to be an essential part of Catholic thought. The words of the Custos of the Holy Land: 'We are indifferent to the political tug-of-war that is raging in Palestine' are in fact, the epitaph of the proposal.

Lastly, there remains the vision of Jerusalem as an 'oasis of peace and prayer', a vision which has found its supreme expression in the idea of the 'Heavenly City'. But the earthly

Jerusalem remains subject to the exigencies of life. 'Jesus,' in the words of Pascal, 'will remain in agony until the end of the world'; and Jerusalem for the world represents not only ultimate peace but also the Cross.

On Good Friday 1971, Pope Paul VI, addressing thousands of pilgrims at the Colosseum, appealed for help to the Christian communities in the Holy Land. This appeal commands universal support; and whilst the proposal for an internationalisation of Jerusalem, so often repeated in the past, is open to the gravest objections – the Churches themselves are divided on the issue – there should be no hesitation anywhere to help preserving and maintaining the rights, the traditions and the full life of the Christian Churches and communities in the Holy Land to whose sanctification throughout the world they have contributed immeasurably.

8 Solemn Declarations and Functional Internationalisation

Apart from the various schemes for internationalising the territory of Jerusalem – wholly or partly – a number of other proposals concerning the Holy Places have been discussed since the end of the Mandate. Some of these are of relevance today.

The Palestine Conciliation Commission and the Declaration of the Arab States

When in 1949 the Palestine Conciliation Commission had to deal with those Sanctuaries which are situated outside Jerusalem and therefore were not included in the scheme of internationalisation, they felt that protection could best be assured by the issue of formal declarations by the governments concerned which should be presented to the General Assembly for approval. Accordingly the Commission submitted to the Heads of the Arab and Israel Delegations the text of such a draft, with the request 'that by this Declaration formal guarantees be given by the respective Arab and Israel Governments with regard to the protection of and free access to, any Holy Places, religious buildings and sites of Palestine situated in the territory which may be placed under its authority by the final settlement of the Palestine problem, or pending that settlement, in the territory at present occupied by it under armistice agreements' and the Commission added that 'this communication would not prejudice in any way the final settlement of the territorial question in Palestine'.

The draft consisted of eight articles. The first five contained the usual and generally accepted points concerning the free exercise of worship, the preservation of the Holy Places, maintaining of existing rights, free access and freedom from taxation. The additional three articles suggested supervision of all arrangements by a Commissioner of the UN; the creation of a permanent Council 'to ensure the preservation of the Sanctuaries', and the provision that disputes between the Commissioner and the respective governments be decided by an International Tribunal.

The Israel representative in a letter of 8 November 1949, expressed agreement with the principles:

My Government has given careful consideration to the draft Declaration and affirms its support for the safeguarding of Holy Places by binding declarations from the Governments concerned. The Government of Israel reiterates its readiness solemnly to give formal guarantees for the free exercise in Israel of all forms of worship; for the preservation of Holy Places, religious buildings and sites in Israel, and for the associated amenities; for the granting of rights of visit, access and non-disturbance; and for appropriate measures in regard to taxation.

He reserved however, Israel's attitude to the legal formulations:

In considering the legal formulation of the matters contained in the Commission's draft Declaration, the Government of Israel has reached the conclusion that there are certain elements involved which have yet to be clarified. For example, the character of United Nations representation in regard to the Holy Places and the methods of settlement of disputes are still undecided. These matters which are of cardinal importance in implementing any guarantees which may be given, are about to be discussed in the General Assembly of the United Nations. On these as well as on the general question of Jerusalem and the Holy Places the Government of Israel intends at an early moment to make specific, positive and helpful proposals.

In these circumstances, my Government considers that it would be preferable to take up the actual formulation of a Declaration in the light of the situation soon to be clarified. The Government of Israel shares the desire of the Commission to achieve appropriate guarantees on the items above indicated. It is of the opinion, however, that it would in the circumstances be in the interests of a constructive and final settlement if the matter of formulation were dealt with after more far-reaching consideration of these problems by the General Assembly.

The Arab Governments went further. They accepted the draft Declaration proposed by the Conciliation Commission, as far as the first five articles were concerned, and reiterated them formally with some small alterations on 15 November 1949. They pledged themselves therefore solemnly to guarantee the free exercise of all forms of worship; to preserve and protect the Holy Places; maintain the status quo, the safety of religious ministers; to grant free access to the Holy Places and freedom from taxation. Like Israel, however, they hesitated concerning the further suggestions about a Commissioner, a Council and the settlement of disputes, and omitted these items in the Declaration which they sent to the Commission in reply to their letter.

The Arab Declaration read as follows:

The Governments of Egypt, the Hashemite Jordan Kingdom, Lebanon and Syria: Conscious of their responsibilities concerning the preservation of the special character of Palestine, whose soil has been consecrated by the prayers and pilgrimages of the three great religions; *Desirous* of implementing the provisions of paragraph seven of the resolution of the General Assembly of the United Nations of 11 December 1948, concerning the protection of and free access to the Holy Places, religious buildings and sites in Palestine outside the area of Jerusalem as this area is defined in paragraph eight of the resolution of 11 December 1948; *Solemnly* undertake by the provisions of the present declaration to guarantee the protection of and free access to the Holy Places, religious buildings and sites of Palestine, situated in the territory placed under their authority by the final settlement of the Palestine problem, or pending that settlement, in the territory at present occupied by them under armistice agreements:

Article 1: The free exercise of all forms of worship shall be guaranteed and ensured in accordance with the Declaration of Human Rights of 10 December 1948.

Article 2: The Holy Places, religious buildings and sites which were regarded as Holy Places and religious buildings on 14 May 1948 shall be preserved and their sacred character protected. No act of a nature to profane that sacred character shall be permitted.

Article 3: The rights in force on 14 May 1948 with regard to the Holy Places, religious buildings and sites shall remain in force.

The Governments of Egypt, the Hashemite Jordan Kingdom, Lebanon and Syria undertake in particular to assure the safety of ministers of religion, those officiating in religious services and the members of religious orders and institutions; to allow them to exercise their ministries without hindrance; and to facilitate their communications both inside and outside the country in connexion with the performance of their religious duties and functions.

Article 4: The Governments of Egypt, the Hashemite Jordan Kingdom, Lebanon and Syria undertake to guarantee freedom of access to the Holy Places, religious buildings and sites situated in the territory placed under their authority by the final settlement of the Palestine problem, or pending that settlement, in the territory at present occupied by them under armistice agreements – and, pursuant to this undertaking, will guarantee rights of entry and of transit to ministers of religion, pilgrims and visitors without distinction as to nationality or faith, subject only to considerations of national security, all the above in conformity with the status quo prior to 14 May 1948.

Article 5: No form of taxation shall be levied in respect of any Holy Place, religious building or site which was exempt from such taxation on 14 May 1948. No change in the incidence of any form of taxation shall be levied which would either discriminate between the owners and occupiers of Holy Places, religious buildings and sites, or would place such owners and occupiers in a position less favourable in relation to the general incidence of that form of taxation than existed on 14 May 1948.
New York, 15 November 1949.[1]

This Declaration to the Conciliation Commission, which covers both the Sanctuaries outside and inside Jerusalem is the only obligation which the Arab states ever undertook concerning the administration of the Holy Places. It formed the basis upon which Jordan administered the Sanctuaries for nineteen years and, as far as the Christian shrines are concerned, this administration did not give rise to any objection from the Christian communities.

The Israel Draft of an Agreement with the United Nations on the Holy Places

On 25 November 1949, Israel submitted the draft of an Agreement on the Holy Places, to be concluded between the United Nations and herself. In substance the draft contained the generally accepted principles, such as the maintenance of existing rights (status quo); the preservation and protection of, and access to the Holy Places, as well as their freedom from taxation. Thus far it was essentially identical with the formal Declaration which the Arab Governments had made a few days earlier on 15 November. Contrary to the Arab Declaration, however, the Israel draft allowed supervision of the arrangements by the United Nations, and in addition contained provisions for the settlement of disputes. But in neither case did the Israel proposals go as far as those of the Conciliation Commission. Thus the Israel draft did not envisage the appointment of a *commissioner* of the United Nations. Such an office, it was felt, would be an infringement of Israel sovereignty. Instead the draft provided for the appointment of a United Nations *representative*.

Israel hereby agrees [reads Section sixteen of the draft] that if the Secretary-General so requests he may appoint and send a representative to Israel to exercise the rights and duties conferred upon the United Nations by this Agreement. In making such appointment the Secretary-General shall have due regard for the accepted international custom relating to the appointment of diplomatic representatives. Such a representative may establish his headquarters in Jerusalem or in some other place agreed between him and the Government of Israel, and shall be accredited to the President of Israel. For the duration of his mission the Convention on the Privileges and Immunities of the United Nations approved by the General Assembly of the United Nations on 13 February 1946, as acceded to by Israel, shall be applicable to him as well as to his staff and to the buildings he occupies, all as is more particularly laid down in the said Convention on the Privileges and Immunities of the United Nations, it being understood that nothing in this agreement shall imply the extension of the provisions of the said Convention to any Holy Place.

The functions of the representative were carefully limited and defined as follows:

The functions of the representative of the Secretary-General shall be limited to matters pertaining to the application and implementation of this Agreement; in particular it is understood that nothing shall authorize the United Nations or the Secretary-General or his representative to intervene in matters which are essentially within the domestic jurisdiction of the State of Israel, or shall require the Government of Israel to submit any such matters to settlement under the Charter of the United Nations or under this Agreement.

Concerning the settlement of disputes between the United
Nations and Israel arising from the Agreement, the draft
suggested a tribunal of three arbitrators, named respectively by
the Secretary-General of the United Nations, the Israel Minister
for Foreign Affairs, and the President of the International
Court of Justice.

As for disputes between religious communities, the draft
proposed:

> Such dispute shall, in the first instance, be referred to the Govern-
> ment of Israel which may, in reaching its decision, seek the guidance
> of the United Nations. If the decision of the Government of Israel
> does not settle the dispute, then either Israel or the Secretary-
> General may refer the matter to the General Assembly.[2]

No steps were taken at that time on this proposal.

The Swedish Suggestion of Functional Internationalisation

When in December 1950 the question of Jerusalem was considered by the Ad Hoc Political Committee, the representative
of Sweden put forward a new proposal[3] based on the conception
of a 'functional rather than territorial internationalisation of the
Holy Places'. In essence the Swedish suggestion was a variation
of the proposals of the Conciliation Commission. Like the latter
it was based on Solemn Declarations – this time called Pledges –
of the Governments in possession of the Holy Places, promising
to deal rightly with the Sanctuaries. Accordingly the Swedish
draft Resolution invited the Governments of Israel and Jordan
to pledge themselves to observe the principles of the Universal
Declaration of Human Rights; to give free access to the Holy
Places, maintaining existing privileges in that respect; to
abstain from measures of taxation detrimental to the Holy
Places; and to respect the property rights of religious bodies.
In addition the Resolution contained detailed and far-reaching
suggestions concerning supervision by a Commissioner of the
United Nations. This Commissioner who was not to be selected
from among nationals of the State of Israel or of an Arab state,
nor from among the residents of the Jerusalem area, was to be
empowered:

(a) to request the Governments in the Jerusalem area to modify, defer or suspend such laws, ordinances, regulations and administrative acts pertaining to the area which in his opinion impaired the protection and free access to Holy Places, or other rights, immunities and privileges.

(b) to request the Governments to take such action or to make such orders or regulations for the maintenance of public security and safety as he deemed necessary to ensure the protection of and free access to the Holy Places or the safeguarding of the rights, immunities and privileges concerned.

The Governments were to carry into effect any action which the Commissioner deemed necessary. He also had the right to employ guards for the performance of his function in Jerusalem as well as to assure his own security and that of his staff; and the Governments in the Jerusalem area were to direct at the Commissioner's request their own police forces to assist the Commissioner in the performance of his duty. Disputes between the Commissioner and one of the Governments of the states in the Holy Land were to be referred to an ad hoc arbitrator. Disputes between religious denominations in connection with a Holy Place were to be decided by the Commissioner on the basis of existing rights and his decision was to be final.

All three proposals described in this chapter have in common that they do not demand a territorial internationalisation of Jerusalem but rely for the protection and welfare of the Holy Places on binding Solemn Declarations by the governments in control of the country. They differ, however, on the issues of supervision and the settlement of disputes between the religious communities. Both the draft of the Conciliation Commission and the Swedish proposal envisage supervision by a United Nations Commissioner to whom the Swedish proposal gives considerable executive and functional power. The Israeli draft, on the other hand, proposes a United Nations *representative* without executive power and of merely diplomatic status. Concerning disputes between the religious communities the Conciliation Commission made no suggestions. The Swedish draft provided that the Commissioner of the United Nations should decide once and for all; whilst Israel proposed that in the first instance the decision should be made by the government of the country and in the second instance be referred to the General Assembly.

145

On the eve of the fighting of June 1967, the position was that the Arab states had made a Solemn Declaration about the Holy Places to the United Nations confirming the substantial proposals of the Conciliation Commission. Israel whilst expressing her agreement in principle had refrained from entering any international obligation in the matter for the time being. Both parties, however, in practice fulfilled their duties concerning the Christian Sanctuaries in their territory.

On 7 June 1967, the Old City of Jerusalem, together with the town of Bethlehem, passed under Israeli control. Less than three weeks later the Knesset promulgated the Protection of Holy Places Law, by which the responsibility for the Sanctuaries was made part of the national law of the country. A few days later, at the beginning of July, Mgr Felici arrived in Israel and negotiations began about an international solution of the issue of the Holy Places, but no agreement was yet reached.

The Lauterpacht Proposals

In 1968, the question was taken up again by Dr Elihu Lauterpacht in a brochure 'Jerusalem and the Holy Places'.[4] This brochure is of special interest since the author is familiar with the thoughts of the Israel Government on the subject and with the tentative negotiations it has been conducting. In fact, he specially mentions in regard to his proposals that 'the Israel Government has already been able to discuss the matter in some detail with some of the principal interested parties on a basis which she understands to be largely acceptable to those immediately concerned'. The purpose of the proposals is to extend Israel's responsibility for the Holy Places from the sphere of the *national* law of the country into an *international* legal obligation. Like the Conciliation Commission of the United Nations in 1948, and the subsequent Swedish draft, he feels that this aim can best be achieved by the issue of a Solemn Declaration in an internationally binding form. He examines the technical question as to whether such a Declaration should be embodied in a treaty (bilateral or multilateral) or be given unilaterally. He submits that for the time being only a unilateral Declaration would be possible, suggests that the Declaration should be accompanied by a Statute 'setting out the status of the

Holy Places in Jerusalem and the rights and privileges of the religious communities actively associated with them', that the Declaration and the Statute should be registered with the Secretariat of the United Nations, and submits a draft of both instruments.

The substance of the proposals naturally comprises the generally acknowledged principles, such as freedom of access, freedom of worship, preservation of the status quo, and freedom from taxation, to which a number of technical details concerning for instance transport, visas and communications are added. Thus far the proposals – like the Israel Draft Agreement of 1950 – are essentially identical with the Declaration which the Arab Governments in November 1949 made to the United Nations. Besides these recognised principles, however, the proposal adds the three suggestions which had been included in the original draft of the Palestine Conciliation Commission, but which were not contained in the Arab Declarations. All three are open to grave doubts. They concern the appointment of a Commissioner of the United Nations for supervision, the creation of a Council of the Holy Places for advice and, most important of all, the determination of disputes between the different religious communities.

COMMISSIONER

In its memorandum of November 1949, the Israel Government had pointed out that if a supervision were necessary, it should be entrusted not to a Commissioner – whose office would infringe the sovereignty of the State – but to a representative of the United Nations who would not wield any executive power. The fact that the new proposal renews the suggestion of a Commissioner shows the deep concern of the author for an internationally agreed solution. Admittedly his proposals do not go as far as those of the Swedish draft of 1950. His Commissioner cannot 'request the Israel Government to modify, defer or suspend Laws and Administrative Acts of which he disapproves'. He cannot ask the Government 'to carry into effect without delay any action which he, the Commissioner, deems necessary for the protection of the Holy Places'. He has no guards of his own, nor can he demand that the Israel Government direct their police force to assist him. Yet he still has

147

important functions, including the duty to settle all disputes between the religious communities over the Holy Places; and this jurisdiction may have far-reaching consequences.

The essential precondition of any jurisdiction must be that the Commissioner *is* – and is *seen to be* – impartial. The Lauterpacht scheme takes this for granted and does not specify any conditions for his selection. But the question of impartiality may provide formidable difficulties. The Swedish draft had laid down that 'the Commissioner should not be selected from among nationals of the State of Israel or of an Arab State or from among the residents of the Jerusalem area'. This had followed the rules of the 1948 Statute for Jerusalem for the Governor of the City. But as far as the Holy Places are concerned this condition misses the essence of the problem. For the issue is not the *national* conflict between Israel and the Arabs, but the disputes between *religious* communities over the Sanctuaries, and these disputes are in no way identical with the political loyalties of the parties. It is irrelevant, therefore, to define the criteria in national terms.

The matter came up again in 1949 in the United Nations. On that occasion the Greek Orthodox Patriarch expressed the view that nobody should be given jurisdiction over disputes concerning the Holy Places who himself belonged to a denomination which had any interests in the Sanctuaries. The principle that no-one can be judge in his own case certainly is in accordance with the general rules of law. In practice it will exclude as Commissioners Roman Catholics, Greek Orthodox and Armenians besides Copts, Jacobites and Ethiopians. It would not rule out the selection of a Protestant but it is noteworthy to remember that when Balfour suggested a Protestant as Chairman of the Special Commission, the *Osservatore Romano* described the proposal as 'simply preposterous'.

All this deals only with the Christian Sanctuaries and disputes referring to them. But what about the Holy Places of Judaism and Islam, the Western Wall, the Dome of the Rock, the El Aksa Mosque and indeed the whole Temple area which are likewise included in the scheme?

Could Israel today accept as Commissioner for the Holy Places a Moslem, even if he is not an Arab but hails from Pakistan, Indonesia or Mongolia? And would Moslems agree to a Jew even if he came not from Israel, but Great Britain, South Africa or the United States? If a person must be found who is neither Roman Catholic, Greek Orthodox, Armenian, Copt, Syriac or Ethiopian, Protestant, Jew or Moslem, he may have to be sought among Buddhist monks, Hindu priests, Japanese Shintoists or perhaps even avowed and confirmed atheists – a choice as humiliating as unacceptable to all who are attached to even one of the Holy Places in Jerusalem.

Moreover, apart from the problem of impartiality, the task of deciding the religious disputes concerning the Sanctuaries of Judaism, Christianity and Islam, under the present conditions, must be considered to be beyond the scope of any individual human being.

COUNCIL

The second suggestion concerns the creation of a Council of the Holy Places. This Council is to consist of the Heads of the religious communities interested in the Sanctuaries, and shall serve as the organ for the representation to the Commissioner of their collective views. However, the suggestion, like that about the Commissioner himself, does not appear to be practical. It is hardly possible to imagine that in the present situation one Council, consisting of Jewish, Christian and Moslem leaders, could reach agreement on any issue, let alone present to the Commissioner collective views or useful advice. It was for that reason that already in 1950, when the conflict had in no way reached its present intensity, M.Garreau as President of the Trusteeship Council suggested, instead of one Commission, the creation of three Commissions for the Holy Places, one for each of the three religions concerned. And similarly, in 1967, the Israel Prime Minister Mr Eshkol announced that 'arrangements at the Western Wall would be determined by the Chief Rabbis of Israel, those in places sacred to Moslems by a Council of Moslem ecclesiastics, and those in places sacred to Christians by a Council of Christian religious dignitaries'. But even if three Councils were established the prospects for a fruitful cooperation are not promising; and as for a Christian Council, Cardinal Gasparri in 1922 predicted that 'a Commission on the Holy Places consisting of the representatives of the Christian denominations could reach no concrete results and there would

149

develop in its midst a bitter internal struggle which would make any objective judgement impossible'.

DISPUTES

The most important of the three suggestions concerns the settlement of disputes about the Holy Places between the different religious communities. It reads as follows:

> Any disputes between the communities as to rights in or over the Holy Places shall be determined by the Commissioner for the Holy Places. Any decision of the Commissioner in this regard shall be recognised as valid and binding under the law of Israel and shall be enforceable by process in the civil courts of Israel.

For hundreds of years the overwhelming majority of all religious disputes in the Holy Land were disputes between the Christian communities about their Sanctuaries arising from the schism of the Church. It is understandable therefore that Israel may have the wish to divest herself for reasons of discretion and tact from the responsibility of such jurisdiction. 'One can see reasons,' says Lauterpacht, 'why Israel should not herself become involved in disputes between various religious communities. In so far as they arise between non-Jewish groups it may be better that they should not be decided by Jewish authorities, and in so far as they affect relations between Jewish and non-Jewish interests, there may again be advantage in having them decided by a non-Israeli body.' These thoughts are certainly persuasive and will probably be shared by many Christians. Nevertheless there are strong reasons for a different attitude. The issues here at stake are not limited to parochial questions in which the government of the country, whoever it may be, could disinterest itself. They have often aroused profound interest abroad and sometimes in fact concerned matters of world-historic dimensions. Thus the Crusades themselves with their wars of nearly two hundred years in a sense were 'disputes about the Holy Places between religious communities'. During the four hundred years of Ottoman rule 'no question more constantly exercised the Moslem rulers of Palestine than the ever recurring disputes of the Christian communities about the Sanctuaries' and they played a great part in the numerous treaties and capitulations between the European Powers and the Ottoman Empire.

Disputes between the Christian communities in the country about the Holy Places in Jerusalem and Bethlehem, combined with the religious passions they aroused in Russia and in France, greatly contributed to the outbreak of the Crimean War. Again, at the Peace Conference of 1919, the Latins demanded the restoration of the Sanctuaries to the status which existed in 1740, and the undoing of what they considered 'the usurpations' by the Orthodox. Religious arguments dominated the deliberations of the League of Nations concerning the Mandate for several years. Up to the present day the conflict between the Western and the Eastern churches about the Holy Places has not yet been solved, and as mentioned above, at Easter 1970, there were even clashes among the Eastern Christians themselves. The status quo is by no means recognised by all, and the reawakened interest of the Russian Church in the Holy Land has added new questions.

Disputes about the Sanctuaries of Judaism and Islam are even more formidable. In 1929–30, Jewish services at the Western (Wailing) Wall led to riots and massacres. Since 1967 the conflict has moved to the Mountain of the Lord itself. There are arguments in the sphere of archaeology. The Islamic Council of Jerusalem has appealed to the Government of Israel for a halt to the excavations which, they feel, endanger the El Aksa Mosque; and similar demands have been made by Orthodox Jews for the sake of the Holiest of the Jewish Sanctuaries. But beyond issues of archaeology there looms the clash of religious claims themselves. The Temple area is holy both to Judaism and Islam. The Moslems fear that Israel ultimately aims at the destruction of the Mosques in order to rebuild in their place the Temple of old; and it was this fear which gave the fire in the El Aksa Mosque a sinister significance in the Moslem mind. Against this the Israel Government protested that the Temple will only be rebuilt in the days of the Messiah and that nothing will be done in the present era to hasten that day. But the fear remains, and Jewish Messianism and Moslem piety face each other in an unsolved confrontation.

One only has to visualise these problems to realise that it would be not only dangerous but impossible for any government to entrust the decision on such explosive issues to an outside agent whose appointment is beyond its control, on whose decisions it has no influence, and who himself may be subjected to political pressure by external forces. No government has ever accepted such proposals and no government will consent to recognise without question, examination or even possibility of appeal 'any decision of the Commissioner on the Holy Places as valid and binding under the Law of the country and enforceable by process in the Civil Courts'.

When in 1949, the Conciliation Commission asked all governments concerned to give formal, binding Declarations concerning their treatment of the Holy Places, the Arabs accepted the substance of the proposals, but ignored the clauses concerning a Commissioner, a Council and the settlement of disputes. This was the result of wisdom and experience. It is suggested that Israel follows their example, but does not go beyond it; and it will be shown that such attitude is not only prudent but also in accordance with the most hopeful developments within the Churches today.

9 United Nations –
United Religions – or
Arab-Israel Condominium?

United Nations

All suggestions for the internationalisation of Jerusalem – be it territorial or functional – which have been put forward hitherto, are ultimately based on the conception of the United Nations. It is indeed tempting to assume that the supreme body of inter-state organisation could be the ideal agency for dealing with a matter of such universal interest. It has been argued particularly that single states are subject to the fluctuations of local politics, which might affect the validity even of the most solemn declarations, whilst an international organisation will enjoy continued stability.[1] But the fallacy of this argument has been exposed by the succesive contradictory resolutions of the United Nations on the very subject of the internationalisation of Jerusalem. Within the three years between November 1947 and December 1950 the matter was put to the vote three times, in every case with a different result. On the first occasion the General Assembly decided for internationalisation by thirty-three votes against thirteen. In December of the following year the General Assembly restated its intention that Jerusalem should be placed under an international regime, but many who had voted for the scheme in the preceding year – including Great Britain, Canada and the USA, now voted against it. In December 1950 the necessary two-thirds majority was no longer available and the scheme had to be abandoned. In fact, several member states, including the United States, changed their attitude to the project at every occasion, voting once for the resolution, once against it, and once abstaining. The shifting majorities of states which are determined in their attitude by

F

their own national interest and their changing views about the international scene, are in no way more stable or reliable than the decisions of a government which represents the permanent identity of the country in whose territory the Sanctuaries are situated. Mgr Collin, himself one of the most devoted advocates of internationalisation, summed up his view on the voting in the United Nations in the following words.

It is not the interest in the Holy Places which determines the issue. The voting is the result of quite different considerations. The transposition of the case of the Holy Places into the global sphere has turned them into stakes in the international game . . . the problem of the Sanctuaries is not presented on the religious plane – its true place – but on the political plane, in the worst sense of the word. The Holy Places, an object of veneration for the whole Christian world, have become the pretext and the object of Machiavellian transactions.[2]

Besides the lack of stability there are, however, more fundamental reasons against placing the responsibility for the Christian Holy Places upon the United Nations. The purpose of the United Nations is essentially the preservation of peace. The preamble of the Charter begins with the words: 'We, the peoples of the United Nations, determined to save succeeding generations from the scourge of war . . . have resolved to combine our efforts . . .'; and Article 1 declares that the first purpose of the Organisation is: 'To maintain international peace and security.'

The Christian Holy Places, however, in no way endanger the peace or security of the world. They are neither the cause nor the object of the present conflict. The conflict between Israel and the Arabs is no re-enactment of the Crimean War in which the rivalry between France and Russia about the control of the Christian Sanctuaries was, in fact, a major issue. The conflict is fundamentally a national struggle and the Christian Sanctuaries are involved only in so far as they are situated in the contested territory.

The situation is different as far as the Jewish and Islamic Holy Places are concerned, because the religious aspirations of both communities clash in the Temple area. In the early days of the Jewish national movement many of its followers, or even leaders, may not have been fully aware of this. Thus Dr

154

Weizmann in his autobiography, referring to the year 1921, writes:

There were no Holy Places in Palestine to which the Jews laid actually physical claim – except perhaps Rachel's Tomb, which was at no time a matter of controversy. The Wailing Wall we did not own, and never had owned since the destruction of the Temple; controversy was later to arise over the Jewish prayers conducted there, but at this time there was no suggestion of even that.[3]

Likewise in 1930, the Jewish representatives disclaimed before the commission which had been appointed by the British Government 'to determine the rights and claims in connection with the Western Wall' any right of ownership in the Wall or in the pavement in front of it. Today the situation is changed dramatically. 'We have returned to the most sacred of our Holy Places never to part from it again' proclaimed General Dayan, and no government of Israel will lightly disown this proclamation.

Others go even further and demand the right of conducting Jewish prayers within the courtyards of the mosques which are sacred to the followers of Islam. The Temple area indeed is a religious issue in the Arab-Israel conflict. But this cannot be said in a similar way of the Christian Sanctuaries. Neither Israel nor the Arabs see in the Holy Sepulchre the centre of their aspirations. All plans to internationalise the Holy City for the sake of the Christian Sanctuaries therefore miss the core of the problem. These plans will not solve the conflict between Israel and the Arabs and are not even designed to do so. In fact, they rather assume the continued existence of the conflict because without it there would be no basis for any international intervention.

The purpose of the measure is to extricate the Sanctuaries from the dangers of the fighting and to preserve the sanctity of the Holy Places. Sanctity, however, is a religious concept, and the United Nations are in no way qualified as a religious body. They are an association of states without regard to the religious affiliations of their citizens. Religion to the United Nations is a personal or private matter which is outside the legitimate concerns of the organisation; and the very word 'religion' is mentioned in the Charter only in a negative sense, in connection with the prohibition of discriminations 'on the ground of race, language, sex and religion', (e.g. Article I, No. 3).

The ideal of peace, of course, is deeply rooted in religious thought, and in particular in Judaeo-Christianity. The medieval visions of universal peace as for instance expressed by Dante's *Monarchia*, were essentially of a Christian character. Others like Dubois[4] aimed at a federation of all Christian states as a means to fight the Infidels. But the unity of Christendom itself had been broken already by the schism between Rome and Byzanz; and the West was furthermore divided by the Reformation and the rise of the national states. Thus religion gradually lost its power as a unifying force, and the efforts to establish general peace shifted to the sphere of reason and natural law.

It was an era of 'a progressive ejection of God from nature and its laws'[5] and Kant in his famous essay on Eternal Peace paraphrasing a passage in the Gospel proclaimed:

> Seek ye first the kingdom of pure and practical reason and of its righteousness, and then will your object, the benefit of eternal peace, be added to you.[6]

The Romantics once more dreamed of a revival of the medieval world, a dream which was beautifully expressed in Novalis' *Europa oder die Christenheit*. But the Holy Alliance after the Napoleonic Wars was the last attempt to base the new order on Christianity. Soon afterwards the lead in the movement for peace was taken by the secular forces, and when the powers of Europe assembled for the first conferences in the Hague to lay the foundations for an international cooperation, the Holy See was not invited.[7] Today the United Nations, like their predecessor the League, are an association of 'states only'. Neither the Pope, the Ecumenical Patriarch, the Archbishop of Canterbury nor the Dalai Lama nor any other religious leader or organisation are members. The United Nations, unlike the British Parliament, do not know any 'Lords Spiritual'. They certainly are not a body specially qualified to deal with religious issues and in particular the preservation of sanctity.

Nevertheless in the early years of the League the majority of the members were nations with a strong Christian life, or at least a long Christian tradition. Of the original forty-one founders only China, India, Japan, Persia and Siam belonged to different worlds. But gradually the picture changed and the influence of Christianity in world affairs declined. In November 1947, when the partition of Palestine was decided, the non-Christian members of the United Nations already formed about twenty per cent, and since July 1967 the long list of member states – beginning with Afghanistan and ending with Zambia – shows a majority of non-Christian nations.[8] The preservation of the sanctity of the Christian Holy Places cannot be considered to be for them a dominant concern and, in the words of the Peel Commission, 'an overriding necessity'.

United Religions

On 24 September 1969, Pope Paul VI sent a message to King Hassan II of Morocco, which contained a new approach to the question of the Holy Places. King Hassan had informed the Pope of the forthcoming Islamic Conference to be held in Rabat to consider the situation which had been created by the fire in the El Aksa Mosque. To this message the Pope replied as follows:

We firstly wish to inform Your Majesty that We were pleased to receive your envoy's assurance of the intentions of the distinguished personalities who are going to meet in Rabat. We particularly appreciate their proposal to encourage pacific methods in the resolution of the painful conflict which is the cause of this meeting and to inspire a belief in God to provide a just and honourable solution to the present situation.

If, in fact, recourse to violence is deplorable everywhere, there is nowhere in the world where it is more injurious to God than in this blessed land of Palestine where are assembled the Heads and the justly cherished sanctuaries of the three great religious groups professing belief in a unique and merciful God.

We therefore think that the representatives of the three mono-theistic religions should agree to recognise the unique and sacred character of the Holy Places and of Jerusalem in particular. The recourse to religious sentiment, far from perpetuating divisions, ought to manifest itself as a unifying principle that can overcome political or military antagonisms and lead to concord and peace.[9]

This message contains a completely new approach to the question of the Holy Places by proposing that a solution may be found not through the United Nations or any other secular agency but by cooperation and agreement between the three monotheistic religions. Seen in an historical perspective the proposal represents an enormous development. In the Crusades the Moslem world appeared to the Christians as a 'vile race of men who do not know God'; and for centuries theological polemics have determined the relationships between the religious communities. Now Christians, Moslems and Jews are called upon to agree among themselves on the basis of their common monotheistic belief.

If the issue were to defend the Holy Places against an attack from outside by a common enemy – be it militant atheism or a belief equally alien to all three of them – there would be no difficulty in reaching agreement for the defence of the common values. This, however, is not the case. The task set by the papal message is not negative defence but positive achievement of mutual appreciation and recognition of the 'unique and sacred character' of the Holy Places. Some of the Sanctuaries are common to all three religions – Judaism, Christianity and Islam alike revere the patriarchs Abraham, Isaac and Jacob. Their tombs therefore could be objects of common veneration. But as far as the major Sanctuaries are concerned the situation is complex. Thus Islam recognises Jesus as the Messiah, although not as divine, and accepts the virgin birth by Mary his mother. But whilst the Christian venerates the Grotto in Bethlehem as the birthplace of the Saviour, the Moslem believes that the birth took place under a palm tree with a streamlet at the Virgin's feet XIX (23/24). Again, Moslems do not accept that the Crucifixion actually took place – 'Yet they slew him not, and they crucified him not, but they had only his likeness' (IV 156). Calvary, to the Christian the holiest of the Holy Places, cannot therefore mean the same to the followers of Islam. Christians on the other hand will find little meaning in the nocturnal journey of the Prophet from Mecca to Jerusalem and thence through the seven heavens. As far as the Temple is concerned, Christians will certainly pay profound respect to its remnants. But since they believe that following the Crucifixion 'the veil of the Temple was rent in twain from the top to the bottom' (Matthew XXVVII. 51) that the Temple was destroyed never to rise again and that the sacrifices of old have been superseded by a new and higher dispensation, they cannot share in the Messianic expectations of Judaism, linked with the Temple Mount. The proposed agreement between the three religions can therefore not be based on the fact that they hold their major Holy Places in common. On the contrary, each of the three religions has its own Holy Places which to its followers are of unique sacredness and the faithful will be reluctant to attach similar – let alone equal – value to the Sanctuaries of other religions, however closely they be linked historically to their own religion. For the agnostic, or indeed any person who himself is not identified with any of the religions concerned, the situation is different. Thus, the British whilst ruling over India, could show the same respect to Hindus and Moslems, to temples and to mosques; and Napoleon I ordered his troops in Egypt 'to have the same tolerance for the mosques and the ceremonies prescribed by the Koran, that you showed for convents and synagogues, for the religions of Moses and of Jesus Christ'.[10] But for the true believer who associates his personal salvation with the Holy Places of his own religion, it is difficult to recognise in the Sanctuaries of other religions – some of which may appear to him strange, irrelevant, outdated or even blasphemous – the same unique and sacred character. He may show politeness, courtesy and respect towards them, but the recognition of their universal sanctity will require great spiritual imagination.

By a strange coincidence, one day before Pope Paul VI sent his message to King Hassan II, Bishop Collin, in an article in *Le Monde*, 23 September 1969, had raised the question whether a conference of representatives of the three monotheistic religions could be called to deal with the issue of the Holy Places. He reached the conclusion that, at least for the time being, such a project would be impracticable. Judaism, he felt, was 'more or less identified with Zionism and it was to be expected therefore that Moslems would *a priori* refuse to meet its representatives'. Islam on the other side had no structural organisation comparable to that of a Church which would be in a position to conduct any negotiations; and he summed up his views by saying that 'the numerous difficulties involved are today and without doubt for a long time to come, insoluble'. It is submitted that the same applies to Pope Paul's proposal to King Hassan. For the time being the responsibility for the

Holy Places of all three religions must rest with the government of the country, and no international body – neither the United Nations nor an association of religious communities – can relieve the government from this duty. This has been the situation throughout history. The Ottoman Empire – like its predecessors – was responsible for the Holy Places from the conquest of Jerusalem in 1517 until its fall exactly four hundred years later. Jordan carried the responsibility during the nineteen years of its rule; and during the time of the Mandate actual control – in spite of the formal but remote supervision by the League of Nations – was in the hands of Great Britain. Never has the power of government over the country been exercised by an international organisation.

The government of the country will naturally try to administer the Holy Places in cooperation with the religious communities concerned. But this cooperation must be negotiated separately with each of the religious groups, Christians, Moslems and Jews. There is no common or universal interest of all three religions in the Holy Places. Each religion has its own sanctuaries and its own profound concern for them. To this the government has to give its attention and to make the utmost efforts to satisfy the demands and requests of the faithful, as far as the corresponding claims of other religious communities permit.

It was in accordance with these principles that on 7 June 1967, the then Prime Minister of Israel, Mr Eshkol, announced: 'Instructions have been given that arrangements at the Western Wall shall be determined by the Chief Rabbis of Israel, those in places sacred to Moslem by a Council of Moslem ecclesiastics, and those in places sacred to Christians by a Council of Christian religious dignitaries.' Similarly Mr Eban in a letter to the United Nations Secretary General wrote on 30 April 1968:

Israel, unlike previous governments in the city, does not wish to exercise exclusive and unilateral control over the Holy Places of other faiths. Accordingly we are willing to work out arrangements with those traditionally concerned, which will ensure the universal character of the Christian and Moslem Holy Places.

After the Pope had sent his message to King Hassan Mr Eban repeated the gist of this statement to the United Nations General Assembly on 29 September 1969.

Condominium

Whilst these lines are being written, it is uncertain which government for the City of Jerusalem will emerge from the Arab-Israel conflict. For Israel Jerusalem is the undivided capital. Most of the Arab states maintain that there can be no peace, until at least the Old City is returned; and some groups within the Resistance Movement demand the destruction of Israel and its transformation into a new secular Palestine. As far as the Christian Holy Places are concerned, all these alternatives would be possible, and they could survive unscathed in any case. They are independent of the political structure of the country. In fact, the Christian Sanctuaries on the whole were safe and protected during the centuries of Islamic rule, and the same can be said of the years under Israel's control. What matters is that the government of the country shows true respect for their sanctity.

Recently grave reproaches have been levelled against Israel for its 'intention to judaise Jerusalem', for the expropriation of Arab land on a vast scale, and for increasing pressure on the Arab population which will reduce their '*Lebensraum*'. Such measures – whatever their merits may be – might still leave the sacred character of the Christian Holy Places as centres of pilgrimages untouched. But they are part of the bitter and tragic struggle between the two nations for the control and the possession of the country. This struggle, naturally, is outside the scope of the present book which is essentially devoted to the issue of the Christian Holy Places. But the writer wishes to put on record his hope that in spite of all difficulties, ultimately a reconciliation between Israel and the Arabs will take place, and an agreement will be reached by which the government over the Old City is shared between them in some form of condominium. Until such an agreement is reached, he believes that the responsibility for the Christian Holy Places must be borne by the Government of Israel which is in control of the City.

10 The Christian Holy Places and the Reunion of the Churches

The End of Litigation – Union in Charity

Eleven months after the Israeli Forces had entered the Old City of Jerusalem, Father A. Arce, OFM, who since 1922 had served in the Franciscan Custody of the Holy Land, wrote as follows:

> During its long life the Custody has been part of the territory of many temporal rulers: the Mameluk Sultans of Egypt, the Ottoman Sultans of Constantinople, the Military Administration and Mandatory Government of Great Britain, the kings of Jordan and the State of Israel. . . . Thank God, it has been able to fit in with them all.[1]

These words clearly mean that the question of who exercises political control over Jerusalem is – from the Christian point of view – of small importance, as long as the minimum requirements regarding free access to the Holy Places, their preservation and the freedom of worship are fulfilled. Temporal government, after all, concerns merely external arrangements, whilst what matters religiously is the internal life of the Church, culminating in the communion with Christ, fellowship and salvation. For many centuries the religious life at the Christian Holy Places has been profoundly affected by the division of the Churches, and the schism has done more harm to the Christian cause than the occupation of the Holy Land by successive Moslem Powers. More than once the conflict between Western and Eastern Christians led to physical violence; but on the whole it took the form of a never-ending legal controversy over disputed rights and titles. A whole literature has been written about the legal problems of the Holy Places, and the Sanctuaries have almost become symbols of division and strife.

162

Once in the long history of the conflict the controversy was submitted for examination and adjudication to the community of nations, when in 1919 both Latins and Greeks laid their memoranda before the Peace Conference at Paris. But the attempt failed, since no agreement could be reached about the composition of the investigating body. Thus the matter remained as it had been before. Catholics from time to time put on record that they do not recognise the status quo as it has existed since 1757; and that they consider the present state as the result of usurpation and violence. The Status Quo, in the words of Baldi is *'un expedient diplomatique'*,[2] and Collin declares: 'For the Catholic Church the Status Quo is no solution. . . . It is not founded on mutual consent and any attempt to base the solution of the problem of the Holy Places upon it is doomed.'[3] The formula of the status quo, therefore, does not represent an agreement between the parties, and below the surface the dispute remains alive as a burning question which at any day may come into the open again.

In these circumstances the question arises whether in spite of the failure of the efforts after the First World War, another attempt could be made to investigate the legal merits of the issue by a special tribunal – whatever its agreed composition might be – in the hope that by historical method and juridical procedure the dispute may be brought to an end, and peace and unity in the Holy Places be established. It would, no doubt, be a formidable task to overcome the weight of an uninterrupted practice of more than two hundred years, recognised and ratified by local law and international treaties. But in a matter which touches the emotions and beliefs of millions the utmost patience and sympathy will be required, and if it should be shown as a result of the investigation, that one of the parties has suffered a grave injustice, the wrong could probably be righted. It is the Catholics who demand a change of the existing situation. What is their case?

Starting from the assumption that the rights which had been established by the Crusaders ceased to exist with the conquest of Jerusalem by Saladin and therefore cannot be invoked now, the claim appears to rest on three foundations: purchase, decrees of the Sultans (firmans) and international treaties.

PURCHASE

Eugene Boré,[4] who during the crisis which preceded the Crimean War was sent by the French Government to Jerusalem to examine the facts and study the documents concerning the Holy Places, states in his report that in 1342 King Robert of Sicily and his wife Queen Sanche bought the Sanctuaries *'pour une forte somme d'argent'*. He adds that this transaction could not be affected by the subsequent conquest of the country by the Ottoman Turks, and claims that accordingly the agreement is still valid. It can be left undecided whether his legal conclusions are correct, since the fact of the purchase itself is not borne out by the evidence. No deed of the transaction is in existence. It is only referred to in two encyclicals of the year 1342. The exact contents of the treaty are not known, but it appears that the purchase in question in reality concerned neither the Holy Sepulchre nor the Basilica in Bethlehem, but the Cenacle on Mount Zion. In addition, the treaty seems to have established a right of the Franciscans to officiate in the Holy Sepulchre and in the Grotto of Bethlehem subject to the rights of others who had acquired the same privilege. This is confirmed by the Fathers Vincent and Abel who in their classic history of Jerusalem sum up the situation as it existed after the purchase as follows:

The Franciscans found themselves in possession of the Cenacle and of the right to officiate in the Holy Sepulchre, in the Grotto of Bethlehem and in the Tomb of the Virgin, always without prejudice to the rights acquired by other denominations enumerated by the pilgrims of the period: Greeks, Abyssinians, Nubians, Maronites, Jacobites, Georgians. These last-mentioned, in fact, held the keys of the Holy Sepulchre and the property of Calvary.[5]

More recent statements accordingly do not maintain any longer the claim of Boré; and the memorandum of the Latins for the Peace Conference of 1919 refers to the purchase only in connection with the 'exclusive property of the Cenacle'. No claim to the property of the Holy Sepulchre or the Basilica of the Nativity can therefore be based on the alleged purchase by King Robert and Queen Sanche.

DECREES OF THE SULTANS (FIRMANS)

The main weight of the Latin claims has always rested on the firmans, i.e. official decrees or instructions by a Sultan, addressed either to his Grand Vizier or to local officials.

It would be impossible [says the memorandum of the Latins] to enumerate the many firmans issued by the Sultans of Egypt and Constantinople in favour of the Custodian of the Holy Land, firmans nearly always obtained by the intervention of one power or another, either through their accredited representatives at the Arab or Ottoman courts or through special envoys.[6]

Undoubtedly some of these firmans were very favourable to the Latins and contained more rights and privileges for them than those which are in force today. This will be particularly true of firmans which, as the Latin Memorandum says, were obtained by the intervention of powerful Western States. But the fact is that these decrees of the Sultans by their very nature were revocable. This was made clear beyond any doubt by the official representative of the Custos himself, Father Simon Bonaventura, in the evidence he gave on behalf of the Custos before the United Nations Special Committee on Palestine (UNSCOP) in Jerusalem on 15 July 1947.[7] The distinguished Canadian lawyer, Mr Justice Ivan Rand of the Supreme Court of Canada, anxious to clarify 'the nature of the proprietorship and of the title of these important shrines in this city', conducted a thorough examination, and although, according to the published minutes, the witness hesitated once or twice because a question might concern the status quo, and this, in the witness' opinion did not fall within the terms of reference of the Committee, he ultimately confirmed that each denomination received and accepted its shrines from the Turkish regime, and that the distribution was made by the Turks alone. 'During the Turkish regime,' he said, 'the Government stated that *this* community should have *this* shrine and *that* community should have *that* shrine. That was the basis of the present Status Quo'; and in reply to a further question by the Judge he added in conclusion that any modification of the existing state had to be made by the Turkish Government.

The revocability of the firmans is beyond doubt. Sometimes

the Turks themselves may have been cynical about this, as for instance the Grand Vizier in his often quoted answer to the Count of Vergennes, mentioned earlier.[8] But there must have been many occasions throughout the centuries of Ottoman rule in which transformations of the European scene made changes within the country advisable or necessary, and the decision about the interest of the state could naturally only lie with the Turkish Government.

The present state of the Christian Holy Places is based on the firman of February 1852 which itself was essentially a confirmation of the arrangements of 1757. It revoked all previous decrees of different content, but in turn has never been revoked itself. In fact, it remained in force until the end of the Ottoman Empire. No firman, therefore, is in existence on which a claim for a change of the Status Quo could be based.

International Treaties (capitulations)

Lastly, there remains the question whether a claim for a change of the status quo could be derived from one of the capitulations, particularly the treaty between France and Turkey of 1740, which has always been considered as a foundation of special rights in favour of the Franciscans. Against this has to be held that all capitulations which Turkey ever entered have ceased to exist. As Collin has pointed out the French religious protectorates since the days of Louis xiv had become 'political instruments for the enlargement of French influence and prestige in the Ottoman Empire'.[9] In Turkey itself the capitulations came to be regarded from the end of the nineteenth century onwards as 'unequal treaties, imposed by colonial and imperialist Powers'. The Young Turks had tried to abolish them but did not succeed. At the beginning of the First World War, however, Turkey declared unilaterally all capitulations null and void. Germany and Austria recognised the abrogation. But the Western Powers considered the action an illegal breach of 'freely entered international obligations' and forced Turkey in the Treaty of Sèvres to restore the capitulations – at least in favour of the victor-states. As is well known, this treaty was never ratified owing to the Turkish national resurgence under Kemal Pasha; and when at last the actual Peace Treaty of Lausanne was signed on 23 July 1923, all powers, including France, agreed 'to accept the complete abolition of all Capitulations on Turkey in every respect'. This brought the matter to an end, as far as the territory of Turkey was concerned.

As for Palestine, the situation was slightly different. At the time when the Treaty of Lausanne was signed, Palestine had already been separated from Turkey, and was under the British Mandatory Government. According to Article 8 of the Mandate 'the privileges and immunities of foreigners, including the benefits of consular jurisdiction and protection as formerly enjoyed by capitulation or usage in the Ottoman Empire' were declared inapplicable in Palestine. But it was provided that those countries which had benefited from capitulations in the past might claim the re-establishment of their privileges at the expiration of the Mandate, provided they had not renounced such right by that time. When in 1948, the Mandate came to an end, France, like all other signatories of the Treaty of Lausanne, had accepted the abolition of the capitulations in Turkey as *a whole*. It would, therefore, have been an anomaly if she had tried to re-establish capitulationary privileges in a territory which had been a *part* of the Ottoman Empire. The United Nations Special Committee on Palestine at the time described such a possibility as anachronistic. In fact, France never did make such a claim, and this could certainly not be done now, more than twenty years after the end of the Mandate, quite apart from the political aspect of the matter. The era of the capitulations has gone and cannot be revived. In the words of Collin, the French right to protect the Christian Holy Places ended with the Treaty of Lausanne.[10]

Neither the purchase by King Robert and Queen Sanche, nor the firmans of the Sultans, nor the capitulations in favour of France can today justify a claim for a change of the Status Quo.

It cannot be expected that any other legal or historical investigation will solve the question of the Holy Places. For the real issue is not *where* the demarcation line between the different Christian communities in the Sanctuaries is to be drawn, but the fact *that* a demarcation line between them is required at all. The real issue is the schism itself. For centuries the arguments about the Christian Sanctuaries have been conducted as if the division was a permanent fact. They were limited, therefore, to the symptoms and did not touch the core of the problem. But now an attempt is being made to attack the schism itself with the aim of ultimate reunion. The historic meeting of Pope Paul VI with the three Orthodox Patriarchs in January 1964 in Jerusalem may open a new era, not only in the general field of the Christian ecumenical movement but for the special problem of the Christian Holy Places. At their meeting in Jerusalem, the spiritual leaders did not engage in arguments about the rights and titles of their Churches, but met 'in a sacred encounter', in common prayer, in the hope that 'the night of separation may end and that Charity may reign more and more between all'.[11] In the face of such spirit juridical arguments lose their significance.

The encounter did not take place without some opposition, particularly in the Greek Church, and during the meeting in Jerusalem a night-vigil was held in the Patraki Monastery in Athens at which cries could be heard such as 'Down with the Pope, Down with Athenagoras'.[12] But both leaders continued in their efforts. For centuries Rome and Byzantium had claimed respectively to be the One Catholic Apostolic Church, and Pope Paul and Patriarch Athenagoras were well aware of the dangers of a 'false union'. They agreed that 'difference in the field of Doctrine, Liturgy and Discipline are to be examined at the right time and place' and that a theological Dialogue may require many years. They were convinced however that a new relationship between the Churches could now be built up immediately in the sphere and the spirit of Charity, whilst the Theological discussions were being prepared and conducted. At the Pan Orthodox Conference in November of the same year, Metropolitan Meliton expressed this conviction in the following words: 'A dialogue requires studies. Charity has no need for studies. It needs practice, initiative, generosity and the spirit of sacrifice. The Dialogue of Charity precedes the Dialogue of the Churches'; and he proclaimed: 'We shall begin ourselves to exercise Charity.'[13]

As described above, Pope Paul VI and Patriarch Athenagoras gave a magnificent example of this spirit when on 7 December 1965, in services held simultaneously in St Peter's in Rome and the Patriarchal Church in Constantinople they removed from the memory of the Church the mutual excommunications of the year 1054, and publicly expressed their regrets for the 'offensive words, unfounded reproaches and condemnable acts which on either side had marked or accompanied the sad events of that epoch'.[14]

It is not impossible that a similar declaration could be made in the Holy Places. At times there has been much hostility, mutual accusations and even violence. A statement of regret and mutual forgiveness would remove the bitterness which has accumulated over centuries.

It is obvious that the government of the country has no part in this most intimate and internal Christian development. But being aware of it, it will avoid any action which – however inadvertently – may impede the progress towards reunion. To achieve this aim it is suggested that the government refrain at the present time from separate arrangements about the Holy Places with any of the Christian communities – since they may tend to perpetuate separation – but rather aim at joint agreements with all interested Churches together. Likewise it appears helpful to discourage disputes about the Sanctuaries among the different Christian communities by refraining from setting up machinery for such disputes. It will be recalled that the Arab Governments in 1949 pursued this line[15] and it is proposed that the Israel Government follow their example.

At present an Ecumenical Institute for Theological Studies is being erected in Jerusalem. It will give new opportunities for cooperation in the field of scholarship. But the Christian Holy Places themselves could become an important factor in the move for reunion. In the past both the Roman and the Orthodox Churches were reluctant to allow any form of common worship. Today common prayer services for unity are considered possible. Pope Paul VI himself on 4 December 1965, four days before the close of the Second Vatican Council, participated in an interfaith prayer service for unity in the Basilica St Paolo fuori le Mura, assisting (not presiding) with Protestants, Catholic and Orthodox in a reading of Scripture lessons. What is possible in St Paolo fuori le Mura should not be impossible in the Church of the Holy Sepulchre; and if one day common prayer services of the Eastern and Western Churches will be held at the Holy Sepulchre – for the peace of Jerusalem – the

Sanctuaries which for so long have been objects of strife, will become symbols of reconciliation and hope and the impact of such development will transcend the borders of Christendom.

Imagination may reach even further. Patriarch Athenagoras I has repeatedly expressed the hope that one day in the future Roman Catholic and Greek Orthodox priests may co-celebrate Holy Mass on the same altar; and Pope Paul VI in an historic letter, dated 8 February 1971, assured him of his determination 'to hasten the day, when at the end of a concelebrated Mass we can communicate together from the same chalice of the Lord'. When this vision is fulfilled, the question of the Christian Holy Places will have found its ultimate solution.

Appendix 1

Gregory, Bishop of Nyssa: About those who go to Jerusalem

Since, my friend, you ask me a question in your letter, I think that it is incumbent upon me to answer you in their proper order upon all the points connected with it. It is then my opinion that it is a good thing for those who have dedicated themselves once for all to the higher life to fix their attention continually upon the utterances in the Gospel, and, just as those who correct their work in any given material by a rule, and by means of the straightness of that rule bring the crookedness which their hands detect to straightness, so it is right that we should apply to these questions a strict and flawless measure as it were – I mean, of course, the Gospel rule of life – and in accordance with that, direct ourselves in the sight of God. Now there are some amongst those who have entered upon the monastic and hermit life, who have made it a part of their devotion to behold those spots at Jerusalem where the memorials of our Lord's life in the flesh are on view; it would be well then, to look to this rule, and if the finger of its precepts points to the observance of such things, to perform the work, as the actual injunction of our Lord; but if they lie quite outside the commandment of the Master, I do not see what there is to command any one who has become a law of duty to himself to be zealous in performing any of them. When the Lord invites the blest to their inheritance in the kingdom of heaven, He does not include a pilgrimage to Jerusalem amongst their good deeds; when he announces the Beatitudes, He does not name amongst them that sort of devotion. But as to that which neither makes us blessed nor sets us in the path to the kingdom, for what reason it should be run after, let him that is wise consider. Even if there were some profit in what they do, yet even so, those who are perfect would do best not to be eager in practising it; but since this matter, when closely looked into, is found to inflict upon those who have begun to lead the stricter life a moral mischief, it is so far from being worth an earnest pursuit, that it actually requires the greatest

171

caution to prevent him who has devoted himself to God from being penetrated by any of its hurtful influences. What is it, then, that is hurtful in it? The Holy Life is open to all, men and women alike. Of that contemplative life the peculiar mark is Modesty. But Modesty is preserved in societies that live distinct and separate, so that there should be no meeting and mixing up of persons of opposite sex; men are not to rush to keep the rules of Modesty in the company of women, nor women to do so in the company of men. But the necessities of a journey are continually apt to reduce this scrupulousness to a very indifferent observance of such rules. For instance, it is impossible for a woman to accomplish so long a journey without a conductor; on account of her natural weakness she has to be put upon her horse and to be lifted down again; she has to be supported in difficult situations. Whichever we suppose, that she has an acquaintance to do this yeoman's service, or a hired attendant to perform it, either way the proceeding cannot escape being reprehensible; whether she leans on the help of a stranger, or on that of her own servant, she fails to keep the law of correct conduct; and as the inns and hostelries and cities of the East present many examples of licence and of indifference to vice, how will it be possible for one passing through such smoke to escape without smarting eyes? Where the ear and the eye is defiled, and the heart too, by receiving all those foulnesses through eye and ear, how will it be possible to thread without infection such seats of contagion? What advantage, moreover, is reaped by him who reaches those celebrated spots themselves? He cannot imagine that our Lord is living, in the body, there at the present day, but has gone away from us foreigners; or that the Holy Spirit is in abundance at Jerusalem, but unable to travel as far as us. Whereas, if it is really possible to infer God's presence from visible symbols, one might more justly consider that He dwelt in the Cappadocian nation than in any of the spots outside it.

For how many Altars there are there, on which the name of our Lord is glorified! One could hardly count so many in all the rest of the world. Again, if the Divine grace was more abundant about Jerusalem than elsewhere, sin would not be so much the fashion amongst those that live there; but as it is, there is no form of uncleanness that is not perpetuated amongst them; rascality, adultery, theft, idolatry, poisoning, quarrelling, murder, are rife; and the last kind of evil is so excessively prevalent, that nowhere in the world are people so ready to kill each other as there; where kinsmen attack each other like wild beasts, and spill each other's blood, merely for the sake of lifeless plunder. Well, in a place where such things go on, what proof, I ask, have you of the abundance of Divine grace? But

I know what many will retort to all that I have said; they will say, 'Why did you not lay down this rule for yourself as well? If there is no gain for the godly pilgrim in return for having been there, for what reason did you undergo the toil of so long a journey?' Let them hear from me my plea for this. By the necessities of that office in which I have been placed by the Dispenser of my life to live, it was my duty, for the purpose of the correction which the Holy Council had resolved upon, to visit the places where the Church in Arabia is; secondly, as Arabia is on the confines of the Jerusalem district, I had promised that I would confer also with the Heads of the Holy Jerusalem Churches, because matters with them were in confusion, and needed an arbiter; thirdly, our most religious Emperor had granted us facilities for the journey, by postal conveyance, so that we had to endure none of those inconveniences which in the case of others we have noticed; our waggon was, in fact, as good as a church or monastery to us, for all of us were singing psalms and fasting in the Lord during the whole journey. Let our own case therefore cause difficulty to none; rather let our advice be all the more listened to, because we are giving it upon matters which came actually before our eyes. We confessed that the Christ Who was manifested is very God, as much before as after our sojourn at Jerusalem; our faith in Him was not increased afterwards any more than it was diminished. Before we saw Bethlehem we knew His being made man by means of the Virgin; before we saw His Grave we believed in His Resurrection from the dead; apart from seeing the Mount of Olives, we confessed that His Ascension into heaven was real. We derived only thus much of profit from our travelling thither, namely that we came to know by being able to compare them, that our own places are far holier than those abroad. Wherefore, O ye who fear the Lord, praise Him in the places where ye now are. Change of place does not effect any drawing nearer unto God, but wherever thou mayest be, God will come to thee, if the chambers of thy soul be found of such a sort that He can dwell in thee and walk in thee. But if thou keepest thine inner man full of wicked thoughts, even if thou wast on Golgotha even if thou wast on the Mount of Olives, even if thou stoodest on the memorial-rock of the Resurrection, thou wilt be as far away from receiving Christ into thyself, as one who has not even begun to confess Him. Therefore, my beloved friend, counsel the brethren to be absent from the body to go to our Lord, rather than to be absent from Cappadocia to go to Palestine and if any one should adduce the command spoken by our Lord to His disciples that they should not quit Jerusalem, let him be made to understand its true meaning. Inasmuch as the gift and the distribution of the Holy Spirit had not yet passed upon the Apostles, our Lord commanded them to remain in the same place, until they should have been endued with power from on high. Now, if that which happened at the beginning, when the Holy Spirit was dispensing each of His gifts under the appearance of a flame, continued until now, it would be right for all to remain in that place where that dispensing took place; but if the Spirit 'bloweth' where He 'listeth', those, too, who have become believers here are made partakers of that gift; and that according to the proportion of their faith, not in consequence of their pilgrimage to Jerusalem.[1]

Appendix 2
St Bernard of Clairvaux: Letter to the English people

I address myself to you, the people of England, in the cause of Christ, in whom lies your salvation. I say this so that the warrant of the Lord and my zeal in his interests may excuse my hardihood in addressing you. I am a person of small account, but my desire for you in Christ is not small. This is my reason and motive for writing, this is why I make bold to address you all by letter. I would have preferred to do so by word of mouth had I but the strength to come to you as I desire.

Now is the acceptable time, now is the day of abundant salvation. The earth is shaken because the Lord of heaven is losing His land, the land in which He appeared to men, in which He lived amongst men for more than thirty years; the land made glorious by His miracles, holy by His blood; the land in which the flowers of His resurrection first blossomed. And now, for our sins, the enemy of the Cross has begun to lift his sacrilegious head there, and to devastate with the sword that blessed land, that land of promise. Alas, if there should be none to withstand him, he will soon invade the very city of the living God, overturn the arsenal of our redemption, and defile the Holy Places which have been adorned by the blood of the Immaculate Lamb. They have cast their greedy eyes especially on the holy Sanctuaries of our Christian Religion, and they long particularly to violate that couch on which, for our sakes, the Lord of our life fell asleep in death.

What are you doing, you mighty men of valour? What are you doing you servants of the Cross? Will you thus cast holy things to dogs, pearls before swine? How great a number of sinners have here confessed with tears and obtained pardon for their sins since the time when these holy precincts were cleansed of pagan filth by the swords of our fathers! The evil one sees this and is enraged, he gnashes his teeth and withers away in fury. He stirs up his vessels of wrath so that if they do but once lay hands upon these Holy Places there shall be no sign or trace of piety left. Such a catastrophe would

175

be a source of appalling grief for all time, but it would also be a source of confusion and endless shame for our generation. What think you, my brethren? Is the hand of the Lord shortened and is He now powerless to work salvation, so that He must call upon us, petty worms of the earth, to save and restore to Him His heritage? Could he not send more than twelve legions of angels, or even just say the word and save His land? Most certainly He has the power to do this whenever He wishes, but I tell you that God is trying you. 'He looks down from heaven at the race of men, to find one soul that reflects, and makes God its aim', one soul that sorrows for Him. For God has pity on His people and on those who have grievously fallen away and has prepared for them a means of salvation. Consider with what care He plans our salvation, and be amazed. Look, sinners, at the depths of His pity, and take courage. He does not want your death but rather that you should turn to Him and live. So He seeks not to overthrow you but to help you. When Almighty God so treats murderers, thieves, adulterers, perjurers, and such like as persons able to find righteousness in His service, what is it but an act of exquisite courtesy all God's own? Do not hesitate. God is good, and were He intent on your punishment He would not have asked of you this present service or indeed have accepted it even had you offered it. Again I say consider the Almighty's goodness and pay heed to His plans of mercy. He puts himself under obligation to you, or rather feigns to do so, so that He can help you to satisfy your obligations towards Himself. He puts Himself in your debt so that, in return for your taking up arms in his cause, He can reward you with pardon for your sins and everlasting glory. I call blessed the generation that can seize an opportunity of such rich indulgence as this, blessed to be alive in this year of jubilee, this year of God's choice. The blessing is spread throughout the whole world, and all the world is flocking to receive this badge of immortality.

Your land is well known to be rich in young and vigorous men. The world is full of their praises, and the renown of their courage is on the lips of all. Gird yourselves therefore like men and take up arms with joy and with zeal for your Christian name, in order to 'take vengeance on the heathen, and curb the nations'. For how long will your men continue to shed Christian blood; for how long will they continue to fight amongst themselves. You attack each other, you slay each other and by each other you are slain. What is this savage craving of yours? Put a stop to it now, for it is not fighting but foolery. Thus to risk both soul and body is not brave but shocking, is not strength but folly. But now, O mighty soldiers, O men of war, you have a cause in which to conquer is glorious and for which to die is gain.

But to those of you who are merchants, men quick to seek a bargain, let me point out the advantages of this great opportunity. Do not miss them. Take up the sign of the Cross and you will find indulgence for all the sins which you humbly confess. The cost is small, the reward is great. Venture with devotion and the gain will be God's kingdom. They do well therefore who have taken up this heavenly sign, and they also will do well, and profit themselves, who hasten to take up what will prove to be for them a sign of salvation.

For the rest, not I but the Apostle warns you, brethren, not to believe every spirit. I have heard with great joy of the zeal for God's glory which burns in your midst, but your zeal needs the timely restraint of knowledge. The Jews are not to be persecuted, killed or even put to flight. Ask anyone who knows the Sacred Scriptures what he finds foretold of the Jews in the psalm. 'Not for their destruction do I pray', it says. The Jews are for us the living words of Scripture, for they remind us always of what our Lord suffered. They are dispersed all over the world so that by expiating their crime they may be everywhere the living witnesses of our redemption. Hence the psalm adds, 'only let thy power disperse them'. And so it is: dispersed they are. Under Christian princes they endure a hard captivity, but 'they only wait for the time of their deliverance'. Finally we are told by the Apostle that when the time is ripe all Israel shall be saved. But those who die before will remain in death. I will not mention those Christian money lenders, if they can be called Christian, who, where there are no Jews, act, I grieve to say, in a manner worse than any Jew. If the Jews are utterly wiped out, what will become of our hope for their promised salvation, their eventual conversion? If the pagans were similarly subjugated to us then, in my opinion, we should wait for them rather than seek them out with swords. But as they have now begun to attack us, it is necessary for those of us who do not carry a sword in vain to repel them with force. It is an act of Christian piety both 'to vanquish the proud' and also 'to spare the subjected', especially those for whom we have a law and a promise, and whose flesh was shared by Christ whose name be for ever blessed.[2]

Appendix 3

Imperial Firman of February 1852, Concerning the Christian Holy Places

To thee, my Vizier, Ahmed Pasha, Governor of Jerusalem; to thee Cadi of Jerusalem; and to you, members of the Medjliss.

The disputes which from time to time arise between the Greek and Latin nations, respecting certain Holy Places which exist both within and without the City of Jerusalem, have now been again revived.

A Commission has in consequence been formed, composed of certain Muchirs and distinguished men of the law, and of other persons, to examine this question thoroughly; and this is the result of the researches and of the investigations of that Commission, and of those of the Cabinet Councils held after the Commission. The places in dispute between the two rites are – the great cupola of the Church of the Holy Sepulchre; the little cupola, which is above the spot called the Tomb of Jesus, on whom may the blessing of God rest, and which is in the church before-mentioned; the Hadjir el Moughtesil; Golgotha, which is also within the inclosure of the Church of the Holy Sepulchre; the Arches of the Holy Mary; the Great Church which is in the village of Bethlehem; as well as the Grotto, which is the true spot where Jesus – may the blessing of God be upon him – was born, and which is situated below that church; and the tomb of the Blessed Mary, whom may God bless.

Seeing that the great cupola above-mentioned applies to the entire church, the Latins have no right to claim exclusive possession either of that cupola, or of the lesser cupola, or of the Hadjir el Moughtesil, or of Golgotha, or of the Arches of the Holy Mary, or of the Great Church of Bethlehem, or of the Holy Manger; all these places must be left in their present state. In former times, a key of the two gates of the Great Church of Bethlehem and of the Holy Manger was given to each of the Greek, Latin, and Armenian nations – a measure which was also confirmed by the Firman delivered to the Greek nation in the year of the Hegira 1170; and that arrangement shall still continue. But as it does not follow from this that it is permitted to alter the existing state of things in that church or to prevent the Latins from officiating there, or in short, to make any new arrangement calculated to incommode other sects, either in the passage from the church to the Holy Manger, or in other respect; the smallest pretension in regard to this shall not be allowed or entertained, on the part of any one whatsoever.

No change shall be made in the present state of the gates of the Church of Bethlehem.

As, according to ancient and modern documents, the two gardens belonging to the Frank Convent at Bethlehem, to which the Latins have also laid claim, are under the superintendence of both parties; they shall remain as at present.

The Latins, on the ground of certain Firmans of which they are in possession have advanced the pretension that the Tomb of the Blessed Mary belongs exclusively to them; but they are not right in this either. Only since the Greeks, the Armenians, the Syrians, and the Copts at present exercise their worship within this holy tomb; that is to say, as the exercise of worship is not confined to a single rite, it has been declared just to uphold and to confirm on behalf of the Roman Catholic Christians the permission which they possess *ab antiquo*, of exercising their worship in a spot where various nations exercise theirs, but upon condition that they shall make no alteration either in the administration or in the present condition of that monument.

As this decision confirms and consolidates the rights which have been granted to the Greek subjects of my Empire by my august ancestors, and confirmed by Firmans invested with Hatti-Scherifs issued from my Imperial throne, it has accordingly obtained my sovereign assent, as I have much at heart to maintain the above-mentioned rights. None of the parties shall allow themselves to contravene this decision.

Furthermore, the Latins at the present day perform service once a year, on Ascension Day, in an oratory at Jerusalem, called Coubet-el-Messad, which is situated on Mount Olivet; and the Greeks perform their devotions outside that oratory. Now this oratory is a Mohammedan temple, and it consequently does not belong exclusively to any Christian sect; and I do not consider it right that the subjects of my Empire who profess the Greek faith should be deprived of the power of worshipping in the interior of the above-named oratory. The Greeks shall therefore not be prevented from exercising their worship in the interior of the Coubet-el-Messad (the Cupola of the Ascension), on condition that they make no alteration in the present condition of that oratory, and that there shall be a

Mohammedan porter at the door, as heretofore. This measure shall be recorded at the head of the copy of the Imperial Firman dated the month of Sheval, 1254 (December 1838).

Such is my decided and sovereign will; and, in conformity with the orders which I have in consequence given, the present Firman, which is furnished with a Hatti-Scherif and issued from my Imperial Divan, has been delivered to the Greek nation.

As soon as my sovereign orders shall become known to you, you will take every care that henceforward my decision and my commands above-mentioned shall not in any way be contravened, either by those who profess the Greek, Armenian, Syriac and Copt religions, or by the Latins.

You will take care to have the present Imperial Edict recorded in the archives of the Mehkémé, to serve constantly and for ever as a permanent rule. Understand this; and give heed to the noble signature with which it is decorated.

Issued about the end of the month of Djemadi-ul-evel, 1268

(February 1852).[3]

Les Lieux Saints de la Palestine: Memoire des Latins a la Conférence de la Paix (1919)

Ce Mémoire a été publié par l'Imprimerie des Pères Franciscains à Jérusalem en 1922, sous le nom de: « *Les Lieux-Saints de la Palestine* » (pro manuscripto), accompagné de documents affirmant les droits des Franciscains sure le Saint-Sépulcre, sur Bethléem, sur le Tombeau de la Vierge, sur le Cénacle et leur préséance sur les autres Rites dans les Sanctuaires. Un tableau « de toutes les œuvres religieuses et charitable des chrétiens tant catholiques que dissidents en Palestine » le complète. Ces documents n'ont pas été reproduits ici.

Du jour où, après l'héroïque mais malheureuse ère des Croisades, la domination musulmane se fut de nouveau affermie en Orient, la question des Lieux-Saints fut toujours une des grandes questions du droit public européen, et, dans tous les temps, elle a occupé la diplomatie des Puissances occidentales. Souverains et Républiques rivalisaient entre elles pour établir leur Protectorat sur les Sanctuaires du Christianisme, Venise, Gênes, Naples, la France, l'Autriche, la Pologne, l'Espagne, l'Angleterre, la Hollande se firent toujours une gloire de protéger les Lieux-Saints et les religieux latins, préposés à leur garde, de leur assurer le libre exercice du culte et de veiller à la sûreté des pèlerins qui visitaient la patrie de Jésus.

Dès le commencement du xive siècle, les Rois d'Aragon, de France et de Naples firent des démarches auprès des Sultans du Caire pour obtenir que des Religieux catholiques fussent établis d'une manière stable dans les principaux Sanctuaires de Judée pour y célébrer les offices du culte. Et de fait, en 1333, après de longues et difficiles négociations, et au prix de sommes énormes, les Souverains de Naples et Sicile, Robert d'Anjou et Sancia, son épouse, obtinrent du Sultan Mélek-en Nasser Mohammed, en faveur des Frères Mineurs, la propriété exclusive du Cénacle et le droit de pouvoir habiter, d'une manière permanente, dans l'Eglise du S. Sépulcre et d'y célébrer l'office divin.

Vers la même époque, les Franciscains prirent possession de la Basilique de la Nativité de Bethléem ainsi que de la Grotte de la Crèche qu'elle recouvre ; puis, un peu plus tard, du Sépulcre de la Ste Vierge dans la vallée de Josaphat, avec le secours de Jeanne, reine de Naples, du Doge de Venise, Lorenzo Celsi, et de Pierre IV, roi d'Aragon.

De son côté Venise qui, dès les premières années qui suivirent la chute du Royaume de Jérusalem, avait entretenu des relations commerciales avec les Sultans d'Egypte, faisait insérer, dans presque tous ses traités et capitulations, passés avec les Souverains sarrasins et plus tard avec la Sublime Porte, des clauses spéciales relatives aux Lieux-Saints. C'est ainsi que, dans la première moitié du xve siècle, et en même temps que la République de Gênes, elle obtint de pouvoir établir ses propres consuls à Jérusalem, pour la protection des pèlerins et des religieux préposés à la garde des Sanctuaires de Palestine.

A son tour, le Roi de France, en 1604, en renouvelant ses capitulations avec le Gouvernement ottoman, y faisait entrer un article relatif à la Protection des Lieux-Saints, article qu'on retrouve ensuite répété dans les capitulations suivantes de 1673 et 1740.

D'autre part, il ne serait pas possible d'énumérer les nombreux firmans émis par les Sultans d'Egypte et de Constantinople en faveur des intérêts de la Custodie de Terre Sainte, firmans presque toujours obtenus par l'intervention d'une Puissance ou d'une autre, soit par le moyen de leurs Représentants accrédités auprès des Souverains Arabes ou Ottomans, soit au moyen d'Envoyés extraordinaires.

En 1633, a lieu la première grave usurpation, de la part des sectes dissidentes sur les possessions et les droits des catholiques dans les Sanctuaires de Jérusalem et de Bethléem ; mais une action diplomatique commune des Princes et Républiques d'Occident oblige la Sublime Porte, dès 1635, à rendre justice aux Religieux Franciscains.

Une nouvelle usurpation s'étant produite peu après, les mêmes Puissances intervinrent de nouveau pour la défense des droits de l'Eglise catholique en Terre Sainte. En 1663, les Envoyés de l'Empereur, en négociant la paix de Wasvarar, demandent la restitution des Lieux-Saints, et le Roi de Pologne, à la paix de Zarowen en 1676, s'emploie au même but ; mais dans toutes ces circonstances, les intrigues des grecs triomphèrent toujours de la justice.

Quand, plus tard, Venise, l'Autriche et la Pologne, étroitement unies dans une sainte alliance, infligèrent aux armées turques les plus sanglantes défaites, au point de contraindre la Sublime Porte, en 1688, à implorer une trêve, les alliés posèrent aussitôt, comme condition de paix, la restitution des Sanctuaires usurpés aux Latins et l'exemption de tout tribut pour les pèlerins qui se rendaient à Jérusalem.

La paix ne fut pas conclue; mais l'intervention de la France obligea la Turquie, en 1690, à remettre les Frères Mineurs en possession de leurs droits.

En 1699, lors de la signature du traité de Carlowitz entre la Sainte Alliance et la Turquie, un article spécial confirmait la liberté de la Réligion catholique dans tout le territoire de l'Empire ottoman et spécialement à Jérusalem. Semblables articles se retrouvent dans les traités de Passarowitz en 1718, de Belgrade en 1739, de Sistow en 1791.

Lorsque, en 1757, se consomma une nouvelle et très grave usurpation au détriment des Religieux Franciscains représentants de la Catholicité en Terre Sainte, les Puissances catholiques, en particulier la France, Venise, l'Autriche et Naples qui avaient leurs représentants à Constantinople, s'employèrent avec une grande activité, pour obtenir de la Sublime Porte, réparation de la grande injustice commise; mais ce fut sans succès, en raison de l'influence des chrétiens de rite grec qui dominait en Turquie.

La question des Lieux-Saints, plusieurs fois traitée dans la première moitié du XIXe siècle, fut reprise de nouveau et avec plus d'énergie en 1850, quand les gouvernements de France, d'Espagne, de Belgique, de Sardaigne et d'Autriche se lièrent ensemble pour exiger de la Sublime Porte que, dans les Sanctuaires de Judée, fussent rétablis les possessions et les droits de la Custodie Franciscaine tels qu'ils étaient en 1757. La bonne volonté, montrée alors par la Turquie, de résoudre selon la justice la question des Lieux Saints, fut, comme on le sait, rendue vaine par l'intervention de la Russie qui appuya la cause des Grecs, prête qu'elle était, comme l'événement le montra, à soutenir, les armes à la main, ses projets d'hégémonie sur tout l'Orient orthodoxe. La Turquie, tiraillée entre des intérêts et des influences contraires, ne put faire autre chose que s'appliquer à maintenir le *Statu quo* dans les Lieux-Saints.

Quelques années plus tard, en 1878, lorsque les Puissances européennes se réunirent à Berlin, la France qui comprenait bien que la question des Lieux-Saints ne pouvait se résoudre à ce moment là par une juste reconnaissance des droits des Latins, préféra la laisser hors de discussion; c'est ce qui résulte de l'article 62 du traité, où il est établi que «aucune atteinte ne saurait être portée au *Statu quo* dans les Lieux-Saints», ce qui indiquait que les catholiques ne renonçaient nullement *à leurs droits*.

Cette grande question des Lieux-Saints ne fut donc pas résolue; et, pour des raisons politiques, elle fut seulement renvoyée à des temps plus favorables.

Et voilà qu'aujourd'hui, après une attente de plus d'un siècle et demi, la Palestine a été soustraite à la domination de l'empire turc. La Catholicité espère donc, et elle s'impose nécessairement, une détermination précise des droits et possessions des diverses communautés chrétiennes qui officient dans les Sanctuaire de Judée.

Aujourd'hui la Custodie de Terre Sainte, comme elle le fit bien d'autres fois à la veille des grands traités de paix entre la Turquie et les Puissances occidentales, adresse ses prières aux Représentants des Nations qui vont se réunir en congrès à Versailles; elle les leur adresse au nom de la Justice depuis trop longtemps foulée aux pieds; au nom de la Catholicité tout entière qui doit avoir dans les Sanctuaires de la Rédemption la place qui lui appartient légitimement; au nom, enfin, du monde civilisé. Car il ne faut pas oublier que c'est précisément l'état d'indetermination dans lequel a été laissée l'étendue des droits de chaque Communauté chrétienne, qui a fait que les pauvres Franciscains se sont vus maintes fois et jusqu'au commencement de ce siècle, exposés sans défense possible, aux agressions de leurs rivaux, au point que plusieurs fois ils ont arrosé de leur sang le seuil du S. Sépulcre et les abords de la grotte de la Nativité. Ajoutons même qu'elle les leur adresse au nom de l'Art, puisque les glorieux monuments, élevés par Constantin et par les Croisés, se trouvent réduits à l'état le plus déplorable, par suite de la jalousie et de la rivalité des sectes dissidentes. Il importe donc, bien plus il est urgent de leur rendre leur beauté primitive, leur ancienne splendeur.

La Custodie de Terre Sainte, en s'adressant au Tribunal suprême des Nations, Tribunal réuni en assises solennelles pour rétablir la justice dans le monde ne demande rien autre chose sinon que justice lui soit rendue. Ce qu'elle demande, c'est qu'on examine une bonne fois toutes les controverses qui ont lieu depuis des siècles entre les diverses communautés chrétiennes ayant le droit d'officier dans les Lieux-Saints; qu'on vérifie la valeur des documents historiques produits par chacune d'elles, et que chacune soit mise en possession définive de la part qui lui revient. Ce qu'elle demande, c'est exactement ce que, vers le milieu du siècle dernier, les Puissances catholiques exigeaient de la Turquie, c'est-à-dire le retour des Lieux-Saints au *Statu quo* existant au moment des usurpations commises par les hétérodoxes en 1757, ce qui revient à dire le retour au *Statu quo* qui s'était établi légalement dans le courant du xIveˢ., après la chute définitive du royaume latin de Jérusalem.

Les nations qui, à cette époque de 1850, s'unirent pour revendiquer la reconnaissance des droits de la Custodie de Terre Sainte, pourraient-elles ne plus vouloir l'accomplissement en Terre Sainte de ce qu'elles exigeaient au milieu du siècle dernier, aujourd'hi surtout, que, grâce à la Divine Providence, Jérusalem, la Ville Sainte, a été délivrée?

On sait en effet comment la France et les autres Nations qui appuyaient son action diplomatique crurent alors plus prudent de ne pas soutenir, pour le moment, les justes revendications de la Catholicité, dans la crainte d'assumer la responsabilité d'une guerre qui, d'ailleurs, ne fut pas évitée. Aujourd'hui, ces louables motifs de prudence n'existent plus. Rien donc ne peut plus empêcher que les catholiques soient réintégrés dans leurs droits et possessions sur les Lieux-Saints.

La Custodie de Terre Sainte demande donc qu'on fasse droit aux demandes que le Gén. Aupick, Représentant de la France à Constantinople, par sa note du 28 Mai 1850, présentait tant au nom de son Gouvernement qu'au nom de la Sardaigne, de la Belgique, de l'Espagne et de l'Autriche, demandes qu'il précisait et détaillait au mois d'Août de la même année, en remettant à la Chancellerie ottomane le *Statu quo* des Sanctuaires possédés exclusivement par les Latins en 1740.[4]

Appendix 5

Memorandum of the Greeks submitted to the Peace Conference in Paris, 1919

The superior of the Franciscan Monks in Jerusalem, Ferdinand Diotallevi, submitted to the Peace Conference in Paris a short Memorandum under the date of the current year, which was written in French and printed in the printing-office of the Franciscan Fathers in Jerusalem, under the following title: 'Memorandum – The Holy Places in the Paris Conference.'

Just from the first page of this memorandum an honourable mention is made of the activities of the Latin Powers in the West, and especially of Venice, Genoa, Naples, France, Austria, Poland, Spain, England and Holland for the interest, care, and protection which they had shown towards the Franciscan Monks in the Holy Places. It is also historically explained that, after the unfortunate period of the Crusades, the Franciscans had settled down in the most important Holy Places, since the fourteenth century through pecuniary means on one hand, and on the other by the intermediation of Kings and Democracies.

The Memorandum is written in such a way by which the Franciscans appear as occupying the Holy Places. Furthermore, they pass over in silence the existence of their Christian communities in these places, and in addition they avoid to state by whom they had been occupied during the previous long centuries; because it is historically and archaeologically proved that the Holy Places existed, since the fourth century. These two points are essential and most important for the understanding of the whole question of the Holy Places.

The Franciscan Monks succeeding through political influences to occupy a position in the Holy Places since the fourteenth century, they never were alone in them, but the Greeks always occupied in the central positions the important Holy Places, and around them in fixed corners, sometimes outside the enclosure of the Holy Places,

Latins and Armenians were stationed. We mention these two Communities only, as the jurisdiction of the smaller Christian Communities in the Holy Places was greatly limited.

But political circumstances and various other influences at different periods, as well as an incontrollable zeal of a national and ecclesiastical strife, have given to the Christian Communities in the Holy Places a hostile character towards each other. Thereupon the monks of the various Christian Communities, who were serving in the Holy Places, have been changed in their real nature and mission to soldiers and guardians of the Holy Places.

The Greek Monks, as possessors and masters of the Holy Places, by virtue of possessory rights and reasons of ethnological nature, from the fourth century till the period of the Crusades, at the eleventh century, have been exclusively the rulers and masters of the Holy Places; erecting repairing, ornamenting, and serving in them. During the period of the Crusaders, however, the position of the Greeks in the Holy Places has been changed into a secondary one, because Latinism has appeared as an enemy to Hellenism in the East generally, and especially in the Holy Places; but after the expulsion of the Crusaders the Greeks by virtue of an official political act of Saladin were recognised as the only rulers and masters of the Holy Places, they continued their mission and traditions, with the only difference that since the fourteenth century and further on Latins and Armenians, as well other smaller Christian Communities, had settled down in fixed positions of the Holy Places.

As a proof of the modern intrusion of the Latins into the Holy Places it is not necessary that we should refer to the positive facts of history, but it is sufficient to observe that all the ancient Monasteries in Jerusalem are occupied by the Greeks, and none of them by the Latins. The few Monasteries occupied by them are principally the Stations of the Via Dolorosa, which are an invention of modern authors, not having any authenticity in connection with the Holy Places. Besides that, the Monastery of the Franciscans itself has been taken from the Greeks, as the history of the event, which is well known, witnesses the fact. But in addition to what has been mentioned, there is another more important fact, that the centre of the Greek Fraternity of the Holy Sepulchre was always and continually the Holy Sepulchre, which was built by them, while the Franciscan Monks had always as their starting point a place on Mount Zion, considered by tradition to be the Coenaculum (Chamber of the Last Supper), which they had occupied temporally by a royal transaction and on payment of a sum of money.

After that period of the Mamluks in the Holy Places, who used to disregard the Greeks, the Turkish sovereignty since the sixteenth century and the Greek revolution at the nineteenth on one hand, and on the other, the influence of the Catholic Powers of Europe on the Sublime Porte, and the large amounts of money of the Latin Church, created severe struggle and almost continual war in the Holy Places, especially between the Greeks and the Franciscans since the sixteenth century. This struggle used to end in favour of the Franciscans whenever the political influence of the West oppressed efficaciously the Sublime Porte leaving no outlet to it.

The Greek Fraternity of the Holy Sepulchre used to march out courageously against these influences and oppressions of so strong powers, and sometimes used to come out of the struggle victorious and sometimes wounded; but the power of duty, the grace drawn from the Holy Places, which she many a time bought off by her own blood, and the conscience of the honour in the service and custody of the Holy Places, strengthened her and exalted her power to an invincible position. Thus the Fraternity of the Holy Sepulchre under the leadership of her Patriarchs, used to have continually a struggle of right against the powerful and strong men of the earth, against money and political influences; but by the grace of God she succeeded, through difficult times, to arrive at these days of liberty at which the rights of the great and small nations and communities are equally recognised.

The other point, in which the memorandum of the Franciscan Monks is deficient, is the passing over in silence of the position of the Holy Places before the twelfth century. The reason for that is very simple. The Latins heavily bear the fact that the Holy Places were Greek, and that their custody and the care about them were intrusted to the Greek Clergy of the Church of Jerusalem. Whenever this question is presented, some of them pass over it attentively with silence, while others, when provoked to discuss this matter, they invent and devise by a judicial way new theories to the effect that the custodians of the Holy Places had not an ethnological character, as these places were under the rule of the Byzantine Empire, which was a Roman Empire, i.e. Latin and not a Greek Empire. Thus a complete bankruptcy of the historic truth is presented and a corruption of the real facts for personal reasons and prospects.

The establishment of the Byzantine Empire was subjectively and objectively Greek, although during its first period there existed some documents written in Latin. But this part also was quickly swept off by predominating the other aspects of the Byzantine period Cosmopolitan Greek spirit. The establishment of the Byzantine Empire meant the great political event of the gradual separation of the Latin West from the Greek East. The centre of the former was Rome, with the traditions and claims of ancient Rome the bearers and apostles of which were the Popes, while the centre of the latter was Constantinople, and therefore it was called New Rome. The political and ecclesiastical events which had followed completed the separation of the West from the East. Greece itself had not at that time a deep conception, not to say something more, of the fact that the Byzantine Empire was the Ark of the further salvation of the Greeks with all their spiritual and moral capital. It was proved later that Constantinople saved Greece and Peloponnesus from continual barbaric invasions. Constantinople as a fortified rampart saved the Greek Church and the Greek literature and education.

When great parts of the body of the Empire had been separated, then it commenced to have a deeper conscience of its national powers that they are Greek powers. The Latin aspect was quickly swept off and hindered by two factors viz. the Greek Church and the Greek Public (Plebs).

But the most important of all is an historic irony. The Latins imagined for a moment, that the Emperor Justinian introduced the new Latin spirit by his code, which was written in Latin, but this phenomenon was upset and reversed by the great scheme of the same Emperor, who built the Cathedral of Constantinople and of the whole Empire 'The Church of Agia Sophia' (St Sophia). This Cathedral was built according to the Greek and Eastern style, with a Greek idea, and a Greek name was given to it (God's Wisdom). The Architects of Agia Sophia worked artistically a miracle of art, in which was incorporated the living spirit and magnificence of the Greek Church.

Besides these important events Hellenism displaced rapidly in Byzantium the administrative system of the Roman Empire. Thus the Proconsul, Praefectus, and Praeses, have been substituted by a General, concentrating in them the highest military and political administration. From the reign of Emperor Heraclius the districts (themata) existed in the administration of the country.

The Issavrian and especially Macedonian Dynasties worked hardly and successfully for the renaissance of the Greek spirit, which was in flourishing state during the Komnenian period. At that time, however, the Crusaders at their invasion showed clearly, in documents and deeds, through the conduct of their leaders, as well as by the behaviour of the army in general, and antihellenic policy, and rude phraseology, that they were inspired by the ambitions and ideas of the Popes.

Therefore Manuel Komnenos deported the Venetians from Constantinople for reasons of national contrast. Kinamos states that this measure has been taken on account of the arrogance of these persons.

On the other hand, in 1147 French Barons and Bishops, incited by national and religious motives, used to request the King of France, Louis VII in alliance with the King of Sicily Rogerus, to conquer Constantinople. The same project occupied the mind of Frederic I at 1190, and afterwards his son Henry VI, and at last the 'Hateful Byzantium' was conquered on the 12–13 of April 1204, with a terrible destruction and devastation, and great indecency, which is beyond any description. Therefore, the brother of the Metropolitan of Athens Niketa characterises them as follows: 'But none of the Graces or Muses was agreeable to these barbarous people, and in addition I think that they were fierce in nature, their anger always outrunning their reason.' The conquerors mocking at the Greeks used to go about in pomp carrying pens, ink-stand, and volumes of books, and with a strange fanaticism used to destroy the decorum of the Christian Churches, and deliver it to the Latin priests.

But with all the efforts for reconciliation, between Latinism of the West and Hellenism of the East, the result was, as it has been expressed by Marius Sandus, of Venice, in his publication under the name of 'Secreta fidelium Crucis', that the strong men of the West have been able to dissolve the Greek Empire, but did not possess the power to maintain it, and that the Union of the Eastern and Roman Churches could not be obtained by force, as it had been proved in several countries of the East, in which the foreign conquerors only and not the natives accepted the Latin doctrine. They killed for a moment the body of the East, but not the spirit, and it was proved that it is impossible for the centrifugal and centripetal forces to meet. In this essential struggle, and in the other factors, which formulate the political character of an independent and self-sufficient government, the Greek character of the Byzantine Empire is clearly and completely revealed. In addition we have before us a better proof of that in the relation of the Byzantine Empire to the Holy Places in Palestine, which have not only been established and maintained by the Greeks, but the most important of all is that, when Palestine was separated from the Byzantine Empire and subjected to the Rulers of Islam, they continued to show the same great interest for the Holy Places. They used to protect them either by making alliances with the conquerors, or by intervention through their ambassadors or special commissioners. This fact has been more clearly manifested during the rule of the Crusaders in the Holy Places.

Many consider as curious fact, and probably even as inexplicable one, that although the Crusaders were the sovereigns in the Holy Places, they showed such intolerance and fanaticism against the Greeks, and always hated and suspected the Byzantine Court, nevertheless many renovations and embellishments have been made in the Church of the Holy Sepulchre, Bethlehem and other Monasteries by the Byzantine Emperor. But this question becomes very simple if the documents of that period are carefully studied. The high chivalry of the Crusaders, corrupted by the selfish tendencies of their hierarchy, became bankrupt and degenerated sooner than it was expected, and unobservedly was found under the vehicle of the regenerated Byzantine Power at the period of the Komnenian Dynasty, which reached the culmination of success and glory during the reign of Manuel Komnenos.

On account of that the Sovereigns of the Crusaders used to give their daughters to the Byzantine Court, and to hold the stirrup of the Emperor's horse. Thereupon, the curious and probably inexplicable question becomes natural and explicable, i.e., how the Emperor of Byzantium repaired, embellished the Holy Places, and extended his protection over them. These acts had been accepted by the succeeding Emperors, who even intervened that Latin Monks may be established in the Holy City. The Greek Patriarchs used to accept these Latin Monks with fraternal love, and grant to them the proper accommodation, considering this act as a Christian duty, although these Monks were ill-disposed, hostile, and had malignant thoughts against the Greeks. The geographical, physiological, and historical contrast between Hellenism, and Latinism which was manifested by many events in the history of the Byzantine Empire, has been transmitted, though in a small scale, to the Greeks and Franciscans at the Holy Places. As at that time the Latins used to curse and hate Byzantium, at present also they never deviate from this principle, but as if by tradition they always hate, and bitterly slander the Greeks in the Holy Places. Nevertheless, with all this contrast, it is necessary that efforts should be exercised for reconcilliation of both parties, and establishment of friendly relations between them. Because it is a well-known fact that this disposition is the best way for the settlement of all differences, and avoiding all misunderstanding, more especially in these days, when many good and beneficial things might be expected from it.

The Greeks work, toil, and keep a vigilant eye in order to preserve the Holy Place, which are in their possession for series of centuries, and to them is due the great honour and glory, that before the appearance of the Latins in the Holy Land, they preserved with the Holy Places the Christian faith, fighting against insurmountable obstacles which used to be presented by the Non-Christian strong factors in Palestine. The Franciscans on the other hand, use all means, in order to take off from the Greeks the Holy Places, which are in their possession, and on account of that, especially since the sixteenth century, a continual severe struggle is taking place in the Holy Places between the Greeks and the Latins. Therefore, whenever the pro-Franciscan political influences were predominating, especially during the war of the Greek independence, they gained many places; but whatever they gain immediately forget and do their level best always in order to extend their possessions and obtain something more. This is the reason of the continued struggle and of the uninterrupted storm at the Holy Places.

These dispositions have appeared again with greater bitterness especially now, when the terrible World War is ended, and while from the blood, which has been shed in torrents, and from the agony of the entire world the ideals of justice and fraternal love have grown up, as principles and not as abstract ideas, notwithstanding these facts, the Franciscan Monks have published a most insulting and indecent pamphlet against the Greeks at the Holy Places, which was even printed in the printing-office of the Pope.

In the memorandum, which was submitted by the superior of the Franciscans to the Peace Conference in Paris, the Franciscans endeavour again to obtain not the share of the lion, but they try by all means to expel the Greeks from the Holy Places. From the seventh page of this memorandum they present two lists in comparison the one with the other, in which they mention the Holy Places belonging exclusively to them, and those which they claim. In both lists the exaggerations and transgressions of the Franciscans are evident. In the first list, in which the Holy Places which belong exclusively to them are noted, some places which have never belonged to them exclusively are included, while the other list contains almost all the Holy Places claimed by them, and which they had usurped at 1740. A similar list to the latter had been submitted to the Sublime Porte by the Ambassador of France in Constantinople at 1850. Thus the aim of the Franciscans is to take for themselves everything and to change, as if by an alchemical method, everything into Latin.

They have observed at what period of the long history of the Holy Places the Franciscans had usurped the greater part of them, and they have stuck to it, considering this usurpation as justice, and requesting therefore the Peace Conference to confirm this point. All their attention concentrated in the year 1740 because during that year the usurpation had reached its highest point. History contains between its pages the tragic occupation of the Holy Places at that time.

Hence the question naturally arises, i.e., why do we concentrate all our attention to one chronological point, that of the year 1740, which was also mentioned by General Aupick at 1850, and we do not refer to the established 'Status Quo' relating to the Holy Places, which is fixed and defined in two official Firmans, which had been similarly recognised and confirmed by two European Conferences, that of Paris and that of Berlin?

The establishment of peace and its consolidation in the Holy Places is obtained by the firm maintenance of the 'Status Quo' relating to the Holy Places. It is the supreme duty of every Christian Nation, whatever might be its sect or doctrines, to do its level best, in order to cause peace and love reign in the Holy Places, between the custodians there, viz. Greeks, Franciscans, Armenians, and the other smaller Christian communities, so that all the Christians might take from these Holy Shrines the best example of Christian love, and practise it in deeds in their own life. Thus also an excellent example is set before the non-Christian nations for imitation.

But if the proper men consider the proposed basis as insufficient, why to confine ourselves to the year 1740, as the Latins claim, and not to examine the long history of the Holy Places during the sixteen centuries, which preceeded the year 1740, as well as their modern history from 1740 to the present day? Then everybody will see clearly for how many centuries the Greeks were alone in the Holy Places and when the Franciscans appeared later in these places by which means they had entered into them as well as the period during which they had made the greater usurpation by diplomatic means and how long they have kept them.

We desire, and believe that it is necessary, that the history of the Holy Places during the first sixteen centuries should be examined and studied. From this study we can see on one hand, what was the position of the Greeks, and what historical, legal and political documents they have in their possession, and on the other hand, when and how the Franciscans entered into the Holy Places, and by what means they had taken the places, which are now in their possession. Furthermore what is the basis upon which the Franciscans depending lay their claims or all the Holy Places, while not only history and the official documents, but also Archaeology and the Christian Art, which is hitherto preserved, present clear and indisputable proofs refuting this basis? Besides that, all the preserved renovations of the important Holy Places, which had been erected by the Greeks, protest energetically against the claims of the Franciscans.

After all the various customs and the daily services which are held by the Greeks, in the Church of the Holy Sepulchre and in the Basilica of Bethlehem, leave no ground to the Franciscans to lay such claims. But what can we say about the other tendency of the Franciscans, who, in order to overshadow the rights of the Greeks, cover with curtains in many of the Holy Places the Greek inscriptions.

G*

At last we request the wise men, who will give their decision about the Holy Places, to take into consideration these facts, which are undisputed truth, containing long history, which we are ready to explain in discussion and publications, and to grant to every one his own right. We earnestly desire that the Greeks and Franciscans may live together in the Holy Places with mutual esteem and love.

In the Holy City of Jerusalem,   Written by the Chief Secretary of
29 June 1919.   the Greek Orthodox Patriarchate.
                                                T. P. Themlis[5]

Appendix 6

Excerpt from a confidential Memorandum 'The Status Quo in The Holy Places' by L.G.A. Cust, former District Officer, Jerusalem. Printed for the Government of Palestine by His Majesty's Stationery Office, 1929.

The Church of the Holy Sepulchre

The whole ensemble of the Church of the Holy Sepulchre, that is to say the Parvis and Entrance, the Rotunda, the Katholikon, the main fabric of the Church, and the commemorative shrines and chapels are subject to the regulation of the Status Quo in a greater or less degree.

The present Church is in outline the Church of the Crusaders erected following the partial reconstruction by the Emperor Monomachus after its destruction by the fanatical Caliph al Hakem and dedicated on 15 July 1149. The indifferent style of much of the architecture and the unsightly decoration are the result of the tasteless restoration after the fire of 1808* and the fetters of the Status Quo account for the state of dirt and dilapidation which is characteristic of many parts of the building.

As in the other Holy Places, the three Patriarchates of Jerusalem alone are considered as having possessory rights in the Church with the exception of the small Chapel in the possession of the Copts. They alone have the right to require the entrance door to be opened on their behalf, to enter in religious procession and to officiate regularly at their will. As is again the case elsewhere, of the Latin Orders, only the Franciscans of the Custodia di Terra Santa have the right to officiate independently. The Copts after a long period of penetration succeeded in establishing an independent foothold in the sixteenth century, but have no formal residence. They do not hold daily services, but have the right of censing at the shrines: similarly, the Syrian Jacobites have no formal residence and officiate only on Holy Days. Neither the Copts nor the Syrian Jacobites may

*The fire is said to have started in the Armenian Gallery and to have been caused by a drunken monk, who endeavoured to put it out by pouring *aqua vitae* over it, which he mistook for water. The danger of fire in the galleries and storerooms is always present.

hold processions unless in company with the Armenians, with the exception that on Good Friday afternoon they each hold a procession independently, after giving prior notification to the Orthodox and the Latins. The Abyssinians have no residence or accommodation of any sort and hold no offices within the precincts of the Holy Sepulchre, excepting their Easter services on the roof of St Helena's Chapel, around which they reside.*

In the various component parts of the Church the position at the present moment can be summarized as follows:—

1 The Entrance Doorway and the Façade, the Stone of Unction, the Parvis of the Rotunda, the great Dome and the Edicule are common property. The three rites consent to the partition of the costs of any work of repair between them in equal proportion. The Entrance Courtyard is in common use, but the Orthodox alone have the right to clean it.

2 The Dome of the Katholikon is claimed by the Orthodox as being under their exclusive jurisdiction. The other Communities do not recognize this, maintaining that it is part of the general fabric of the Church, and demand a share in any costs of repair. The Orthodox, however, refuse to share payment with any other Community. The same conditions apply *mutatis mutandis* to the Helena Chapel, claimed by the Armenians, and the Chapel of the Invention of the Cross claimed by the Latins.

3 The ownership of the Seven Arches of the Virgin is in dispute between the Latins and the Orthodox, of the Chapel of St Nicodemus between the Armenians and the Syrian Jacobites, and of the Deir al Sultan between the Copts and Abyssinians. In these cases neither party will agree to the other doing any work of repair or to divide the costs.

4 The Chapel of the Apparition, the Calvary Chapels, and the Commemorative shrines are in the sole possession of one or other of the rites, but the others enjoy certain rights of office therein. Any projected innovation or work of repair is to be notified to the other rites.

5 The Katholikon, the Galleries and the Chapels in the Courtyard (other than the Orthodox Chapels on the West) are in the exclusive jurisdiction of one or other of the rites, but subject to the main principles of the Status Quo as being within the ensemble of the Holy Sepulchre.

The three Patriarchates of Jerusalem are each represented by a Superior and clergy permanently resident within the precincts of the Church, and no other rite is entitled to be thus represented.

*History relates, however, that all these rites as well as others, such as the Georgians, Nestorians, and Maronites, had possessions at one time or another in the Church, which they lost in the course of time, principally from their inability to pay the heavy dues imposed on them by their Turkish masters.

The hours of the services of the various Communities are normally agreed on between the Superiors concerned, and only on rare occasions where festivals coincide is any difficulty caused.* Each rite holds its fixed offices daily, but it is unnecessary to specify these in detail. The Orthodox, however, have the right to say the Liturgy at night before the Latins and Armenians officiate.

As a general rule, when minor difficulties arise over the hours of the service agreement is arrived at between the Superiors, who readily co-operate to ensure good order and avoid misunderstanding.

THE PARVIS

The Courtyard or Parvis is entered from the Muristan on the east, and down a flight of steps from the Christian Street on the west. The remains of the twelfth century arcade, which stood along the north front of the Hospital of the Knights of St John, are still visible facing the Church.

The Courtyard is surrounded by Chapels and Monasteries belonging to the different rites. On the south side is the Orthodox Convent of Gethsemane and the Courtyard of the Omariyeh Mosque.† On the west, the Orthodox Chapels of St James, St Mary Magdalene, and of the Forty Martyrs.‡ On the north, the Orthodox Chapel of St Mary of Egypt, beneath the Latin Chapel of St Mary's Agony. On the east, the Chapel of St Michael, below the Chapel of the Four Persons, both at present under Coptic control, the Armenian Chapel of St James and the Orthodox Convent of Abraham.§ The whole of the Parvis, including the entrance, and all the Chapels on the north and east sides and the exterior of the Orthodox Chapels on the west are subject to the regulations of the Status Quo.

In 1927, at the time of the Orthodox Ceremony of the Washing of the Feet, the Abyssinians protested against the Copts lighting a Lamp in the Chapel of St Michael, but it was decided that this was the usual practice.

---

*Naturally, complications would be more frequent were the Orthodox Patriarchate of Jerusalem to adopt the Gregorian Calendar, as has been the case elsewhere.

†The true Mosque of Omar, built on the traditional site where Omar prayed before the Holy Sepulchre.

‡Actually the lower storey of the belfry. For a long time the belfry was disused, as the use of bells was forbidden by the Moslems.

§In 1885, the Patriarch Nicodemus assigned to the Church of England the Chapel of Abraham on the upper terrace of the Orthodox Convent of this name for the celebration of Anglican services. This act conveyed a privilege but no right of any description.

The pavement and the two external doors are the common property of the three Patriarchates. The Orthodox sweep the Courtyard and keep it clean and hold the keys of the external doors, but all repairs are to be conducted at the joint expense of the three Patriarchates concerned, or failing that, by the local authorities. In 1921 the Orthodox Patriarchate repaired the latch of the eastern entrance door, claiming that this was their sole right. The Latin Patriarch objected, and after investigation which showed that similar work had been done previously by the Municipality in 1879 and 1906,* the above ruling was given.

The steps leading up to the Chapel of St Mary's Agony are Latin property. The question as to who was to clean the lowest step, which is barely above the level of the Courtyard, was in 1901 the cause of a sanguinary encounter between the Latin and Orthodox monks.† The position now is that the Latins brush it daily at dawn, and the Orthodox at times together with the rest of the Parvis.

In front of the entrance to the Church is the Tombstone of the English Crusader, Philip d'Aubigny, tutor of Henry III, Governor of Guernsey, and one of the signatories of the Magna Charta, who died in Jerusalem in AD 1236. Thanks to the fact that for a long period it was protected by a stone divan built over it for the use of the Moslem guards, the Tombstone is in a tolerably good state of preservation. To protect it from further damage the Pro-Jerusalem Society in 1925 arranged for it to be sunk below the level of the Parvis and covered with an iron grill.‡ The necessary funds were provided by the Daubney family, the lineal descendants of the Crusader, and by the Island of Guernsey. §

Instrumental bands are not allowed to enter the Parvis. When this ruling was given in 1925 the Latin authorities objected, citing instances before the war when bands had been admitted. It was established, however, that on these occasions the Turkish Government had protested and held the practice to be irregular.

National flags, if unfurled, are similarly forbidden, and neither flags nor bands are allowed within the precincts of the Church.

*On this last occasion, the Municipality put in iron locks, but this was objected to as an innovation and the wooden ones were replaced.

†In this affray several Spanish and Italian monks were injured, and their respective Consuls took measures to obtain satisfaction on their behalf. This was objected to by the French representatives, who maintained that this was their prerogative in view of the protectorate exercised by France over all Roman Catholics in the Ottoman Empire. They were not, however, successful in their pretensions.

‡During the operation, the bones and some of the accoutrements of the Crusader were discovered and the stone was replaced exactly above them.

§Reference District Commissioner's letter, No. 4025, of 11 June 1925.

THE ENTRANCE

The Church of the Holy Sepulchre is entered from the Parvis* by a single portal, closed by a massive wooden door in two leaves. Originally it was a double entrance, but the eastern portal was walled up by Saladin.†

Above the portals are sculptured tympana of twelfth century work.‡ The left-hand panel is in a badly damaged condition.§

In May 1927, it was noticed that a further fragment had recently disappeared. Whether this was due to wilful damage or to the effects of the heavy snowfall that was experienced that year was uncertain. Protective work was carried out by the Government at the joint expense of the three Patriarchates.

Above the doorway runs a classical cornice, a relic of the Byzantine buildings. This is reached from the windows of the Armenian Chapel of St John, and this Community has the use thereof on the occasion of the festival ceremonies that take place in the Courtyard. The upper cornice is used in the same manner by the Orthodox. These two cornices are in a damaged condition and the whole façade is badly weather-beaten and requires expert attention.

The keys of the entrance doors are in the custody of Moslem janitors, who occupy a divan just within. According to tradition, the origin of the appointment of Moslem guardians dates from the time of the Caliph Omar. It is a recorded fact that the Arab Conqueror refrained from entering the Anastasis and entrusted it to the Patriarch Sophronius, placing it at the same time under the protection of Moslem guards. After the Saracens had finally recovered control of the Holy City from the Crusaders in 1289, the custody of the keys was given to the family of El Insaibi to prevent disputes between the various Christian Communities over their possession. Suleiman the Magnificent and other Turkish Sultans confirmed this

*This is the only entrance to the floor of the Church. Another entrance existed previously from the west and the arches may still be seen near the Christian Quarter Police Station.

†The hope is held in Latin (and some Anglican) circles that one day this other portal may be reopened; the Orthodox on the other hand would oppose this, as thereby the sites of the Tombs of the Latin Kings which were covered over at their instigation at the beginning of the last century would be opened up.

‡The frieze is of French marble and was probably worked in France. The left-hand panel depicts scenes from the life of Our Lord, the Raising of Lazarus, the Triumphant Entry, and the Last Supper, and the right-hand one is composed of a mythological subject. Formerly there were mosaics over both lintels.

§A portion was acquired by the French archaeologist Clermont-Gannaud some years ago and is now in the Louvre. It has been suggested to the French Government that the missing fragment should be returned and replaced, but only a cast was offered.

practice. Ibrahim Pasha divided the guardianship with the Judeh Family, and this is the position at the present time, the Judeh Family holding the keys and the Insaibi having charge of the actual opening of the door.

The right of requiring the door to be opened is confined to the three Patriarchs of Jerusalem. For each time one leaf of the door is opened a payment of eighty *mils* is made to the janitors, and for each time both leaves, a hundred and eighty *mils*. They receive as well some gratuities from the Copts and the Jacobites. Two-thirds of the payments made are assigned to the Insaibi Family and one-third to the Judeh. The door is opened by the different rites in turn; thus in Easter week, on Maundy Thursday, the door is opened by the Orthodox, on Good Friday by the Latins, and on Easter Eve (the day of the Holy Fire Ceremony) by the Armenians. The Community which desires the doors to be opened knocks on the small 'guichet' in the door, the key of which is kept by the Orthodox. The Orthodox servant notifies the Moslem custodians who come and open the door, a ladder, which is common property, being passed out for this purpose through the small 'guichet'. No dispute has been brought to notice regarding the opening and closing of the doors. Apart from his other functions, the Moslem janitor has always been treated as the neutral and disinterested authority on matters concerning the rights of the various Communities in the Holy Sepulchre.*

The three Patriarchs of Jerusalem alone have the right of entering the Church of the Holy Sepulchre in sacerdotal procession. Visiting ecclesiastics and pilgrimages of these rights are permitted to enter in procession, but provided no sacerdotal vestments are worn; in the other event, the Patriarch must accompany the procession himself. Thus, on several occasions cardinals have visited the Church.

In 1927 the Roumanian Patriarch and Co-Regent Miron Cristea, who was making an official visit to Jerusalem, entered the Church in procession, and after vesting within, was received at the entrance to the Tomb by the Patriarch Damianos. The Latin Patriarch protested that the entrance of the Roumanian Patriarch and his act in giving an address in Roumanian by the Tomb constituted breaches of the Status Quo, in that the Roumanian Orthodox Church had no connection with the Greek Orthodox Church, and that a comparison with the visits of the Cardinals who are all of the same Church as himself was not relevant. The Government decided that the Status Quo had not been violated by the Patriarch's entrance, nor by the

---

*Hence the sealing by him of the door of the Tomb during the Ceremony of the Holy Fire.

use of the Roumanian language, as there is no one universal tongue in the Eastern Orthodox Church.*

If a visiting ecclesiastic of note of the Coptic, Jacobite, or Abyssinian rites desires to visit the Holy Sepulchre, notification is made to the Armenian authorities, who arrange for the opening of the door, after informing the Orthodox and Latins, and receive him at the entrance, placing a carpet for him before the Stone of Unction. Two Armenian clergy also accompany the visitor to the Tomb.†

THE STONE OF UNCTION

Just within the entrance lies the Stone of Unction, commemorating the spot where Our Lord's Body was anointed before entombment. The Stone is of native red limestone, nine feet long by four feet six inches wide and one foot high, and has, it is asserted, been placed there to protect the real stone underneath.

The first mention of the Stone of Unction as a feature of the Church of the Holy Sepulchre is in the narrative of Saewulf, who made the pilgrimage to Jerusalem in the twelfth century. It was at that time in the Chapel of the Virgin, which existed on the site of the present belfry; at another time it was in the Chapel of St Mary, somewhere on the site of the present Courtyard.

The Stone with the floor surmounting it is common property, and before it all genuflect on entering the Church. The Lamps suspended above it belong to the various rites as follows:– four to the Orthodox Community; one to the Latin Community; two to the Armenian Community; one to the Coptic Community.

The great candlesticks belong two to each of the three principal communities.

Turning to the left the door on the left leads up to a room with a curious window, which is used by the Copts. The room opposite is Orthodox.‡

*See Deputy District Commissioner's letter, No. 10/60, of 24 June 1927, to the Chief Secretary. The possibility that the Patriarch of Jerusalem might endeavour to make a departure in favour of the Patriarch of Roumania so as to influence the Roumanian Government in the matter of the confiscated properties of the Jerusalem Patriarchate in Bessarabia was not overlooked: on the other hand, the Jerusalem Patriarchate are intensely jealous of their privileges and rights in the Holy Places, *vis-à-vis* the other Orthodox Churches and could be entrusted to preserve them with the utmost vigilance.

†A breach of these provisions was reported in April 1927, when a Coptic procession entered the Church wearing vestments and censing.

‡This room is used as a First Aid Post during the great festivals.

THE STATION OF THE HOLY WOMEN

Between the Stone and the Rotunda is a circular slab in the floor covered by a metal cage. This is said to mark the spot where the women waited and beheld the Crucifixion, and where the Virgin Mary stood while the Body of Our Lord was being anointed for Burial. The Armenians have charge of this part of the Church, their Priory is here and a steep staircase leads up to their portion of the Gallery and to their Chapel of St John the Almoner.* As mentioned previously, the windows of this Chapel lead out to the cornice overlooking the Courtyard.

THE ROTUNDA

Eighteen columns support the iron Dome and Galleries that enclose the Edicule covering the Tomb. The Dome is the common property of the three rites and was reconstructed in 1866 after fifteen years of diplomatic negotiations at the joint expense of the Turkish (as representing the Armenians), French and Russian Governments.†

The floor of the Rotunda within the circle of pillars is common property. No fixed furniture is permitted in it, and it must be kept free for circulation at all times. The three principal rites clean and sweep it in turns by weeks.

The portion of the Rotunda between the Edicule and the Orthodox Katholikon is known as the Latin Choir. Within this space the Latins hold regular services and the benches, lectern and other pieces of furniture and the hangings on the pillars, as well as the small room in the northern pillar, are their property. In February, 1928, the Orthodox objected to the Latins repairing alone one of the benches, but it was shown that these benches bear their distinctive marks and are their absolute property. This space is subject to the principles of the freedom of passage in the Rotunda and the two other principal rites have the right to hold religious offices here. When an office is being held it is accepted that the rites that are not worshipping and the general public refrain from passing in front of the Tomb.

The large candlesticks in front of the Edicule are the property of the three communities, two to each.

In 1573 the Copts, despite the protests of the other rites, were

---

*He was Patriarch of Alexandria at the time the Church was destroyed by the Persians and despatched money, tools and workmen to assist in its rebuilding. He was the Patron Saint of the merchants of Amalfi, who founded the hostelry in Jerusalem, which gave rise to the Order of Hospitallers of St John.

†The wooden Dome that previously covered the Rotunda was consumed in the 1808 fire. In the reconstruction, however, the dimensions were accurately reproduced.

able to build the small Chapel they own against the west end of the Edicule. This Chapel is their exclusive possession except that its exterior is subject to regulation under the Status Quo. The Register of the Armenian Priory of the Holy Sepulchre contains an entry dated 4 August 1901, to the effect that the Copts, in return for the construction of a drain under the area in their occupation, were granted 'as a favour' the right to sweep and wash the roof and exterior of this Chapel, which privilege would be withdrawn 'in the event of their creating disorders or trying to acquire new rights'. For a long time, i.e., between 1920 and 1924, the right of passage by the entrance of this Chapel was the subject of a prolonged and bitter dispute between the Copts and the Latins. When the Copts are celebrating their Mass the passage way, which is very narrow, becomes blocked by the worshippers. The servants of the Franciscan Convent of the Holy Sepulchre bearing food-stuffs, etc., are accustomed to cross by this way to avoid passing in front of the Edicule. When this occurred at the time the Coptic service was being held, the Copts refused to allow the servants to pass. The Latins accordingly refused to allow the Coptic Deacon to exercise his right of censing in the Latin Chapel of the Apparition. The Copts for their part attempted to pass through the Latin service in their Choir in front of the Edicule, and on another occasion assaulted the Friday procession at the Ninth Station near the entrance to the Coptic Convent.* After many efforts on the part of the Government to effect a compromise had failed, it was decided that the right of passage must be upheld and the obstruction was forbidden.† The Latins also have the right to pass benches by this way for use during their services on Palm Sunday and Good Friday. The benches have to be removed immediately after the conclusion of the services.

In 1920 the Orthodox placed tables with images thereon round the Edicule. It was complained that this was an innovation and the practice was forbidden.

All round the Rotunda are small rooms in the occupation of various rites and opening into it. These are constructed in the ambulatory that originally encircled this part of the Church. The columns also, together with the intervals between them, belong to different rites. With the exception mentioned below, the proprietorship of each column is indicated by the picture or ikon hanging

---

*On another occasion a dispute occurred between these two Communities over the position of the Chair of the Coptic Convent Kavass, which it was complained impeded the worshippers at this station. Instructions were given that the Chair was to be placed on the doorstep of the Convent when the procession was in progress.

†See Despatch No. Pol. 171 of 11 March 1924, in file No. 4773.

on it. Beginning from the east, columns eighteen to fifteen are Armenian; then until column twelve Orthodox. The Copts have the use of the next two rooms, but columns eleven and ten are Armenian, as also Nos. nine and eight in front of the Chapel of St Nicodemus. The big pictures on columns ten and eleven are however Coptic. From column eight to column five is Orthodox property. Between columns five and four a common passageway used for the storage of furniture leads past a walled-in Byzantine column to the closed-up entrance of St Mary. Columns five to one are Latin.

A dispute arose in 1924 about the right of the Copts to dust the doors leading into the room they occupy between columns eleven and ten. The Armenians claimed the exclusive right, as the Copts only have the use of the room by their permission, and by virtue of their situation as their subordinates (*cf.* the Jacobites). The Armenians produced documentary evidence in support of their claim* and the Government decided that the exclusive right to dust the doors was enjoyed by them†

THE EDICULE

The Edicule which encloses the Chapel of the Angel and the Tomb was erected in the place of the Crusaders shrine after the fire of 1808; the architect was a certain Commenus of Mitylene, whose name is inscribed just inside the inner doorway.

The Edicule is the common property of the three rites. In 1926, the Government, after much preliminary negotiation, undertook with the consent of the Patriarchates and at their joint expense an investigation into its structural condition. The report showed that, whereas the construction was very indifferent, there was no immediate danger of collapse, and it was not found necessary to do any repair work.‡

The lamps and fixtures that hang on the exterior are the property of the three principal communities in specific proportion.

On certain of their Feast Days, the three communities decorate the Edicule with heavy cornices and other ornamentations, in carefully regulated quantities. In 1920, at the instance of the Inspector of Antiquities, they were requested to desist from the practice, owing to the insecure state of the building, but it has now been resumed.

The interior of the Sanctuary is open at all times to pilgrims and visitors. In the centre of the Chapel of the Angel is a pedestal supporting a portion of the Stone on which, according to tradition,

*Letter of Mutesarrif to Armenian Patriarch, dated Mad. 29 1315 (1901).
†District Governor's letter, No. 4025/2, of 17 September 1924.
‡See District Commissioner's letter, No. 5745/D.C., of 18 June 1926.

the Angel sat. From this Chapel two staircases lead up to the roof of the Edicule. The one on the right of the entrance is used exclusively by the Latins, and that on the left by the Orthodox and Armenians.

The Tomb chamber itself is entered by a low doorway. The Tomb* is covered by a marble slab, and over it hang forty-three lamps that are always kept burning.† Of these the Orthodox, Latin, and Armenians have thirteen each, and the Copts four.

The ledge above the slab is divided between the three rites; the centre portion is Orthodox; the left angle is Latin and the right angle Armenian, while the two projecting ends are Orthodox. The votive candles of each Community are supposed to be kept on the portion of the ledge allotted to it. The pictures and candlesticks all belong to the three principal rites and they alone have the right to officiate regularly within the Sanctuary.

THE CHAPEL OF ST NICODEMUS

At the west end of the Rotunda is the Chapel of St Nicodemus. The Chapel, which is really the western apse of the Church, is entered by a doorway between Pillars eight and nine opposite the Coptic Chapel and consists of an antechamber, the Chapel with an altar and beyond a cave containing some old Jewish Tombs. Two of these are venerated as the Tombs of Nicodemus and Joseph of Arimathea, following the tradition that the last named made arrangements that when he and his friend died, their bodies were not to be laid in the Tomb in which Our Lord's had lain, but in this tomb near by. The presence of these tombs is considered a powerful argument for the historicity of the site of the Holy Sepulchre, as the Jews always buried their dead outside the City Walls.‡

The possession of this Chapel, which is open to visitors at all times, has been for some time in dispute between the Armenians and the Syrian-Jacobites, and much bad feeling has been thereby caused between these Communities.§ The Armenians say the Chapel is their property, and the Syrian-Jacobites enjoy the right of officiating there on Sundays and on certain other fixed days with their permission and by virtue of the fact that they are there 'sub-ordinate

*Of the original Tomb little can have survived the restoration of Constantine or the destruction of El Hakem.

†Except for the Ceremony of the Holy Fire.

‡Curzon holds this view: see *Monasteries in the Levant* Chap. 13.

§As an instance, a fracas occurred between these Communities at the conclusion of the Holy Fire Ceremony, in 1927, when the Syrian-Jacobite Patriarch placed his chair in such a way as to prevent the exit of the Armenian procession: see Deputy District Commissioner's letter, No. 1900 10/22, of 25 June 1927, to the Chief Secretary.

adepts'* in all matters relating to the Holy Places. The Syrian-Jacobites, however, do not accept this position and claim that the Chapel is theirs, and any rights the Armenians have in it have been obtained by force.

There is little historical evidence that can be brought to bear on the question. Travellers in the latter half of the fifteenth century tell of a Chapel belonging to the Jacobites adjoining or behind the Tomb. On the other hand, the Dutch traveller, Rauwolf, who visited Jerusalem in 1575, states that the Jacobites owned (as they do now) the Convent of St Mark, but does not assign them any special locality in the Holy Sepulchre. Cornelius de Bruyn, the Dutch painter, visiting Jerusalem in 1691, says the Syrians like the Abyssinians have ceased to be resident in the Church.

The map of the Holy Sepulchre and its surroundings drawn up by Dr Shick in 1885 denotes this Chapel as belonging to the Jacobites.

Serious quarrels broke out on two or three occasions between the contending parties under the Turkish Government, in 1874, on account of the repair of one of the doors by the Armenians, in 1881, over one of the clothes-presses, and again in 1889, when the Armenians white-washed the ceiling; on this last occasion, the Armenian picture over the Altar was torn to pieces. In every case, according to the Armenians, the enquiries instituted by the Government resulted in their favour,† and in 1890, the Mejliss Idara submitted to Constantinople a full report on the whole subject, with the conclusion that the Altar, the lamps and the upper chamber belong to the Armenians, while the Syrian Jacobites 'as the "Yamaks" of the Armenians' say Mass in the Chapel on appointed days, and have the use of the upper room in Easter Week.

Once again, to continue the Armenian version of this story, in 1900, when the 'Armenian question' had encouraged the Syrians to renew their pretensions, the Turkish Government ordered the matter to be looked into afresh,‡ and the local Mejliss Idara in a second report,§ confirmed the substance of the report made ten years before.

No satisfactory solution to the dispute was found by the Turkish Government, and the matter was left in the position that no repairs were to be conducted by either party except with the consent of the other, and after notification to the Government, and in the case of

---

*In Turkish 'Yamaklak,' meaning 'client' or more literally 'hem (of a garment)'.

†Letter of Mutesarrif to Minister of Justice, dated 18th Teshrin Seni, 1298 (1882), letter of Minister of Justice to Jacobite Vicar in Constantinople, 22nd Teshrin Awal, 1305 (1888), and report of Mutesarrif of 13th Teshrin Sani, 1306 (1889).

‡Letter of Grand Vizier, of 26th Hegira, 1317 (1900).

§Dated 18 August, 1900.

their disagreement any essential work was to be carried out by the Government at public expense. This the Turkish Government naturally avoided as much as possible, and the consequence has been the dilapidated state of the Chapel at the present time.

Since the British Occupation disputes have continued to occur. In 1926, the Armenians repaired the floor after giving notification to the Orthodox and the Latins. The Jacobites immediately protested and asked for the floor to be restored to its former state, as they feared that, to further their claims of proprietorship, some of the new stones had been inscribed on the underneath by the Armenians. It was ruled that the Armenians had acted incorrectly in carrying out the work without the authority from the Government. At the same time what had been done undoubtedly constituted an improvement and was therefore allowed to remain.*

There was in 1926 a recrudescence of trouble in this as in other matters of dispute between these two Communities.†

The Armenians claimed that the Jacobites were causing wilful damage to the upper room during their use of it, and were deliberately tearing the Armenian picture on the Altar and defacing its inscription (in Armenian): the Jacobites said the picture was theirs and the rent was made by the Armenians as in this corner there was an inscription in Syriac.

The Armenian arguments are set out at great length in a memorandum dated 4 July 1927, in which they quote the official documents mentioned above. They adduce in proof of their rights of possession the facts that:–

1 They own the doors and keep the keys and do all the cleaning in the Chapel;
2 They are at liberty to officiate in the Chapel whenever they desire;
3 The Altar and the picture on it belongs to them;
4 The twelve lamps all belong to the Armenians, two of them are always kept alight by them, and they light three others during the celebration of the Syrian-Jacobite Mass on Sundays, and the remainder on festival days;
5 The pictures on the outer wall of the Chapel and between the Pillars are all Armenian.

On the other hand, the Syrian-Jacobites have, according to them been granted the right of:—

*Acting District Commissioner's letter, No. 4025, of 12 October 1926, to Armenian Patriarch.
†The question of the ownership of this Chapel came into special prominence in 1926 during the time that the Syrian Jacobite Patriarch of Antioch, Ignatius Elias III, was on a visit to Jerusalem

1 Hanging three mobile pictures on the walls of the Chapel;
2 Keeping their vestments in two clothes-presses allotted them by the Armenians;
3 Officiating in the Chapel every Sunday;
4 During Holy Week using the room of the Armenians above the Chapel, the key of which has to be returned on Easter Monday.

The Syrian-Jacobites' point of view is detailed in a memorandum dated 5 March 1927. They claim that the fact that they have the right to officiate on Sundays and other Holy Days is sufficient proof of their rights of possession, of which they have been deprived by force. They argue in the same way as regards the upper chamber, which they state they have improved and repaired on several occasions and quote documents they hold which show that a monk of their Community, by name of Yacub, lived there in the fifteenth century.*

The Syrian-Jacobites have never been able to produce convincing evidence in support of their claim to the proprietorship of this Chapel. Moreover, the picture over the Altar clearly bears an Armenian inscription. In the Holy Sepulchre their position *vis-à-vis* the Armenians is the same as in the Church of the Nativity and the Church of the Virgin. At the same time the Armenian assertion that the Syrian-Jacobites are their Yamaklak or subordinates, and should only deal with the local authorities in any matter concerning the Holy Places through them, is now a dead letter, though once it may have been a fact, in the same way that the Armenian member on the Mejliss Idara was considered as the representative in administrative matters of the lesser Orthodox Churches.

The Status Quo therefore as regards this Chapel is such at the present time as it was under the Turkish Government, as described above.

THE KATHOLIKON

The great Katholikon or Chorus Dominorum, in the middle of which is the stone marking the Centre of the World, is, as it has been since the fourteenth century at least, Orthodox property; at the same time, being within the ensemble of the Church, any important or structural innovation should properly be notified to the other two rites. Thus, when in 1922 the Orthodox regilded the gates leading into the Rotunda considering they had exclusive authority over this part of the Church, the Latins objected and the Government ruled that this principle of the Status Quo should be held to apply.†

The Orthodox also claim that the twelfth century central lantern

*See Deputy District Commissioner's letter, No. 1400/10/22, of 25 June 1927, to the Chief Secretary. The pictures have now been glazed.
†See District Governor's letter, No. 4025/G., of 14 November 1922.

and Dome over the Katholikon are included within their exclusive jurisdiction, especially as the only access to its exterior, and to the top gallery within it, is from their Patriarchate. In the time of the Patriarch Nicodemus, however, the right to carry out work on the Cross surmounting it was strongly contested by the Latins. When the question of its urgent repair arose after the earthquake in 1927, the Orthodox notified the Government of their intention to restore it. It was decided, however, that as the Dome was part of the main fabric of the Church and the right of the Orthodox to repair it at their sole expense was disputed, the work of reparation should be undertaken by Government. It was subsequently decided that the costs should be defrayed by the Orthodox Patriarchate in view of the authority granted to the Armenians and the Latins to carry out certain works of repair.*

THE COMMEMORATIVE SHRINES

Since very early days shrines commemorating the various incidents of the Passion have been a feature of the Church of the Holy Sepulchre, and no pilgrim can have felt the lack of devotional suggestiveness. They are mentioned by Saewulf, and are frequently referred to in documents of later date.

To the North of the Rotunda, between the Rotunda and the Khankah Mosque lies the Franciscan Convent and the Chapel of the Apparition of the Virgin, approached by a vestibule dedicated to St Mary Magdalene. In the Chapel is preserved a portion of the Pillar of the Flagellation, and in the vestibule two stones mark the traditional spots where the risen Lord and Mary respectively stood when He appeared to the latter and she mistook Him for the gardener. All this area is Latin property, but the provisions of the Status Quo apply.

Thus in 1922, when, as mentioned previously, the Orthodox regilded the gates of the Katholikon, the Latins were permitted on their part to carry out some new work of decoration in this Chapel.†
Further, the Orthodox, Armenians, and Copts have the right to cense before the right-hand Altar in the Chapel of the Apparition, provided there is no Latin service in progress.‡

*See Deputy District Commissioner's letter, No. 2541/10/1, of 12 July 1927, to the Chief Secretary, and Chief Secretary's letter, No. 1938/27 of 23 November 1927.

†See letters of Latin Patriarch Prot. 522/22, of 25 September 1922, of Orthodox Patriarch No. 1487, of 6 October 1922, and Governor No. 4025/G., of 9 October 1922.

‡During their dispute with the Copts about the right of passage by the Coptic Chapel, the Latins for a time prevented the Copts from censing at this Altar.

The part lying north of the Katholikon is known as the Seven Arches of the Virgin, consisting of vestiges of the structural alterations carried out at different times.*

The ownership of this part of the Church is in dispute between the Orthodox and the Latins. Ladders are kept here, but absolutely no alteration by either party is permitted. The pictures are Orthodox. The Latins hold Firmans and *hojjets*, principally of the seventeenth and eighteenth centuries, which refer to the Arches as in their possession, but at this period the possession of the Holy Places alternated several times between the contending parties. Shick's map assigns it to the Orthodox. No recent incidents regarding this area are recorded, but the Status Quo is rigorously adhered to.

The Galleries above are exclusively in Latin use as store-rooms.

An entrance leads from the North Transept to the great latrines, which are common property.

Just to the east lies the Prison of Christ, a low Chapel, originally a Tomb or cistern. It is in Orthodox possession but claimed by the Latins. At the entrance two round holes in a marble slab, 'The Stocks', are shown.†

Entered from the great eastern ambulatory are, beginning from the north, the Chapels of St Longinus, Orthodox; of the Parting of the Raiment, Armenian; and of the Derision or Mock Coronation, Orthodox.‡ These Commemorative Chapels are first mentioned in connection with the reconstruction of the Emperor Constantine Monomachus in the eleventh century.

Between the Chapels of the Parting of the Raiment and of the Derision is the stairway leading down to the Chapels of St Helena and of the Invention of the Cross. The stairway and the Chapel of St Helena belong to the Armenians.§ The walls of the Chapel are of solid rock, though the roof is of construction, originally Crusader. The floor is some sixteen feet below that of the Rotunda. There are two altars in this Chapel, that to the north being dedicated to the Penitent Thief, and that to the South to St Helena. Near the latter is shown the stone seat on which the Empress is said to have rested while she was watching the excavations in search of the True Cross

*It may be that the Byzantine Pillars mark the northern boundary of Constantine's great court. Some Greek inscriptions are clearly visible. See Vincent and Abel '*Jerusalem*'.

†A similar 'holy site' is to be found in the Convent of the Prison of Christ in the Via Dolorosa.

‡Formerly Abyssinian.

§Though formerly to the Abyssinians. Casola AD 1494, however, found the Armenians in possession of a Chapel 'which goes down by many steps under Mount Calvary'. Ten years previously it is said to have belonged to the Georgians. See Luke *op. cit*. pp. 42 and 43.

in the Cave below. The Armenians were given authority to carry out the restoration of this Chapel in 1929.*

The Grotto of the Invention of the Cross, which is a cavern reached by a rough rock-hewn staircase, much worn by the feet of pilgrims and worshippers, leading from the Helena Chapel, is in two parts, the shrine with a marble slab the spot where the Crosses lay, and an altar adjacent commemorating the visit to Jerusalem, in 1850, of the ill-fated Archduke Maximilian, afterwards Emperor of Mexico.

The Latins claim exclusive possession of the Grotto of the Invention and of the stairway approaching it, and in 1929 they were authorised to place an iron grill staircase over the old stairs.† The Orthodox, however, claim certain rights over the actual Place of the Invention, and some disagreement has occurred about the placing of candles thereon. The Orthodox, however, now refrain from the practice.

The Armenians and Syrian-Jacobites hold services here on the Feast of the Invention of the Cross.

The shrines mentioned above are all visited by the various Communities so entitled and censed during the litanies and other offices.

CALVARY

The Calvary Chapels lie to the right of the main entrance, and are reached by two steep staircases, the northern belonging to the Orthodox and the southern to the Latins.‡ Below are the Orthodox Chapel of Adam, where the rent in the rock may be seen, and the Orthodox vestry; also the sites of the Tombs of Godfrey de Bouillon and Baldwin I, which were destroyed in the reconstruction after the fire of 1808.§

From the time of Constantine the traditional scene of the Crucifixion has been the object of veneration, and chapels have at various times been built on the site. Originally the Church of Calvary, called the Martyrion, was separate from the Church of the Anastasis.‖ The Crusaders enclosed Golgotha as part of their great cathedral on the flank of the southern transept; the shrine was

*See Chief Secretary's letter, No. 1938/27, of 23 November 1927.

†*Ibid.* Some years previously the Latins had attempted to place an iron staircase over the steps by night.

‡The semi-circular seat between the two staircases has a line marked on it to indicate the dividing line between the area of the two Communities.

§See Curzon: *Monasteries in the Levant*, Chap. 8.

‖The two Constantinian Churches are depicted in mosaic in the Church of St Pudenziana in Rome.

two-storied, and of much the same appearance as at the present time.

The Orthodox have possession of the northern portion, known as the Chapel of the Plantation or Exaltation of the Cross, where the hole in which the Cross was fixed is shown, and the Latins of the southern, that of the Crucifixion. The altar between the two, that of the 'Stabat', is Latin. A grill looks out on to the Latin Chapel of the Agony. The mosaic pavement belongs to the twelfth century, and was repaired by the Latins in 1929.* At one time during the Middle Ages, the Calvary Chapel belonged to the Armenians and at another to the Georgians. The Latins claim that, in 1740, they had part possession of the northern Chapel as well.

The Chapels are visited and censed during their offices by the rites so entitled in the same manner as the other commemorative shrines. On Good Friday, the Latins hold a ceremony on the Orthodox altar. In 1920, a disagreement arose with the Orthodox about the removal of the Orthodox altar-cloth before the Latin altar-cloth is placed in position, the Orthodox attitude being that this act implied a form of possessory right to which the Latins were not entitled, and it was decided that, until the matter had been cleared up, the Orthodox altar-cloth should not be removed for this ceremony.†

All the living and store-rooms and passages behind the Calvary Chapel, and the two doors leading to them, are exclusively Orthodox.

THE UPPER PORTIONS OF THE HOLY SEPULCHRE

The Gallery on the south side above the Rotunda is Armenian property as far as the southern divided Column. It is said that they acquired this portion in the fifteenth century, after the Georgians took their place in the Calvary Chapel. The rest of the Gallery is Latin and contains several portraits of Roman Catholic Sovereigns and Princes. An Armenian and a Latin picture are hung on the divided column.

The topmost Gallery under the Dome is Orthodox, and can only be reached from the Orthodox Convent.

The terrace above the Gallery of the Rotunda is under Orthodox control on the south, while the northern section is comprised within the precincts of the Khankah Mosque. The rest of the roof and the belfry is in general under Orthodox control, but as being part of the main fabric of the Church the provisions of the Status Quo apply as regards any important structural alterations.

*See Chief Secretary's letter, No. 1938/27, of 23 November 1927.
†For similar occurrences in the middle of last century, see Consul Finn's *Stirring Times*, Vol. I.

THE CONVENT OF DEIR AL SULTAN

The Convent of Deir al Sultan is adjacent to the Church of the Holy Sepulchre on the east side. It consists of a Courtyard with a Dome in the middle, and a cluster of hovels occupied by Abyssinian monks, under a Coptic guardian. The Dome is the lantern of the Chapel of St Helena. The Convent occupies the site of the cloisters of the Augustinian Canons of the Latin Kingdom, ruined in the sack of the City by the Charismians in 1245, traces of whose buildings are still visible. The Chapel of St Michael, which opens on to the Parvis of the Holy Sepulchre, and of the Four Martyrs are attached to the Convent. The big Coptic Convent lies to the north.

The Copts and Abyssinians both claim possession of the Deir al Sultan, the Copts maintaining that the Abyssinians living there do so as their guests and on their sufferance. The story of this dispute is long and complicated, and it is especially regrettable in that the Coptic and Abyssinian churches are of one communion, for the Abyssinian church is a daughter church of the Coptic Patriarchate of Alexandria by whom its Primate or Abuna, who is always a Coptic Ecclesiastic, is appointed.

Several medieval writers bear witness to the presence of Coptic and Abyssinian (or Nubian) monks in the Holy Sepulchre, and undoubtedly the Abyssinians at one time had important rights in the Holy Places. In the fourteenth century the Abyssinians owned the small Chapel of St Mary of Egypt, and in the fifteenth the Chapel of the Derision in the Ambulatory. At another period, they owned the Chapel of St Helena. In the seventeenth century, however, together with the other smaller Christian Communities who could not afford to pay the exactions of the Turkish Governor, they lost their holdings in the Church itself, when, as they claim, they obtained possession of the Deir al Sultan which they have occupied till the present time.

The Copts assert that the Deir al Sultan has always been their property, and that out of charity they took in their co-religionists when they were expelled from their possessions, and their pilgrims needed a place of rest. In the same way they were permitted to officiate in the Chapel of the Four Martyrs.*

The dispute over this Convent is first heard of early in the last century. It is not clear how the established order that had been the rule hitherto became upset or why these sister churches, whom it might have been thought would have been close allies in all matters

---

*A pamphlet in support of their claims has been published for the information of the Holy Places Commission by the Coptic Patriarchate, and the Abyssinian's point of view has been set out in a brochure entitled: '*Abyssinians and the Holy Places*,' by A. Devine (1926).

that concerned the Holy Places, quarrelled. The Copts hold a document dated 17 October 1820, consisting of an inventory made by the Cadi of the furniture of the Abyssinians 'when expelled from the Sultan Monastery'. They can produce four or five other documents relating to repairs carried out by them at this period, with official approval. They also possess one document of earlier date which makes reference to their occupation of this Convent.

In 1838, there was a calamitous plague in Jerusalem and the Abyssinians, it is related, all died out. This was during the occupation of the City by Ibrahim Pasha, and the Copts appear to have profited by the occasion in obtaining the Pasha's assent to the burning of the Abyssinian documents and library, including their title deeds, on the ground that they were infected with plague. They also secured the keys of the churches and the Convent. The wrangling between these two Communities continued throughout the nineteenth century. In 1863, the Abyssinians had apparently recovered possession of the keys. An enquiry was ordered by the Turkish Government and the verdict was favourable to the Copts. The Abyssinians refused to give up the keys and accordingly new locks were provided, the keys of which were entrusted to the Copts. This incident occurred just at the time when King Theodore was involved in war with Great Britain and the Abyssinians were consequently at a disadvantage.

The next incident occurred in 1889, when the Copts received permission from the Municipality to enlarge the northern gate. They had desired to pull down the whole north wall, but this was not allowed by the Turkish Government in view of the Status Quo. The Abyssinians violently opposed the right of the Copts to carry out any alterations, and insulted the Coptic Archbishop. The Copts thereupon refused the Abyssinians their *ab antiquo* right of officiating in the Chapel of the Four Martyrs.*

The matter came before the Turkish Government who refrained from compelling the Copts to reopen the Chapel to the Abyssinians, but allowed the latter to open a door for their exclusive use in the east wall of the Convent: and at the same time despite the objections of the Copts, the Abyssinians obtained permission to erect a tent on the terrace of the Convent for the celebration of their Easter services. The Abyssinians redoubled their efforts after this adverse decision, but to no purpose, and it is evident that the Turkish Government in this troublesome matter was predisposed towards the Copts.† At the

---

*The Abyssinians never had the right to officiate in the (lower) Chapel of St Michael.

†This may have been due in part to the fact that the Abyssinians were not 'Rayahs', and had always resisted Turco-Egyptian pretensions of suzerainty over them.

same time, the Abyssinians could never produce any documentary evidence in support of their claims.

Mention has been made of the destruction of the Abyssinian documents in 1838. The legend, however, grew up that the title deeds were still in existence in Abyssinia. The uncertainty arising from the reputed existence of these title deeds provided an acceptable occasion for foreign intervention. Russia saw in the matter an opportunity to further her designs on the Holy Places and sponsored the Abyssinian claims, on the understanding that a portion of what Abyssinia expected to recover would be handed over to her ally. Accordingly in 1893, at the request of the Russian Ambassador acting on behalf of the Abyssinians, the Porte ordered a fresh enquiry into the case of the Deir al Sultan. The Jerusalem local authorities replied that the matter had already been thrashed out and prayed that it be not re-opened. Again in 1902, the Italian Consul in Jerusalem made representations to the local authorities at the request of the Emperor Menelik. Once again in 1907, the Turkish Government informally raised the matter, but the British Occupation found the position the same as after the 1889 dispute, i.e., neither party will permit the other to do any act which may convey an implication of proprietorship, and neither agrees to pay any share of the cost of work done for fear of weakening its position.

In 1919, and again in 1927, it has been necessary for repairs to be carried out to the Convent, which on account of the disputed ownership is in a very bad condition. These were done by the Municipality while, in 1923,* the pruning of the trees was effected by the Department of Agriculture.

On the occasions when the Government has had to intervene, the Abyssinians have made reference to the existence of their title deeds in Abyssinia, and requested leave to produce them. Accordingly, in 1920, His British Majesty's Consul-General in Addis Ababa was asked to institute enquiries.

The information obtained was that the alleged title deeds were said to have been formerly in the possession of a certain Baron Nicholas Chef d'oeuvre, a Russian domiciled in Abyssinia, who had endeavoured to part with them for a very high price to the Emperor Menelik. Some such documents were produced in 1925 at H.B.M.'s Consulate-General at Constantinople for certification. On the other hand, there is a local version that they were sold to the Copts by the agency of a member of the Orthodox Synod of Jerusalem. At all events, it is clear that the Regent Ras Taffari gave little credence

*See District Governor's letter, No. 4408/A/1, of 9 February 1921, to the Mayor of Jerusalem, with copies to the Coptic and Abyssinian Superiors.

to the fable of the deeds, and correspondingly small encouragement to the intrigues on their account.*

The situation of the Abyssinians in Jerusalem is now much improved in that, in addition to a Convent in the Old City, they possess a Convent with a handsome Cathedral outside the Walls, besides other urban property of considerable value.

It has here to be mentioned that His Highness Ras Taffari, at the time of his visit to Jerusalem in 1924, obtained from the Orthodox Patriarch the cession of a cellar under the Convent of St Abraham, adjoining the Holy Sepulchre, in exchange for an amount of gold and certain properties in Abyssinia. The matter roused strong protest in lay Orthodox circles and in the Holy Synod. The real importance of the transaction lay in the fact that the cellar was partly situated under the Deir al Sultan, and, as it was intended to close the existing staircase leading from the Orthodox Convent, the only means of communicating with the cellar would have been to construct a staircase leading down to it from the Deir al Sultan. The Government viewed the matter in the light of an infringement of the Status Quo and intimated to His Beatitude that the transaction could not take place, requesting that His Highness be so informed, and in February 1925, His Beatitude informed the Government that he had taken the action required through the medium of His Highness' Greek physician.

The Church of the Nativity at Bethlehem

The Basilica of the Nativity, dedicated to St Mary, is one of the noblest Christian monuments in existence, and is probably the building of greatest antiquity still in constant use for Christian religious worship. Originally built by Constantine in AD 330, it was restored and enlarged in the sixth century by Justinian, who added the three great apses and built the belfry.† Most of the early travellers testify to its glory and magnificence. To instance a few, Archlf refers to the 'Great Church of St Mary'. Willibald, the cousin of St Boniface, calls it 'a glorious building in the shape of a cross'. Bernard the Wise tells of 'a very large Church of St Mary, with a crypt and two altars', and the accounts of pilgrims generally present a

---

*A Russian Mission under the leadership of the Grand Duke Alexander has been one of the principal parties.

The title-deeds have also been brought into negotiations regarding the Lake Tsana and Alcohol Concessions. See Secretary of State's Despatches, Confidential A, of 14 and 28 September 1925.

†The belfry was destroyed by an earthquake in 1575. The lower story that survived is now part of the Orthodox Convent. Its massive proportions give an indication of the magnificence of the belfry before its destruction.

striking uniformity of admiration. It was especially prominent during the Latin Kingdom of the Crusaders.* The Byzantine Emperor Manuel Komnenus restored it thoroughly in the twelfth century, from which period the mosaics date. Of particular interest also is the fact that in 1482, Edward IV of England supplied the lead for the roof.†

The ensemble of the Church is strictly governed by the Status Quo and the arrangements regarding the services of the different Communities are most complicated. The Basilica has had the same vicissitudinous history as the other Holy Places. The Latins hold many documents, principally of the seventeenth and eighteenth centuries, which show that for long periods the *praedominium* was theirs, but at the present moment the Orthodox enjoy by far the most privileged position. Thus the Orthodox alone hold processions round the Nave. In the North transept is the Armenian Church. In the Nave the rights of the Armenians are limited to passage to their Church.

Latin Christianity has a special interest in the Church too by reason of its connection with Saints Jerome and Paula, who lived and died at Bethlehem in the fifth century. The Grotto in which, according to tradition, St Jerome made his translation of the Vulgate and the Tombs of the Saint and of Paula and Eustachia are exclusively in Latin possession, but subject to the general principles of the Status Quo.‡ The modern Church of St Catherine,§ which commemorates Our Lord's appearance to St Catherine of Alexandria, is their absolute property. In the main Church the privileges of the Latins are limited to the possession of the altar of the Manger ‖ and the right of passage from the main entrance to the door of their Convent and from their Church in a straight line across the north transept to the north door of the Grotto. They may hold no religious ceremony in the body of the Church, and take no part in the general cleaning.

The official cleaning of the Church takes place in January and lasts about two hours. The Orthodox Patriarch notifies the Government

*Baldwin I was crowned here on Christmas Day 1101: his brother, Godfrey de Bouillon was crowned in the Church of the Resurrection.

†This roof was removed by the Turks in the early part of the seventeenth century for the manufacture of ammunition.

‡These shrines were shown to pilgrims in medieval times. Paula and her daughter Eustachia were two patrician Roman ladies who were converted by St Jerome and accompanied him to Bethlehem. These grottoes are connected by a wooden door with the Grotto of the Nativity. A similar series of caves exist under the south wall of the Nave, but no especial significance is attached thereto.

§Built adjoining the Basilica to the north by the Franciscans in 1881.

‖Acquired through the influence of the Emperor Napoleon III.

of the date, and a Government representative is present. The date is notified by the Government to the other communities. Whenever the Government uses implements belonging to one or other of the communities, formal notice is given that no form of right in favour of that community is thereby conveyed.

THE PARVIS

The Orthodox claim the sole ownership, but no work can be carried out except with the consent of the other Communities. The same applies to the cisterns, the water of which is used by the Bethlehem Municipality. The Status Quo applies to the northern face of the Armenian Convent which lies on the south side and on the east, to the outside wall of the Church as far as its junction with the new building of the Casa Nova: the opening of new doors and windows or the enlargement of existing ones can only be done with the consent of the three Communities, and efforts that the Armenians have made to enlarge the windows of their convent have been opposed.

On the north side lies the Orthodox Cemetery. The Orthodox have the right to erect buildings only in the northern part of the cemetery, and so as not to come higher than the level of the railings.*

The three Patriarchs enter the Church in solemn procession at the Christmas festivals, being accompanied from Jerusalem by an escort of mounted police. Distinguished personages are met outside the District Offices by the clergy in sacerdotal robes with religious banners and conducted to the entrance. The Roumanian Patriarch in 1927 thus made an official visit to the Church. The Latins alleged that a breach of the Status Quo had taken place. As in the case of His Beatitude's visit to the Holy Sepulchre, it was difficult to find a precedent, as no distinguished personage of the Orthodox faith had visited Bethlehem in recent years. It was decided, however, by the Government that a breach of the Status Quo had not occurred.†

THE ENTRANCE DOORWAY

This small opening is the only direct entrance into the Church. The remains of larger entrances are visible and the retrenchment was

---

*In 1924 a portion of the cemetery was surrendered, after some opposition from the Lay Orthodox Community, to enable the approach road from the north to be widened.

†The Grand Dukes Serge and Paul of Russia made an official visit to Bethlehem several years ago and were received in this manner.

due, apart from reasons of security, to the necessity of preventing animals, etc., being brought into the Church.

The key of the door is kept by the Orthodox, though the Latins also formerly possessed a key.* The door is opened and closed daily immediately after the Latin bells ring, the time varying according to the season of the year, i.e., earlier in summer than in winter. On the request of the Latins, the door is opened earlier or kept open later on account of their services, especially during the month of November and the fortnight before Christmas. On the Latin Christmas Eve, the door is opened at 9.30 pm, on the Armenian at 10 pm, and on the Orthodox Christmas Eve it is kept open all night.

THE NARTHEX

This is the space between the Nave and the entrance door. It is Orthodox property and cleaned daily by them, with the exception of the two steps leading to the Armenian Convent to the south, which are cleaned by the Armenians. The room on the left is Government property, being intended for the use of the Guard. The lamp in the centre belongs to the Orthodox and the other to the Armenians.

THE NAVE

The plan of an early Christian Basilica can here be seen untouched. Four rows of Corinthian pillars, eleven in each, support architraves bearing a wall thirty-two feet high with clerestory windows. An unsightly wall built across the east end by the Orthodox in 1842 was removed at the instigation of the Military Governor in 1919, thereby restoring the symmetry of the building.

All the ikons, lanterns and lamps in the Nave belong to the Orthodox. The lamp inside the door is kept burning day and night. The floor of the Basilica and the pillars up to the cornice are dusted daily by the Orthodox, and the marble slabs under the lamp in the centre and in front of the east door in the north aisle, known as the 'common door', is washed by them every Saturday. The Font is Orthodox property, but now unused. The big processions take place in the Nave on festivals and other Holy Days.†

The Latins have the right of passage from the entrance to their Convent door between the first and second pillars of the northern rows. Any attempted departure from this practice is immediately objected to by the other Communities.

*See the Firmans of 1852 and 1853.

†In Greek ἐσοδοι: they are divided into big, medium and small. Of the former five take place every year, and four and thirty-four of the other two respectively. For a detailed statement and description see Abdullah Eff. Kardus' memorandum, pp. 53, 54.

The Armenians have the right of passage through the Nave to their Church, after notifying the District Officer who informs the Orthodox authorities in writing, on the occasion of weddings, baptisms and funerals, and certain feast days; they pass straight up to the steps of the Katholikon and then turn north and go through the 'common door'.*

The Orthodox close the 'common door' every day after sunset, but the Armenians also have a key and can open the door at their will.

The cleaning of the Nave, including the windows and roof, is done exclusively by the Orthodox, though formerly the Armenians used to attempt to take part. With regard to the question of repairs, this matter came into prominence in 1926, when it was found necessary to make the roof watertight. The Armenians and Latins demanded to share the expenses with the Orthodox, but the latter refused, claiming the exclusive jurisdiction. As the matter was of great urgency, the repairs were carried out by the Government in the presence of representatives of the three Communities, and the incidence of the costs held in suspense.†

THE KATHOLIKON

As in the case of the Church of the Holy Sepulchre, this part of the Church is exclusively used by the Orthodox, though the principles of the Status Quo apply as regards innovations or alterations, and any intended change of furniture must be notified to the Government.‡ Cleaning may not, however, take place while the Armenians are holding a service in their Church. The Orthodox Patriarch has on more than one occasion requested permission to repair the pulpit, and to put a railing between the Nave and the Katholikon on the alignment of the wall removed in 1919. His Beatitude was asked to submit a design, but this has never been received.

---

*Previously, the Government had to give final permission, adding the phrase '*à titre contesté*' as the Orthodox maintained a formal objection. In the same way, the Armenians used to register a formal protest against the cleaning of the Nave by the Orthodox.

†See District Officer, Jerusalem's letter of 18 December 1926. A similar situation had arisen under the late Government, when the Orthodox replaced some broken window panes. The Latins strongly objected, and satisfaction was given by Government sending up a mason with another pane, who pretended to break the one replaced by the Orthodox.

‡See letter of D.C. Bethlehem to the Orthodox Bishop, No. BM/9, of 24 March 1924. By an ingenious contrivance the great chandeliers are made to swing during the festivals.

Appendix 6

THE CHURCH OF ST NICHOLAS

This Church in the south transept is exclusively Orthodox, as well
as the door leading into the south aisle of the Nave. Here also,
however, the principles of the Status Quo apply.

THE ARMENIAN CHURCH OF THE NATIVITY

This is situated in the north transept. In the north-west corner
is the door leading to the Latin Church and the Latins have the
right of passage in a straight line thence to the north door of the
Grotto, and to clean the passage way. This right has been established
only after many incidents between the two Communities in the past.

On the Armenian Christmas Eve, the Latins at the request of the
Armenians close the door leading into their Church for twenty-four
hours from 10 am when they complete their sweeping till the morning
following. The Armenians then are permitted to place carpets and
chairs in the whole of the Church.*

At the time of the Orthodox Christmas Festivals the Copts and
the Syrian-Jacobites hold services in the Armenian Church, the
former at the main altar and the latter at the side altar. Neither,
however, are permitted to place any Church vessels or furniture of
their own on the altars, excepting a Chalice. They also descend to
the Grotto and officiate. The Syrian-Jacobites follow the Copts
down to the Grotto, a regulation which was infringed in 1927, partly
owing to the Coptic procession being late.† The Syrian-Jacobites
claim that the altar at which they officiate is their own property
and that they have the right to use vessels of their own. Under
the present circumstances, however, their position *vis-à-vis* the
Armenians in the Church of the Nativity is the same as in the
Church of the Holy Sepulchre and in the Church of the Virgin.

The arrangements for the cleaning of this part of the Church are
very complicated. In places where the possessory rights are in
dispute, the cleaning is done by the Government.

THE GROTTO

The Grotto of the Nativity is situated under the Katholikon, and
entered by stairways from the north and the south. The cavern

*In this Church a chain will be noticed suspended from the ceiling, but without
any lamps. This is due to an unfortunate omission, as by mistake authority to
suspend a chain was only obtained from the Turkish Government.

†See p. 4 of Deputy District Commissioner's letter to Chief Secretary, No.
1900/10/22 of 25 June 1927.

is really continuous with the series of caves comprising the Tomb of St Jerome, etc., but is divided from them by a wall.

As early as the days of Justin Martyr, in the second century, a cave was shown as the scene of Our Lord's Birth, and the present spot has been the object of devotion and veneration without interruption from the days of Constantine. Traces are still visible of the medieval decoration. The shrine consists of two parts, the Altar of the Nativity, belonging to the Orthodox and the Armenians, and at which the Copts and Syrian-Jacobites officiate, and the Altar of the Manger which is exclusively in Latin use.

The order of the services is very complicated; arrangements in their regard are made between the Superiors concerned. If a Community desires to hold any office other than what is customary prior notice is to be given to the Orthodox Superior. Any such office is interrupted for the ordinary office or ceremony to take place. The lamps and furniture are the property of the three rites; the existing position of the hangings has to be most scrupulously adhered to.

The southern door is used exclusively by the Orthodox, no clergy of the other communities being permitted to enter the Grotto by this way in sacerdotal dress. In a private capacity, however, any person is at liberty to use the staircase at any time.* The curtains along the steps belong to the Orthodox. Of the two lamps that are suspended above them, the one nearer the door is Latin and the other Orthodox. There are also two ikons on the east wall, one Orthodox and the other Armenian.

The hanging round the main walls is Latin property.† Of the pictures on it, six are Orthodox and six Armenian. Many of them are very faded, but under present conditions their replacement would be a matter of great difficulty. The floor is cleaned alternately by the Orthodox and the Latins, an equal number of persons of each Community participating.

The northern entrance is used principally by the Latins and Armenians. The hangings along the side of and above the northern flight of steps are Latin. The Latins clean this set of steps daily. Above this door are two ikons and two lamps, belonging one each to the Orthodox and Armenians. The steps leading down to the door are cleaned alternately by the Latins and the Armenians.

The actual Grotto is in two sections: the lower section where

---

*See District Officer of Bethlehem's letter to the Orthodox Superior, No. BM/9, of 20 March 1924.

†The hanging is made of asbestos on account of the fact that tapestries hung there previously were set on fire.

there is the Star of the Nativity, and the upper where there is the Altar.

The silver Star was in the early part of the last century, on more than one occasion, the cause of international contention. It was more than once stolen, the last time by the Orthodox in 1847, on account of its Latin inscription.* Harried by the Ambassadors at his Court, the Sultan eventually replaced it himself.† Again, when at the beginning of this century, some of the nails were lost, they were replaced by the Government. As the result of the disputes and aggressions that were continually taking place in the Grotto, the Turks stationed a guard here, and the British Government has maintained the practice.‡

The Star is dusted daily by the Orthodox. It is washed by the Orthodox and the Armenians, twice a week each; the Altar above is cleaned by the Orthodox alone.

On the Altar above the Star there is a small Orthodox ikonostasis; the other ikons belong to the Orthodox and Armenians in equal proportions. The purple embroidered strip is Orthodox. The iron railing in front is opened and closed by the Orthodox at fixed hours. The other hangings here are Orthodox.

At Christmas, 1928, the Latins objected to the retention of the Orthodox ikon on the Star during the Latin night mass. The ikon was removed, but it was subsequently established that the ikon should remain until the morning. §

In 1924, a member of the Polish Consular Staff was married in the Grotto. The Orthodox Patriarch protested that this was a breach of the Status Quo, but the right of the Latins (as of either of the other Communities) to hold such a ceremony was upheld.

Stringed musical instruments may not be introduced into the Grotto. ||

In 1928 the Latins made application to bring electric lamps into the Grotto, but authority was not given. ¶

Hic de Virgine Maria Jesus Christus natus est. See Consul Finn's *Stirring Times*, Vol. I.

†See Khatt-i-Sherif of 1269 (1853) quoted by Themeles.

‡The Turkish sentry was formally relieved by a British Guard on our occupation of the Town. A Police Guard is stationed there now.

§ See Acting Deputy District Commissioner's letters Nos. 14330/10/2 of 19 July 1929.

||See Deputy District Commissioner's letter 11576/10/2 of 10 September, and Latin Patriarch's reply of 5 September 1928.

¶See Deputy District Commissioner's letters to the three Patriarchs of 6 September 1928.

THE MANGER

This is exclusively in Latin use. The hangings all belong to them. The hanging near the steps can only extend to half the width of the pillar between it and the Orthodox hanging. A dispute occurred about this hanging in 1921, and its exact position has to be regulated to the nearest inch.

In front of the Manger, there is a pillar which is cleaned by the Latins. The hanging which falls down this pillar should not, however, fall lower than the cross carved on it. The three candlesticks in front of the pillar belong one to each rite.

The floor of the Manger is cleaned exclusively by the Latins. Efforts have been made by them on more than one occasion to repair it, but this has not been permitted by the other rites, in view of the application of the Status Quo to the whole of the Grotto. When the Armenians desired to replace a very dilapidated picture in their Church, the Latins only consented provided that they were allowed to repair this pavement. To this the Armenians did not agree, as they claimed under the Status Quo certain rights as regards the floor of the Manger, whereas the picture, they maintained, was their exclusive possession.

References

Introduction

1 Security Council Official Records, Twenty-Second Year Supplement for July, August and September 1967, pp. 232 ff., Document S/8146 Report of the Secretary General, para. 111.
2 *Jerusalem Post*, 18 August 1969.
3 *Jerusalem Post*, 22 October 1969.
4 Security Council, 12 September 1969, S/PV 1510.

Chapter 1. The Nature of the Christian Attachment to the Holy Places.

1 St Jerome, Epist. 46, *Migne Patrologia Latina* (MPL) xxii, col. 489.
2 St Augustine, Epist. 78, MPL xxxiii, col. 268–9.
3 St John Chrysostom, *Ad Populum Antiochenum* V, *Migne Patrologia Graeca* (MPG) xlix, col. 49.
4 St Gregory of Nyssa, MPG lxvi, col. 1010–15; see Appendix 1.
5 St Jerome, Epist. 47, MPL xxii, col. 493.
6 St Jerome, Epist. 46, MPL xxii, col. 491.
7 St Jerome, *Praefatio Hieronymi in Librum Paralipomenon*, MPL xxiii, col. 1324.
8 St Jerome, Epist. 46, MPL xxii, col. 489.
9 St Jerome, Epist. 22, MPL xxii, col. 416.
10 St Jerome, Epist. 58, MPL xxii, col. 581.
11 Steven Runciman, *A History of the Crusades*, Vol. i, Cambridge 1954, pp. 32–3.
12 M. Villey, *La Croisade*, Paris 1942, p. 65.
13 Walter Norden, *Das Papsttum und Byzanz*, New York 1958 (Reprint of the original edition Berlin 1903), p. 39, note 2.
14 *Urban and the Crusaders*, in Translations and Reprints from the original sources of European History, edited by Dana Carleton Munro, published by the Department of History of the University of Pennsylvania, Philadelphia, 1894–1908; Vol. i, no. 2. pp. 2–5.

15 Norden *op. cit.*, p. 51, note 1.
16 *Urban and the Crusaders, op. cit.*, pp. 5–8.
17 See Carl Erdmann, *Die Entstehung des Kreuzzuggedankens*, Stuttgart 1935, 1955; *Cambridge Mediaeval History*, Vol. IV, p. 333 ff. Adolf Waas, *Geschichte der Kreuzzuege*, Freiburg 1956; Baldwin Setton, *History of the Crusades*, University of Pennsylvania Press, Vol. I, 1955.
18 Runciman, *op. cit.* Vol. I, p. 115.
19 St Bernard of Clairvaux, *Letters*, translated and edited by Bruno Scott James, Burns Oates London, 1953; nos. 391 and 392; see Appendix 2.
20 About the similarity of Christian and Islamic thoughts on war during the Crusades: E. Sivan, '*La genèse de la contre-croisade*', *Journal Asiatique*, Tome CCLIV, 1966, p. 197; Albrecht Noth, *Heiliger Krieg und Heiliger Kampf in Islam und Christentum*, Bonner Historische Forschungen, 1966.
21 Valmar Cramer, *Kreuzpredigt und Kreuzzugsgedanke von Bernhard von Clairvaux bis Humbert von Romans*, in *Das Heilige Land in Vergangenheit und Gegenwart, Gesammelte Beitraege und Berichte zur Palestina Forschung*, Koeln 1939, p. 73.
22 Cramer *op. cit.*, pp. 74–5.
23 *Digressio qua lamentatur auctor Jerusalem ab infidelibus captam*, MPL 204, 350 and Cramer *op. cit.*, pp. 79 ff.
24 Cramer, *op. cit.*, pp. 180–81.
25 Cramer, *op. cit.*, p. 181.
26 Ursula Schwerin, *Die Aufrufe der Paepste zur Befreiung des Heiligen Landes von den Anfaengen bis zum Ausgang Innozenz IV*, Berlin 1937, pp. 97 ff.; Waas, *op. cit.*, pp. 1 ff.; Erdmann *op. cit.*, p. 308.
27 Waas, *op. cit.*, p. 8.
28 Waas, *op. cit.* pp. 7–8.
29 Cramer, *op. cit.*, p. 131.
30 Cramer, *op. cit.*, pp. 101–2.
31 Walter Hilton, *The Ladder of Perfection*, translated by Leo Sherley-Price, Penguin Classics, London, p. 154.
32 *Le Collège de France (1530–1930)*, Livre Jubilaire, Les Presses Universitaires de France, Paris 1932, pp. 27–50.
33 *Treaties between Turkey and Foreign Powers 1535–1855*, compiled by the Librarian and Keeper of the Papers, Foreign Office, London, 1855, p. 171.
34 Treaties, *op. cit.*, p. 181.
35 Treaties, *op. cit.*, p. 186.
36 Treaties, *op. cit.*, p. 334.

37   Gottfried W.Leibnitz, *Consilium Aegyptiacum and De expeditione Aegyptica Regi Franciae proponenda Leibnitii justa Dissertatio*; see also O.Klopp, *Leibnitz 'Vorschlag einer Expedition nach Aegypten'*, Hanover 1864.

38   Harold Temperley, *England and the Near East – The Crimea*, London, 1936, reprinted 1964, pp. 283–4, and n. 418.

39   Paul Hazard, *La Pensée européenne au XVIIIe siècle de Montesquieu a Lessing*, Paris, 1946; translated by J.Lewis May under the title *European Thought in the 18th century*, Penguin Books, London, 1965, pp. 8 and 57.

40   John E. Howard, *Letters and Documents of Napoleon*, London, 1961, Vol. I, pp. 244–5, Document 309.

41   Howard, *op. cit.*, p. 248, Document 315.

42   E.E.Y.Hales, *Napoleon and the Pope*, London, 1962, pp.7–8.

43   Howard, *op. cit.*, p. 246, Document 311.

44   Howard, *op. cit.*, pp. 299–300, Document 409.

45   Howard, *op. cit.*, p. 282, Document 382.

46   Fauvelet de Bourrienne, *Mémoires sur Napoléon*, Paris, 1830, Vol. II, p. 218.

47   Franz Kobler, 'Napoleon and the Restoration of the Jews to Palestine', *The New Judaea*, Sept. 1940, pp. 189–90; October–November, pp. 18–19; December, pp. 36–8; February 1941, pp. 69–70.

48   Christopher Harold, *Bonaparte in Egypt*, London 1963, p. 294.

49   Novalis (Friedrich von Hardenberg), *Die Christenheit oder Europa*, 1799.

50   Friedrich Sieburg, *Chateaubriand*, London 1961, pp. 153 and 161.

51   *Le Pape et Jérusalem – Solution de la Question Italienne et de la Question Orientale*, E.Dentu, Libraire-Editeur, Paris 1861.

52   Nicolas Zernov, *Eastern Christendom*, London 1961, p.140.

53   Feodor Dostoevsky, *Diary*, July 1876 and March 1877.

54   Laurence Oliphant, *The Land of Gilead*, London 1880, p. 503.

55   Stephen Graham, *With the Russian Pilgrims to Jerusalem*, London 1913, pp. 4–5.

Chapter 2. The Holy Places and the Division of the Church

1   Philip Sherrard, *The Greek East and the Latin West*, Oxford University Press, Oxford 1959, p. 5.

2   Steven Runciman, *A History of the Crusades*, Vol. I, Cambridge 1954, p. 5.

3   Walter Norden, *Das Papsttum und Byzanz*, New York 1958. (Reprint of the original German edition Berlin 1903), p. 38.
4   Norden, *op. cit.*, pp. 38–9.
5   Norden, *op. cit.*, p. 42.
6   Norden, *op. cit.*, p. 49.
7   Norden, *op. cit.*, p. 63.
8   Nicephore Moschopoulos, *La Terre Sainte*, Athens 1957, p.132.
9   Runciman, *op. cit.*, p. 288.
10   D.C.Munro, *The Fourth Crusade*, Translations and reprints from the original sources of European history, Vol. III, Pennsylvania, p. 14.
11   Bernardin Collin, *Les Lieux Saints*, Paris 1948, pp. 74 ff.
12   Treaties between Turkey and Foreign Powers 1535–1855, compiled by the Librarian and Keeper of the Papers, Foreign Office, London 1855, p. 31, Art. 7; p. 37. Art. 7 and p. 46, Art. 9.
13   Treaties, *op. cit.*, 192–200 (*Articles Nouveaux*, Art. 1).
14   Treaties, *op. cit.*, pp. 384–5, Art. 7.
15   Treaties, *op. cit.*, p. 54, Art. 13.
16   Treaties, *op. cit.*, p. 73, Art. 11.
17   Treaties, *op. cit.*, pp. 229 ff.
18   Bernardin Collin, *Le Problème Juridique des Lieux Saints*, Paris 1956, p. 38.
19   Treaties, *op. cit.*, pp. 463 ff, esp. Arts. 7, 8, 16.
20   Moschopoulos, *op. cit.*, p. 223.
21   According to Heinrich von Treitschke, *Deutsche Geschichte im 19. Jahrhundert*, Bd 5, 3. Auflage 1895, pp. 120–21, the memorandum had been written at the King's request by his friend, the General Joseph Maria von Radowitz, an original and imaginative thinker, who besides producing political works of the Romantic School, wrote on subjects as varied as the iconography of the saints, and the different stages in the development of church music.
22   Derek Hopwood, *The Russian Presence in Syria and Palestine 1843–1914*, Oxford 1969, p. 13.
23   *Lettre encyclique de SS. Pie IX aux Chrétiens d'Orient (6 Jan. 1848)*; and *Encyclique responsive des Patriarches et des Synodes de l'Eglise d'Orient*, translated from the Greek by Dr D.Dallas, Paris 1850.
24   See Appendix 3.
25   Comte J.A. de Huebner, *Neuf ans de Souvenirs d'un Ambassadeur d'Autriche à Paris sous le seconde Empire 1851–1859*, Paris 1904, p. 165.

Chapter 3. The Struggle about a Legal Investigation

1   George Antonius, *The Arab Awakening*, London 1938, p. 247.
2   M.Erzberger, *Erlebnisse im Weltkrieg*, Stuttgart und Berlin, 1920, pp. 82–91.
3   Pascal Baldi, *La question des Lieux Saints*, I, Rome, Imprimerie Pontificale de l'Institut Pie IX, 1919, second edition Jerusalem 1954 pp. 93–95, 96; Collin, *Problème Juridique des Lieux Saints*, Paris 1956, pp. 74–75.
4   Clemenceau during the Peace Conference in Paris once tried to impress T.E.Lawrence with France's historic rights to Palestine by asking whether he knew that it was mainly the French who had fought in the Crusades. The reply was: 'Yes, but the Crusaders were defeated and the Crusades were a failure.' (F.Z.N.Zeine *The Struggle for Arab Independence*, Beirut 1960, p. 65, note I).
5   Appendix 4.
6   Appendix 5.
7   Published in Collin *op. cit.*, Paris 1956. Part II, pp. 223–9.
8   18th Session of the Council of the League of Nations, 13 May 1922.
9   *Osservatore Romano*, 30 June 1922; English translation in *The Tablet* 8 July 1922, p. 49.
10 Note of the British Government of 1 July 1922, Cmd 1708.
11 *The Times*, 25 July 1922.
12 Collin, *op. cit.*, Part II, p. 230.
13 Memorandum submitted by Lord Balfour to the Council of the League of Nations on 31 August 1922.
14 20 Session of the Council of the League of Nations, 4 October 1922.
15 Papal Allocution *Vehementer Gratum*, 11 December 1922, *Acta Apostolicae Sedis* XIV, 1922, pp. 610–11.

Chapter 4. Government for the Sake of the Holy Places

1   Palestine Royal Commission Report, July 1937, Cmd 5479, Chapter 22.
2   Yearbook of the United Nations, 1947–8, pp. 229–31.
3   *Acta Apostolicae Sedis* XL, 1948, pp. 433–6.
4   Bernardin Collin, *Le Problème Juridique des Lieux Saints*, Paris 1956, p. 138.
5   *Acta Apostolicae Sedis* XXXXI, pp. 161–4.
6   Bernardin Collin, *op. cit.*, p. 140.
7   Yearbook of the United Nations, 1948–9, p. 192.

8 Yearbook, *op. cit.*, p. 193.
9 United Nations General Assembly, 2nd Session, Supplement 11 UNSCOP Report, Vol. III, Annex A, Verbatim Record of the thirty-first meeting held in Jerusalem, 15 July 1947, p. 14.
10 *Cahiers de l'Orient Contemporain* XXIII, pp. 90–1.
11 *Proche Orient Chrétien (POC)* 1951, pp. 139–40.
12 *Christian News from Israel*, Government of Israel, Ministry of Religious Affairs, April 1951, p. 6.
13 *POC* 1953, pp. 372–3.
14 *Règlement du Patriarcat Grec Orthodoxe de Jérusalem, POC* 1958, pp. 227–36.

Chapter 5. New Developments in the Churches

1 *Christian News from Israel*, September 1966, p. 4.
2 *POC* 1964, p. 232.
3 *POC* 1964, pp. 20–42.
4 *POC* 1965, p. 95.
5 *POC* 1965, p. 104.
6 *POC* 1966, pp. 41–3.

Chapter 6. We Came to Jerusalem Not to Possess Ourselves of the Holy Places of Others

1 Security Council Official Records, Twenty-Second Year Supplement for July, August and September 1967, pp. 232 ff., Document S/8146, Report of the Secretary General, paragraph 111.
2 Khadduri Majid, *The Law of War and Peace in Islam*, London 1940, p. 94.
3 *Christian News from Israel*, July 1967, pp. 10–11.
4 *op. cit.*, July 1967, pp. 12–13.
5 *op. cit.*, July 1967, pp. 19–20.
6 *op. cit.*, July 1967, p. 22.
7 *op. cit.*, December 1967, pp. 20–21.
8 *Jerusalem Post*, 9 October 1968.

Chapter 7. 'An Oasis of Peace and Prayer'

1 *POC* 1967, p. 330.
2 *Cahiers de l'Orient Contemporain*, October 1967, p. 22.

3   *POC* 1967, p. 331.
4   *Journal de Genève*, 31 July 1967, p. 1.
5   *POC* 1967, p. 331.
6   *Cahiers de l'Orient Contemporain*, October 1967, p. 23.
7   Bernardin Collin, *Le Problème Juridique des Lieux Saints*, Paris 1956, Part II, p. 211, and above Chapter III, note 9.
8   Bernardin Collin, *op. cit.*, I, p. 129.
9   *Osservatore Romano*, 16 July 1967, and *POC* 1967, p. 250.
10   *The Tablet*, 22 July 1967, p. 789.
11   *Cahiers, op. cit.*, p. 23.
12   *POC*, 1968, p. 86.
13   *New York Times*, 12 July 1967, and *Christian News from Israel*, July 1967, pp. 22–3.
14   Introduction, Note 1.
15   Jewish Telegraphic Agency, 10 May 1968.
16   *Osservatore Romano*, English Weekly Edition, 2 January 1969.
17   *POC* 1969, p. 377.
18   *Le Monde*, 8 October 1969.
19   *POC* 1967, p. 339.
20   *The Times*, 27 April 1970, p. 4; *Jerusalem Post*, 28 April 1970; *POC* 1970, pp. 197–8. About the historical background of this conflict see Appendix 6, section 'The Convent of Deir al Sultan'.
21   D.P.O'Connell, *International Law*, 1965, Vol. I, p. 379 ff.
22   Further examples Appendix 6, section 'The Chapel of St Nicodemus'.
23   *Jerusalem Post*, 13, 14, 15 March 1968; Monthly Bulletin of the Moscow Patriarchate, April 1968, pp. 4, 6 and 7.
24   Ciprotti Pio, *Il problema dei Luoghi Santi nel momento attuale*, address given in Rome on 27 March 1968 to the Ordine Equestre del Santo Sepolcro di Gerusalemme.
25   *Eastern Churches Review*, Spring 1970, pp. 91–3; W. Zander, 'The Russian Church in the Middle East – New Developments', *The New Middle East*, July 1970.
26   Bulletin of the Moscow Patriarchate, Department of External Ecclesiastical Affairs, 17 April 1970.
27   *Le Monde*, 21 May 1970, p. 13.
28   *Eastern Churches Review, op. cit.*, pp. 95–8.
29   *Le Monde*, 29–30 March 1970.
30   *The Times*, 27 May 1970.
31   Henry Musset, 'Hellenism and Slavism', *POC* 1951, p. 225.
32   *POC* 1953, pp. 372–3.
33   *POC* 1968, pp. 86–7.

Chapter 8. Solemn Declarations and Functional Internationalisation

1   UN Doc. A/1113.
2   UN Doc. A/AC. 31 – L. 42.
3   UN Doc. A/AC. 38 – L. 63.
4   Elihu Lauterpacht, *Jerusalem and the Holy Places*, pamphlet published by the Anglo-Israel Association, London, October 1968.

Chapter 9. United Nations – United Religions – or Arab-Israel Condominium?

1   *Yearbook of the United Nations* 1948–9, p. 193, and B.Collin, *Le Monde*, 26 December 1969, p. 6.
2   Bernardin Collin, *Le Problème Juridique des Lieux Saints*, Paris 1956, p. 150.
3   Chaim Weizmann, *Trial and Error*, London 1950, p. 355.
4   Pierre Dubois, *De recuperatione terrae sanctae*, translated under the title *The Recovery of the Holy Land*, by Walter I. Brandt, Columbia University Press, New York 1956.
5   Carl J. Friedrich, *Inevitable Peace*, Cambridge, Mass., 1948, p. 92.
6   Immanuel Kant, *Zum ewigen Frieden*, 1795, translated by W. Hastie, Boston 1914.
7   See Walter Schuecking, *Die Organisation der Welt*, Festgabe *fuer Laband*, Tuebingen 1908, Vol. I, p. 592: '*Religion ist heute schon immer mehr Privatsache geworden, und wenn dieser Satz leider auch noch nicht im Innern der Staaten ueberall durchgedrungen ist, so gilt er doch fuer den Verkehr nach aussen, fuer die Staaten untereinander*'.
8   *United Nations Yearbook* 1967, pp. 1015–20.
9   *Christian News from Israel*, October 1969, pp. 25–6.
10 See above p. 27.

Chapter 10. The Christian Holy Places and the Reunion of the Churches

1   *Christian News from Israel*, May 1968, p. 36.
2   Pascal Baldi, *La Question des Lieux Saints*, I, Rome, Imprimerie Pontificale de l'Institut Pie IX (no year given), p. 85.
3   Bernardin Collin, *Le Problème Juridique des Lieux Saints*, Paris 1956, p. 186.
4   Boré Eugène, *Question des Lieux Saints*, Paris 1850, reprinted by Collin, *op. cit.*, part II, pp. 120–56.

5   Hugues Vincent et F.M.Abel, *Jerusalem*, Paris, Gabalda 1914, Vol. II part III, p. 979.
6   See Appendix 4.
7   United Nations General Assembly, 2nd Session, Supplement 11 UNSCOP Report, Vol. III, Annex A, Verbatim Record of the thirty-first meeting held in Jerusalem 15 July 1947, pp. 13–19; see also Temperley, *England and the Near East – The Crimea*, London 1936, p. 287.
8   See above, p. 47.
9   Bernardin Collin, *Les Lieux Saints*, Paris 1948, pp. 82–3.
10 Bernardin Collin, *Le Problème Juridique des Lieux Saints*, Paris 1956, pp. 72–3.
11 See above, p. 93.
12 Ernst Benz, *Die Russische Kirche und das Abendlaendische Christentum*, Muenchen, 1966, p. 68.
13 See above, pp. 95.
14 See above, p. 96.
15 See above, p. 152.
16 The Documents of Vatican II (London 1967), p. 352.

Appendices

1   *Select Writings and Letters of Gregory, Bishop of Nyssa*, translated by William Moore and Henry Austin Wilson, Oxford and New York, 1893. (Vol. V of *A Select Library of Nicene and Post-Nicene Fathers of the Christian Church*, Second Series).
2   Printed by permission of Messrs. Burns Oates Ltd, from *The Letters of Saint Bernard of Claivaux*, edited by Bruno Scott James, London 1953.
3   English text from British State Papers, Eastern Papers I (1854), Vol. LXXI, *Correspondence respecting the Rights and Privileges of the Latin and Greek Churches in Turkey*, No. 40, enclosure 2.
4   Published in Jerusalem, 1922, by l'Imprimerie des Pères Franciscains.
5   This English text was published in *Nea Sion*, Jerusalem 1920.

Index

235

Index

Armenian Church of the Nativity, *221*
Arnauld de Pomponne, Simon, 25
Ascension, Sanctuary of the, *179–80, 216*
Assad El-Iman, Sheik, 89
Athenagoras I, Patriarch, 134, 170
  meets Pope Paul VI in Jerusalem, 93–4
  1965 declaration re schism, 96, 168–9
  hope for reunion of Churches, 93, 94, 170
  exchanges visits with Paul VI, 113–15
Athens:
  as possible seat of Ecumenical Patriarchate, 136
  Patraki monastery in, 168
Augustine, St, 6, 8
Augustinian Canons, *213*
Aupick, Gen., 53, 59, 61, *185, 192*
Austria: and Turkey, 45, 46
  1642 treaty, 45
  1699, 46
  1739, 46
  supports Latin claim to Holy Places, *181, 182, 183*
Auvergne, Council of, 12

Baldi, Pascal, *La Question des Lieux Saints*, 55–6, 132, 163
Baldwin I, Emp., *217*
  tomb of, *211*
Balfour, Earl of, 63–4, 66, 67, 68–9, 105, 148
  Balfour Declaration, the, 64
Basilica of the Nativity, Bethlehem
see Nativity, Basilica of the
Bayle, Pierre, 26
Belgrade, Treaty of, 46, *183*
Benedict XV, Pope, *Causa Nobis*, 63, 64
Benedictos I, Patriarch:
  meets Pope Paul VI, 93
  meets Prime Minister Eshkol, 103
Berlin *1878* Congress of, 34
  Treaty, 54, 61, *183*
Bernard of Clairvaux, St, letter to the English People, 14–15, *175–7*
Bernardos, Georges, 56
Bessarabia, 47, *201 n*
BETAR (Jewish National Youth Movement), 2
Bethlehem:
  early pilgrims to, 5–6, 7

no religious significance to Jews, 3
Christmas celebrations in, 131, *219*
  1967, 106–8
  Orthodox, *218, 219, 221*
internationalisation of, proposed, 72–4; *see also* internationalisation
  1948, taken by Arabs, 76
  1967, taken by Israelis, 102
Basilica of the Nativity,
  see Nativity, Basilica of the
Bible, the; study of, 7–8, 9, 22
  pilgrimage in, 5, 6, 16
Boemund, Prince, 42
Bonaventura, Father Simon, 165
Boré, Eugene, *Question des Lieux Saints*, 164
Britain:
  1675 treaty with Turkey, 25
  given Mandate over Palestine, 63–4, 65–6, 67, 105
  assumes Mandate, 68–9
  first report on Mandatory Government, 69–70
  see also Mandate for Palestine
  memo on Status Quo, 70–1
  quoted, *195–224*
Bruyn, Cornelius de, *206*
Byzantine Empire:
  relations with West, 9–11
  army destroyed at Manzikert, 10–11
  and Roman, 38–40
  Norman attacks on, 41
  in Crusades, 40–3
  Greek view of, 60, *188–91*
  Russia as heir and successor of, 33
Byzantium, *see* Constantinople

Caesarea, 10
Cahiers de L'Orient Contemporain, 113
Cairo: Feast of the Prophet in, 28
  Apostolic pro-Nuntio in, 117
Calvary, *see under* Holy Sepulchre, Church of the
Calvin, John, 21
Carlowitz, treaty of, 46, *183*
Casola, *210 n*
Catholic church, the:
  19C. position of Papacy, 31–3
  and Orthodox church, 38–40, 92–7, 168–9, 170
  1848 Encyclical *In Suprema Petri* to Eastern Christians, 50–1

Index

Cluny, Order of, 10
Collin, Bernardin:
    article in *Le Monde*, 159
    Les Lieux Saints, 44, 113, 163, 166
    Le Problème Juridique des Lieux Saints, 130, 154, 167
Commission: Special, re Holy Places, proposed; in Mandate, 62–8, 70
    1950 Commissions for Holy Places, 149–50
Conciliation, *1948*, 79–80, 139–42, 145, 152
Commissioner for Holy Places, 70, 140–1, 144–5, 147–9, 150, 152
Constantine the Great, 9, *216*
Constantinople (Byzantium, Istanbul):
    under Justinian, 60
    at outset of Holy War, 11, 41
    Western attacks on, 42–3, 61, *190*
    sacked, *1204*, 43, 61, *190*
    Turks take, *1453*, 21, 33
    and Greece, *189*
    and Russia, 33–4
    Russian church established in, 47
    Ecumenical Patriarchate in, 48, 50, 134–6
    Hagia Sophia Cathedral of, 33, 40, 60, *189*
    Pope Paul vi in, 113, 114
    see also Byzantine Empire *and* Istanbul
consuls in Israel; 182
    French, 49
    Soviet, 91
Coptic church, the:
    in Easter celebrations, 110
    disputes with Abyssinians, 121, *213–15*
    with Franciscans, *203, 209 n*
    and Syrian-Jacobites, *221*
    Status Quo rights in Holy Sepulchre, *195–6, 197, 200, 201, 202–4, 209*
    in Basilica of Nativity, *221, 222*
    Chapel in Edicule, *202–3*
    Chair of Convent Kavass, *203 n*
Coubet-el-Messad oratory, *179*
Council for Holy Places, 101–2, 140–1, 147, 149, 152
Council of Christian religious dignitaries, 101
Council of Europe, Consultative Assembly:
    1967, 106

Council of Moslem ecclesiastics, 101
Crimean War, 54, 123, 151, 154
Cristea, Miron, Patriarch, *200*
Croix, La, 132–3
Crusaders:
    on *1099* conquest of Jerusalem, 1, 13, 121–2, 136
    Latin Kingdom of, 36, 42, *217*
    in Greek memo, *187, 189, 190–1*
Crusades, the, 9–19
    as Holy War, 9–11
    call for First, 11–13, 41
    on capture of Jerusalem, *1099*, 13–14
    at loss of Jerusalem, *1187*, 15–16
    theology of, 15–19
    romanticised, 30, 132
    as attempt to reunite Christian church, 40–3
    mentioned, 60, 136, 150, *229*
Cust, L.G.A., Status Quo memo by, *195–224*
Custos of the Holy Land, *see* Franciscan Custody of the Holy Land
Cyril, Patriarch, 50

Damascus, Apostolic Nuntiatur in, 117
d'Aubigny, Philip, tomb of, *198*
Dayan, Gen. Moshe, 98, 101, 155
Deir al Sultan, Convent of, *213–16*
Derdérian, Yeghishe, Patriarch, 93
Diderot, Denis, 26
Diotallevi, Ferdinand, 186
Disputes, settlement of, 54, 57–9, 61–2, 64–70, 76, 83, 140–1, 143–5, 147–52, 169
Dome of the Rock, *see* Omar, Mosque of
Dostoevsky, Feodor, 34, 56
Dubois, Pierre, 156
Dutch, the, *see* Netherlands, the

Easter celebrations, 131
    in Status Quo memo, *196, 200*
    of *1968*, 109–10, 131
Eban, Abba:
    at Council of Europe, *1967*, 106
    letters to UN, *1968*, 106, 160
    visits Pope Paul vi, 116–17
Eckhart, Master, 19
Ecumenical Council (Vatican ii), 92–3
Ecumenical Inst. for Theological Studies, 169
Edward iv, King of England, *217*

238

Index

Index

Jaffa, 28, 73, 119
James of Compostella, St, Sanctuary of, 10
Jammes, Francis, 56
Jerome, St, 5–6, 7–8, 9, 36, *217*
Jerusalem:
  Holy Places of, internationalisation of, monks of, Patriarchs of, pilgrimage to, *and* population of, *see those headings*
  in Byzantine Empire, 9
  at different conquests of, 99–100, 121–2
  683, Arab, 9, 99–100
  Moslem rule of, 11, 100
  in Crusades, 9–18
  1099, Christian, 1, 13–14, 42, 136
  Latin kingdom of, 36, 42, 121–2, *217*
  in Greek memo, *187*, *189*, *190–1*
  1187, Moslem, 1–2, 15–16, 100, 122
  1517, Turkish, 21, 122
  1948, Arab, 76, 100
  under Jordanian rule, 89
  1967, Israeli, 2, 98–9, 100, 101, 104, 146
  Israeli administration of, 101–5, 108–10
  theological significance of, 137–8
  to Crusaders, 16–19, 20
  proposed as Holy See, 31–2
  proposed sub-division of, 81, 86
  Orthodox Patriarchal election in, 50
  Islamic conference at, *1953*, 89
  Moscow Patriarch visits, 90
  Russian church in, 91–2
  Pope Paul VI visits, 93–4
  1968 New Year reception in, 108–9
  1968 Easter celebrations in, 109–10
  Old (Walled City):
    government of by condominium, 4, 129, 161
    in proposed subdivision, 81
    internationalisation of, proposed, 128–9
Jerusalem the Golden, 20
Jewish National Home in Palestine, proposed, 63, 64
Jewish National Movement, 2, 154–5
Jews:
  and Arabs, *see* Arab-Israeli conflict
  persecution of, 14, 177
  at Christian conquest of Jerusalem, Synagogue of, 1, 13
  Napoleon appeals to, 28
  attend Christian services, 106, 108
  Passover Night, 109
  and Moslems and own Holy Places, 2–3, 99, 151, 145
  see also Israel, Judaism *and* population of Jerusalem
John, St, Gospel of, 6
John the Almoner, St, *202 n*
John Chrysostomus, St, 6, 8
John XXIII, Pope, 92
Jordan:
  administration of Jerusalem, 142, 160
  1951 appointment of Guardian, 87–9
  and Greek Orthodox Church in, 89
  opposes internationalisation of, 80, 85, 118, 129
  Arab Christians in, 107
  see also Arab Declaration on Holy Places
Joseph of Arimathea, *205*
Judaism:
  and Christianity, 100–1, 158–9
  Holy Places of, 2–3, 99, 148, 151, 155
  and pilgrimage, 5
Judeh family, the, *200*
Justinian, Emp., 60, *189*, *216*

Kant, Immanuel, *Zum ewigen Frieden*, 156
Kemal Pasha, 62, 166
Kempis, Thomas à, *Imitatio Christi*, 20
Knesset (Israeli Parliament), Protection of Holy Places Law, 102, 146
Komnenos, Manuel, Emp., *189*, *191*, *217*
Koran, the, 15, 38, 88
Kutchuk-Kainardi, treaty of, 47

language, proposed, for Jerusalem, Bethlehem, etc., 74
Latin Kingdom of Jerusalem, 36, 42, *217*
Latin language, study of the, 7, 22
Latin Patriarch appointed for Jerusalem, 50
Latins:
  Memo to Peace Conference, *1919*, 57–9, *181–5*

Index

Moslems—*cont.*
and Christians: *10C.*, 10
20C., 89
and Jews, and own Holy Places, 2–3, 99, 148–9, 151, 154, 158
Council of Ulemas in Jerusalem, 89
guards of Church of the Holy Sepulchre, *199–200*
and internationalisation of Jerusalem, 136
see also Arabs *and* Islam
Mount Olive, Ascension Sanctuary on, *179–80, 216*
Mount Zion; Cenacle on, Franciscans and, 57, 164, *187*
see also Temple, the
Mourad IV, Sultan, 44–5
mysticism, Christian, 19–20

Naples, *14C.*, kings of, support French claims, 57, *181, 182*
Napoleon Bonaparte:
in Egypt, 26–8, 48
in Palestine, 28–9
attitude to religions, 27–8, 159
Napoleon III, Emp., 54, *217*
Narkiss, Gen. Uzi, 108
Nativity, Basilica of the (Bethlehem):
rights in acquired, 44–5, 57–8, 61, 100, 164, 178–9
disputes and damage in, 48, 53, 124 *223*
Christmas celebrations in, *see under* Bethlehem
in Status Quo, 70–1, *216–24*
history of, *216–17*
cleaning of, *218*
Armenian Church of the Nativity, *221*
Church of St Nicholas, *221*
Entrance doorway, *219*
Grotto, 44, 45, 158, *222–3*
tapestries of, 124
Star of, 53, 124, *223*
Katholikon, *220–1*
Manger, *224*
Narthex, *219*
Nave, *219–20*
Parvis, *218*
see also Holy Places
Nazareth, 10
Napoleon at, 28–9

internationalisation proposed for, 72, 73, 74, 79, 111
Nestorians, the, *196 n*
Netherlands, the:
and France, 25
treaties with Turkey;
1598, 24
1612, 25, 120
1680, 25
New York Times, The, 115
Nicephorus, Emp., 10
Nicodemus, Patriarch, *209*
Niehuhr, Dr Reinhold, 115
Niketa, 190
Nikodeme, Metropolitan, 124, 134
visits to Jerusalem, 91–2
statement on religion in Russia, 135
Normans, the, attack Byzantine Empire, 41
Novalis, 29–30, 156

Observer, The, 107, 108
Oliphant, Laurence, *Land of Gilead*, 34
Omar, Caliph, 89, *199*
on taking Jerusalem, *638*, 9, 99–100
Omar, Mosque of (Dome of the Rock):
the true, *197 n*
and Christians (Templum Domini), 1, 122, 136
and Jews, 2, 99
Orthodox church:
and Catholic, *see* Christian church, Greek clergy and Arab laity of in Palestine, 89, 90
Ecumenical Patriarchate, seat of, 91, 134–6
in Jerusalem; Patriarch of, 50, 91, *201 n*
under Jordanian rule, 89
and internationalisation of Jerusalem, 82, 83, 114
representation on League of Nations, 68
1964 Pan-Orthodox conference, 94–95, 168
1967 Christmas celebrations, 108
Easter celebrations, 131
1968, 109–10
Patriarchs of Constantinople, Alexandria, Antioch and Jerusalem declare Pope Pius IX heretic, 51–3

244

Index

population, of the Holy Cities:
  Christian,
    independent régime proposed for, 72
    oppose internationalisation, 136–7
    and internationalisation, 72–8, 83–6, 128–31, 137
    language of, 74
    and neutralisation, 125–6
    and right to self-government, 74, 126–7
Proche-Orient Chrétien, 116–17
'protection', notion of, 122–3
  of Holy Places in peace-time, 123–5
  in war-time, 125–6
Protestants, 63, 115
  access to Jerusalem, 25, 120
  proposed as Chairman of Commission on Holy Places, 67–8, 148
Prussia, proposals of re Jerusalem, *1841*, 49, 72

Rabat, Islamic conference in, 157
Rachel, tomb of, 107, 131, 155
Radowitz, Gen. Joseph Maria von, *228*
Raghib Pasha Al-Nashashibi, 87–8
Ramle (Arimathea), 73, 119
  Napoleon at, 28
Rand, Mr Justice Ivan, 165
Ras Taffari, Regent, *215–16*
Rauwolf, the traveller, *206*
Reformation, the, and pilgrimages, 21 156
religion, and UN, 155–7
  and peace, 156
religions, three monotheistic, relations between, 157–60
Renaissance, the, 22
repairs, to Holy Places, 122, *206–7, 209, 220, 224*
revolution, *19C.*, 31–3
Rhodes, Orthodox conference in, 94–5
Richelieu, Duke of, 48
Robert, King of Sicily, 164, *181*
Robert the monk, 12–13, 41
Rogerus, King of Sicily, 61, *190*
Roman Catholics, *see* Catholic church, the
Roman Empire, 9, 39, *188–9*
'Roman question', the, 31
Romantic movement, the, 29–31, 156
Rome: as Holy See, 31–2, 39
  St Peter's church in, 96–7, 111

Rumanian church, 95
  Patriarch of, visits Jerusalem, *1927*, 200–1, *218*
Runciman, Steven, *A History of the Crusades*, 10, 13, 39, 42
Russia:
  as heir to Byzantium, 33
  and Turkey, 47–8
  champions Orthodox church, 33–4, 47–8, 49, 53, 55, *183*; *see also* Crimean War *and* Russian Orthodox church
  supports Abyssinians, *215*
  pilgrims from, 34–5, 92, 134
  1917 revolution, 35, 90
  influence in Middle East, 133
  and internationalisation of Jerusalem, 133
  see also Soviet Union
Russian Orthodox Church:
  return of to Middle East, 33–4, 90–2
  increasing influence of, 133–4, 135–6
  emancipation from Constantinople, 500th anniversary of, 90–1
  in America, 134–5
  in Jerusalem and Israel, 47, 49–50, 89, 91, 133–4
  Russian Church Mission in Jerusalem, 50, 91–2
  Chapel of Mary Magdalen, 92
  complaints about attacks on property, 124
  and dissident White émigrés, 90, 91
  in Turkey, *18C.*, 47
  offers sacraments to Roman Catholics, 134
  see also Moscow *and* Orthodox church

Saewulf, narrative of, *201, 209*
St Catherine, Catholic church of (Bethlehem), 107, 131, *217*
St Paolo fuori le Mura, Basilica of, interfaith prayer service in, 169
St Peter, Church of (Rome):
  excommunication revoked in, 96
  Pope Paul VI addresses pilgrims, in, 111
Saladin, the Saracen, 60, *199*
  1187 conquest of Jerusalem, 1–2, 17, 100, 122, 163
sanctuaries, *see* Holy Places

Index